# TRADIVOX

VOLUME XIX

# TRADIVOX

## *CATHOLIC CATECHISM INDEX*

VOLUME XIX

Germany

*Edited by*
*Aaron Seng*

SOPHIA INSTITUTE PRESS
MANCHESTER, NEW HAMPSHIRE

South Bend, Indiana
www.Tradivox.com

This book is an original derivative work comprised of newly typeset and reformatted editions of the following Catholic catechisms, once issued with ecclesiastical approval and now found in the public domain:

Bishops of Germany. *A Catholic Catechism*. Freiburg: Herder & Co., 1957.

Scripture references follow the Douay-Rheims Bible, per the imprint of John Murphy Company (Baltimore, 1899).



Cover and interior design by Perceptions Design Studio.
Unless otherwise noted, all illustrations are in the public domain.



Sophia Institute Press
Box 5284, Manchester, NH 03108
1-800-888-9344

www.SophiaInstitute.com

Sophia Institute Press® is a registered trademark of Sophia Institute.

ISBN 978-1-64413-386-6
LCCN 2024932779

Dedicated with love and deepest respect
to all the English Martyrs and Confessors.
*Orate pro nobis.*

# CONTENTS

# ACKNOWLEDGMENTS

THE publication of this series is due primarily to the generosity of countless volunteers and donors from several countries. Special thanks are owed to Mr. and Mrs. Phil Seng, Mr. and Mrs. Michael Over, Mr. and Mrs. Jim McElwee, Mr. and Mrs. John Brouillette, Mr. and Mrs. Thomas Scheibelhut, Mr. and Mrs. Kyle Barriger, as well the visionary priests and faithful of St. Stanislaus Bishop and Martyr parish in South Bend, Indiana, and St. Patrick's Oratory in Green Bay, Wisconsin. May God richly reward their commitment to handing on the Catholic faith.

# FOREWORD

The Catholic faith remains always the same throughout the centuries and millennia until the coming of our Lord at the end of the time, likewise "Jesus Christ is the same yesterday, today and forever" (Heb 13:8). The Catholic faith is "the faith, which was once delivered unto the saints" (Jude 1:3). The Magisterium of the Church teaches us solemnly the same truth in the following words of the First Vatican Council: "The doctrine of the faith which God has revealed, is put forward not as some philosophical discovery capable of being perfected by human intelligence, but as a divine deposit committed to the spouse of Christ to be faithfully protected and infallibly promulgated. Hence, too, that meaning of the sacred dogmas is ever to be maintained, which has once been declared by holy mother Church, and there must never be any abandonment of this sense under the pretext or in the name of a more profound understanding. May understanding, knowledge and wisdom increase as ages and centuries roll along, and greatly and vigorously flourish, in each and all, in the individual and the whole Church: but this only in its own proper kind, that is to say, in the same doctrine, the same sense, and the same understanding (cf. Vincentius Lerinensis, *Commonitorium*, 28)."[1]

An authentically Catholic catechism has the function of learning and teaching the unchanging Catholic faith throughout all generations. The Roman Pontiffs indeed, taught: "There is nothing more effective than catechetical instruction to spread the glory of God and to secure the salvation of souls."[2] Saint Pius X said, that "the great loss of souls is due to ignorance

[1] Vatican I, Dogmatic Constitution *Dei Filius de fide catholica*, Ch. 4

[2] Pope Benedict XIV, Apostolic Constitution *Etsi minime*, n. 13

of divine things."[3] Therefore, the traditional catechisms have enduring value in our own day and age, which is marked by an enormous doctrinal confusion, which reigns in the life of the Church in the past six decades, and which reaches its peak in our days.

I welcome and bless the great project of the "Tradivox" in cataloguing and preserving the hundreds of long-lost Catholic catechisms issued with episcopal approval over the last millennium. This project will convincingly show the essentially unchanging nature of the apostolic doctrine across time and space, and so I invite the faithful of the entire world to support this historic effort, as we seek to restore the perennial catechism of the Church. The project of a catechism restoration on behalf of "Tradivox" will surely be of great benefit not only to many confused and disoriented Catholic faithful, but also to all people who are sincerely seeking the ultimate and authentic truth about God and man, which one can find only in the Catholic and apostolic faith, and which is the only religion and faith willed by God and to which God calls all men.

+Athanasius Schneider, O.R.C.,
Titular Bishop of Celerina
Auxiliary Bishop of the Archdiocese of Saint Mary in Astana

[3] Cf. Pope St. Pius X, Encyclical *Acerbo nimis*, n. 27

## *SERIES EDITOR'S*
# PREFACE

SOME are surprised to find that when a given Catholic is asked to "look something up in the catechism," he may well respond: "Which one?" The history of the Catholic Church across the last millennium is in fact filled with the publication of numerous catechisms, issued in every major language on earth; and for centuries, these concise "guidebooks" to Catholic doctrine have served countless men and women seeking a clear and concise presentation of that faith forever entrusted by Jesus Christ to his one, holy, Catholic, and apostolic Church.

Taken together, the many catechisms issued with episcopal approval can offer a kind of "window" on to the universal ordinary magisterium — a glimpse of those truths which have been held and taught in the Church *everywhere, always, and by all.* For, as St. Paul reminds us, the tenets of this Faith do not change from age to age: "Jesus Christ yesterday and today and the same for ever. Be not led away with various and strange doctrines" (Heb 13:8-9).

The catechisms included in our *Tradivox Catholic Catechism Index* are selected for their orthodoxy and historical significance, in the interest of demonstrating to contemporary readers the remarkable continuity of Catholic doctrine across time and space. Long regarded as reliable summaries of Church teaching on matters of faith and morals, we are proud to reproduce these works of centuries past, composed and endorsed by countless priests, bishops, and popes devoted to "giving voice to tradition."

## *In This Volume*

This penultimate volume of the Tradivox collection represents the last catechism to be issued by the German bishops before the opening of the Second Vatican Council in 1962. First appearing as an illustrated "German unified catechism" in 1955, the *Katholischer Katechismus der Bistümer Deutschlands* was adopted throughout Germany and other German-speaking dioceses, and soon became the basis for several translations and derivative works in Spanish, French, Italian, Dutch, Portuguese, Japanese, and other languages abroad. Although we have omitted the period illustrations of Professor Albert Burkart, this volume faithfully reproduces its first English edition of 1957—Herder and Herder's *A Catholic Catechism*—without any change to that body text, which appeared under the Nottingham imprimatur of W. E. Grasar, later bishop of Shrewsbury.

As the most chronologically recent of the many historical catechisms featured in the Tradivox series, several aspects of this text are worthy of special remark. The first is the various nominations of some of the sacraments, reflecting the changing parlance of the time: the last sacrament is variously named as "holy anointing," "anointing of the sick," "extreme unction," and "last anointing." Bishops are said to partake in the sacrament of holy orders as both "consecrated" as well as "ordained." Regarding the Eucharist, contemporary English readers should not mistake the translation of the German *brotbrechung* ("bread-breaking"); far from being diminished, the true presence of Jesus Christ in the consecrated species is clearly emphasized in Lessons 75, 76, and 79.

The most notable quality of this catechism is its unique and eminently useful structure, demonstrating an extensive consultation with experts in both teaching and pastoral ministry. Within the overarching five-tier format, each lesson reflects the markedly German penchant for organization and didactic attention. Nearly every lesson begins with a thematic scripture reference, and is followed by a more expanded catechesis, reflection questions, points for apologetics and making personal resolutions, resonances within scripture, history, and liturgy, student activities, and a concluding verse or exhortation. Such a systematic presentation, remaining concise while also varied in its many elements, proved immediately useful not only to instructors in the classroom, but also parents, pastors of souls, and students of the period.

Another outstanding feature of this catechism is its employment of classical terms and explanations, which it maintains as intelligible, relevant, and suitable even for "a pupil's book." In this, the German bishops present an admirable balance of theological precision and contemporary examples for understanding: a hallmark of the best Catholic catechetical tradition over the centuries.

Interestingly, this same approach of teaching concrete doctrinal formulations in classical terms would be widely abandoned—if not flatly rejected—by many Rhineland bishops within the decade, as the Dutch bishops would assert in 1965: "The renewal which found expression in the Second Vatican Council...required a new type of book. ... [Our *New Catechism* is therefore] an effort to enunciate God's ineffable mystery in the language of our times." Standing as a kind of historical marker on the threshold of this major methodological shift, we are pleased to offer readers this new edition of *A Catholic Catechism.*

## *Editorial Note*

Our *Catholic Catechism Index* series generally retains only the doctrinal content of those catechisms it seeks to reproduce, as well as that front matter most essential to establishing the credibility of each work as an authentic expression of the Church's common doctrine, e.g., any episcopal endorsement, *nihil obstat*, or *imprimatur*. However, it should be noted that especially prior to the eighteenth century, a number of catechisms were so immediately and universally received as reliably orthodox texts (often simply by the reputation of the author or publisher), that they received no such "official" approval; or if they did, it was often years later and in subsequent editions. We therefore include both the original printing date in our Table of Contents, and further edition information in the Preface above.

Our primary goal has been to bring these historical texts back into publication in readable English copy. Due to the wide range of time periods, cultures, and unique author styles represented in this series, we have made

*Woodcut depicting an early method used in the production of Catholic catechisms, circa 1568.*

a number of editorial adjustments to allow for a less fatiguing read, more rapid cross-reference throughout the series, and greater research potential for the future. While not affecting the original content, these adjustments have included adopting a cleaner typesetting and simpler standard for capitalization and annotation, as well as remedying certain anachronisms in spelling or grammar.

At the same time, in deepest respect for the venerable age and subject matter of these works, we have been at pains to adhere as closely as possible to the original text: retaining archaisms such as "doth" and "hallowed," and avoiding any alterations that might affect the doctrinal content or authorial voice. We have painstakingly restored original artwork wherever possible, and where the rare explanatory note has been deemed necessary, it is not made in the text itself, but only in a marginal note. In some cases, our editorial refusal to "modernize" the content of these classical works may require a higher degree of attention from today's reader, who we trust will be richly rewarded by the effort.

We pray that our work continues to yield highly readable, faithful reproductions of these time-honored monuments to Catholic religious instruction: catechisms once penned, promulgated, and praised by bishops across the globe. May these texts that once served to guide and shape the faith and lives of millions now do so again; and may the scholars and saints once involved in their first publication now intercede for all who take them up anew. *Tolle lege!*

Sincerely in Christ,
Aaron Seng

# TRADIVOX

## VOLUME XIX

# A CATHOLIC CATECHISM

HERDER AND HERDER
DISTRIBUTORS
BURNS & OATES
LONDON

# A CATHOLIC CATECHISM

HERDER AND HERDER
DISTRIBUTORS
BURNS & OATES
LONDON

# Introduction

It is our great good fortune that we are Christians. We have received God's grace abundantly, and we know what our business in the world is to be, and what a marvelous goal awaits us.

## *LESSON 1*

### *Of the Glory of Our Calling and of Our Task on Earth*

Before baptism, the priest asks the person to be baptized: "What do you desire of God's Church?" The candidate answers: "Faith." Then the priest asks: "What does faith hold out to you?" to which the candidate replies: "Eternal life." The priest reminds the candidate: "If you would enter into life, keep the commandments: you must love the Lord your God with your whole heart and your whole soul and your whole mind, and your neighbor as yourself."

When we were brought to be baptized, the priest received us in the name of God's Church. Through the words of the priest, we were made welcome by the whole fellowship of the believers, the countless numbers of the saints, as well as by Jesus Christ, our Savior and Lord, who will bring us to the Father through the Holy Spirit.

By means of baptism, the rich treasures of God's Church were opened to us: faith, which Christ gave us; the sacraments, through which he bestows on us his divine life; the commandments and his own example, which point out the way to heaven.

At baptism, we professed the faith through our sponsors, we renounced Satan and the life of sin, and we promised to live as children of God.

Now we are to carry out our task in the world as children of God: to acknowledge him, to grow in the knowledge of him, to love him with all our heart, to adore him, and to serve him with all our might.

If we are God's children in this world and do his will, we shall one day live forever with him.

*Consider.* 1) Who received us when we were brought to be baptized. 2) What treasures were opened to us through baptism? 3) What did our sponsors do in our stead at baptism?

1. **Why are we on earth?**

We are on earth to learn to know God, to love and serve him, and so one day to live with him forever.

*For my life.* I shall always be thankful to God that I am a Christian. I shall often ask myself: "What is it that God wants from me?"

*From holy scripture.* "The scene of your approach now is Mount Sion, is the heavenly Jerusalem, city of the living God; here are gathered thousands upon thousands of angels, here is the assembly of those firstborn sons whose names are written in heaven, here is God sitting in judgment on all men, here are the spirits of just men, now made perfect; here is Jesus, the spokesman of the new covenant..."[1]—"Fight the good fight of faith, lay thy grasp on eternal life, that life thou wert called to..."[2]—"It is written, the Lord thy God shalt thou adore, and him only shalt thou serve."[3]

*The teaching of the saints.* "Man was created to praise God, his Lord, to give him honor, and so to save his soul."[4]

*Things to do.* 1) On what occasions are the vows of baptism renewed? 2) What words can you use to thank God for the gift of faith?

No treasure more wondrous
No honor or good of this world is greater
than the Catholic faith.[5]

1 Heb 12:22-24
2 1 Tm 6:12
3 Mt 4:10
4 Ignatius of Loyola, *Spiritual Exercises*, "First Week"
5 Augustine

## LESSON 2

### *The Church Is the Guardian and Teacher of Our Faith*

Our Lord Jesus Christ once chose seventy-two disciples and sent them ahead into every city and place whither he himself was to come. And he said to them: "He who hears you, hears me, and he who despises you, despises me; and he who despises me, despises him that sent me."[6]

It is the holy Catholic Church which instructs us in the faith we have received in baptism. The Church is the guardian and teacher of our faith. She sends us priests and teachers who make known this faith in her name. She puts into our hands the books which help us to learn more about our faith: the Bible, the catechism, the missal, and the prayer book.

Christ, who is God's Son, has given the Church full authority to teach us. He said to the apostles: "Go ye into the whole world, and preach the gospel to every creature."[7] Christ himself it is who teaches us through the mouth of the Church. He has said: "He that heareth you, heareth me."[8] The Church has put the most important truths of faith together in the Apostles' Creed. It is God's will that we should listen to the Church. We are to believe what she believes, and what she teaches us to believe. Thus we walk in the way of truth, and shall come to everlasting life.

*Consider.* 1) Who teaches us in the name of the Church? 2) Name the books which the Church gives us. 3) Who has given the Church authority to teach? 4) Where do we find a summary of the truths of faith?

2. **Who is the guardian and teacher of our faith?**
The guardian and teacher of our faith is the holy Catholic Church.

3. **Who teaches us through the mouth of the Church?**
Christ our Lord, the King of heaven, teaches us through the mouth of the Church.

[6] Cf. Lk 10:1-16
[7] Mk 16:15
[8] Lk 10:16

4. **Recite the Apostles' Creed.**

I believe in God the Father Almighty, Creator of heaven and earth;
and in Jesus Christ, his only Son, our Lord;
who was conceived by the Holy Ghost, born of the Virgin Mary;
suffered under Pontius Pilate, was crucified, died, and was buried.
He descended into hell; the third day he rose again from the dead;
he ascended into heaven; sitteth at the right hand of God the Father Almighty;
from thence he shall come to judge the living and the dead.
I believe in the Holy Ghost;
the holy Catholic Church; the communion of saints;
the forgiveness of sins;
the resurrection of the body;
and life everlasting. Amen.

*For my life.* I intend to live and die in the faith of the Church.

*From holy scripture.* "If anyone preaches to you what is contrary to the tradition you received, a curse upon him."[9]

*From the life of the Church.* The Church's instruction has been called the "catechesis" from the earliest times: its teacher is the "catechist," and the book used is the "catechism."

*The sign of the cross.* The whole of our faith is summed up and expressed in the sign of the cross: when we make this sign, we acknowledge our faith in the Father and the Son and the Holy Spirit, and in the saving which has been accomplished by means of the death of our Lord.

Faith of our fathers! Holy faith
We will be true to thee till death.

[9] Gal 1:9

# LESSON 3

## The Joyful News of God's Kingdom

One day, Jesus spoke to the people in parables saying: "The kingdom of heaven is likened to a king, who made a marriage for his son. And he sent his servants to call them that were invited to the marriage; and they would not come... Then he saith to his servants: 'Go ye therefore into the highways, and as many as you shall find, call to the marriage.' And his servants going forth into the ways gathered together all that they found, both bad and good; and the marriage was filled with guests."[10]

On the last day, God will no longer hide himself, but will appear, showing us his power and his love in all its glory. He will give to Christ, his Son, the glory which is due to him before the world, and will gather about Christ his children from all peoples. He will make them happy forever in his love, and fill the world with the glory of heaven. "I will create new heavens and a new earth."[11] That will be the completion of the kingdom of heaven in all its splendor. It has been compared with a marriage feast: God is the King, Christ is the bridegroom, mankind redeemed is the bride, and the new-made creation is the place in which the marriage is held.

God wills that all of us should belong to his kingdom. For this reason, he has sent his Son into the world. Jesus has proclaimed the kingdom of God to us, has saved us, and made us God's children.

In Christ, the kingdom of God has already come among us. God rules over us like a kind father, and gives us his grace. Christ, the heavenly bridegroom, is present among us; in the Eucharist, we already take part in his heavenly wedding feast. But the glory of God's kingdom is still hidden from us.

When Christ comes on the last day, we shall see the kingdom of God in the fullness of its glory. The enemies of God will have no part in the

[10] Mt 22:2-10
[11] Is 65:17

banquet of heaven, but the children of God will "shine in the kingdom of their Father like the sun,"[12] and celebrate the wedding feast of the Lamb.[13]

The kingdom of God is not only something God gives us, but something we must strive to build. The Christian who has been called to the kingdom of God must try with all his might to develop this kingdom in himself and in the world around him: "Thy kingdom come."

*Consider.* 1) What will God do on the last day? 2) Who is the King at the heavenly marriage feast; who is the bridegroom and who is the bride? 3) What is the room in which the feast is to be held? 4) What has God done that we may have a place in his kingdom? 5) In what sense can we say that the kingdom of heaven is already with us? 6) What will happen when the kingdom of God comes in all its splendor?

5. **When will the kingdom of God appear in all its glory?**
The kingdom of God will appear in all its glory on the last day.

6. **How has the kingdom of God already appeared among us?**
The kingdom of God has already appeared among us in Jesus Christ; but its glory is still hidden.

*For my life.* The kingdom of God must be of more importance to me than all the riches in the world.

*From holy scripture.* "And over all the earth the Lord shall be king."[14] "I will create new heavens and a new earth."[15]—When God's kingdom has been brought to completion on the last day, the saints in heaven will sing, "Alleluia! the Lord our God, the Almighty, has claimed his kingdom; let us rejoice and triumph and give him praise; the time has come for the wedding feast of the Lamb."[16]—"The kingdom of heaven is like unto a

[12] Mt 13:43
[13] Cf. Apoc 19:7
[14] Zac 14:9
[15] Is 65:17
[16] Apoc 19:6-7

treasure hidden in a field; which a man having found, hid it, and for joy thereof goeth, and selleth all that he hath, and buyeth that field."[17]

*Things to do.* 1) In what prayer do we ask that God's kingdom may come? 2) What must we do that God's kingdom may always grow? 3) At what time of her year does the Church direct our attention most particularly to the coming of God's kingdom? 4) In what parables has Jesus spoken of the kingdom of God?

[17] Mt 13:44

*SECTION I*

# Of God and Our Redemption

## God Our Father in Heaven

"I believe in God, the Father Almighty,
Creator of heaven and earth."
(1st Article of the Creed.)

Wonderful are the ways by which God leads us to his everlasting kingdom. When we consider them, we come to know God better, and to love him more deeply.

### *LESSON 4*

### *God Speaks to Us*

"Moses…was doing shepherd's work,…deep into the desert he led his flock, until he reached God's own mountain of Horeb. And here the Lord revealed himself through a flame that rose up from the midst of a bush. It seemed that the bush was alight, yet did not burn. 'Here is a great sight,' said Moses, 'I must go up and see more of it, a bush that does not waste by burning.' But now, as he saw him coming up to look closer, the Lord called to him from the midst of the bush: 'Moses, Moses'; and when he answered: 'I am here at thy command,' he was told: 'Do not come nearer; rather take the shoes from thy feet, thou art standing on holy ground.'

"Then he said: 'I am the God thy father worshipped, the God of Abraham and Isaac and Jacob.' And Moses hid his face; he dared not look on the open sight of God."[18]

God who is great and holy has bent down through love for us men, and has spoken to us. Under the old covenant, he spoke by means of the patriarchs and the prophets. Under the new covenant, he has spoken to us through his Son, Jesus Christ, and his apostles: "In old days, God spoke to our fathers in many ways, and by many means, through the prophets; now at last in these times he has spoken to us with a Son to speak for him."[19]

God has spoken to us to tell us who he is and what he does; what we are and what we are to do. He has opened to us truths which otherwise would have remained forever secret; God has revealed himself. What God has revealed, he lets us know by means of his Church. He speaks through her; repeating for all men what he once said. He gives us light and strength to receive his word, to understand, and to do it.

When God speaks to us, we catch sight of everything which exists: God himself, our life, the world; and we see everything in a new light. We cannot fully understand the secrets of God, but they can fill our hearts with reverence and thankfulness, with joy and with strength.

*Consider.* 1) Why has God spoken to us? 2) What does *revelation* mean? 3) What has God revealed to us? 4) How has God arranged for his revelation to be proclaimed? 5) What benefits do we receive when God speaks to us?

7. **Through whom has God revealed himself to us?**
God has revealed himself to us under the old covenant through the patriarchs and prophets, and under the new covenant through Jesus Christ and the apostles.

*For my life.* I shall believe what God has said, no matter what else I may hear.

[18] Ex 3:1-6
[19] Heb 1:1-2

*From holy scripture.* "No lamp like thy word to guide my feet, to show light on my path."[20]—When Samuel heard God calling to him, he answered: "Speak on Lord, thy servant is listening."[21]

## *LESSON 5*

### *God Is Truthful and Faithful, Eternal, and Changeless*

"It is not for God to gainsay himself, as men do, to alter like the things of earth; must he not make good his word, fulfill his promise?"[22]

God always speaks the truth. Men can be mistaken and deceive others. God can neither err nor lie. "God is light, and in him there is no darkness."[23] God is truthful.

God keeps his promises. He has sent the Savior whom he had promised under the old law. He will also keep to what he has promised us. God is faithful.

God fulfills what he threatens when men will not listen to him. He had threatened the flood, the plagues of Egypt and other punishments, and let them come upon the men who had refused to do penance. He will punish us as well, if we sin and do no penance. "Make no mistake about it: you cannot cheat God."[24]

Once there was no world and no men. But God always is. He always was and he always will be. He has no beginning and no end: there is no yesterday or tomorrow with him. God is eternal. "Before the hills came to birth, before the whole frame of the world was engendered, from eternity to eternity, O God, thou art."[25]

The world and men change. But God remains ever the same: he never grows old and never changes. God is changeless. "Heaven and earth will perish, but thou wilt remain; they will all be like a cloak that grows

[20] Ps 118:105
[21] 1 Kgs 3:10
[22] Nm 23:19
[23] 1 Jn 1:5
[24] Gal 6:7
[25] Ps 89:2

threadbare, and thou wilt lay them aside like a garment, and exchange them for new; thou art unchanging, thy years can never fail."[26]

*Consider.* What do we call God, meaning that he never changes?

8. **Why do we say: "God is truthful"?**

We say that God is truthful because he always speaks the truth: he can neither be mistaken nor tell lies.

9. **Why do we say: "God is faithful"?**

We say God is faithful because he always does what he has promised.

10. **Why do we say: "God is eternal"?**

We say God is eternal because he always was and always will be: he has no beginning and no end.

*For my life.* I shall always speak the truth and keep my word, because God my Father in heaven is always truthful and keeps his promises.

*From holy scripture.* "With the Lord, a day counts as a thousand years, and a thousand years as a day."[27] — "With God is no change, no swerving from his course."[28]

*The teaching of the saints.* "Consider how quickly men change and how little one can rely on them. Therefore, hold fast to God who cannot change."[29]

*Things to do.* 1) Search the Bible to find occasions when: a) God promised something and then kept his promise; b) God threatened something and then carried out his threat. 2) In what prayers of the Mass do we speak of the "eternal God"?

Infinite thy vast domain,
Everlasting is thy reign.

[26] Ps 101:27-28
[27] 2 Pt 3:8
[28] Jas 1:17
[29] Teresa of Avila

## LESSON 6

### *God Reveals Himself through the Created World*

The writer of the book of Wisdom says that men who do not know God must be very foolish. They see the things that have been made, but take no notice of him who made them. If men are delighted by the beauties of creation, they should realize that the master of creation is even more glorious, for it was the source of all beauty who made things beautiful. And if men wonder at the power and efficacy of natural things, they ought to be able to see that he who made these things is even more powerful. For the greatness and beauty of creatures reveals to man the Creator of them all.[30]

When we look upon the universe about us, the stars of heaven and all that is on the earth, we must marvel at the wonderful order which is in them all. All things, every creature, has its place in the great world. There must be someone who has thought out and brought this order into being; there must be an all-wise and all-powerful Creator to have made all this.

Each living thing is a work of art. Plants and animals are so made that they can live and grow and multiply. The human body too is formed marvelously, every part fitted to its purpose. These living beings cannot have given themselves such wonderful arrangements; they were the gift of an all-wise and all-powerful God.

Within each of us is the voice of conscience. It tells us what is good and what is evil. Conscience speaks to us, whether we like it or not. We have not given ourselves a conscience; we have not received it from others, either. It must have been a holy lawgiver and just judge who put it into our hearts.

But from created things we cannot learn about God's own inner life, nor about his plans for our salvation; these are God's secrets which we come to know only from his revealing them.

*Consider.* 1) How do we come to know God: a) from the marvelous order in the world about us; b) from the purposeful dispositions of living

[30] Cf. Ws 13:1-5

things; c) from the voice of conscience? 2) What is it that we can know only from revelation?

11. **Through what things does God make himself known?**
God makes himself known: 1) through the world we see around us; 2) through our conscience; 3) above all, through his revelation.

*For my life.* When I see the beautiful world, I shall think to myself: "God, you are much greater and more beautiful than anything I can see."

*From holy scripture.* "See how the skies proclaim God's glory, how the vault of heaven betrays his craftsmanship!"[31]—"The very beasts will tell thee, the birds in the air will be thy counselors; the secret is known in every cranny of the earth, the fish in the sea will make it known to thee; none doubts, I tell thee, that all this is the Lord's doing."[32]—"As for the gentiles, though they have no law to guide them, there are times when they carry out the precepts of the law unbidden, finding in their own natures a rule to guide them in default of any other rule; and this shows that the obligations of the law are written in their hearts; their conscience utters its own testimony."[33]—"The fool hath said in his heart: 'There is no God.'"[34]

*Things to do.* Name some of the examples from nature from which you see very clearly that an all-wise Creator must have made everything.

Creation is a book
Wherein who wisely reads
Can ever find the line
That to its author leads.[35]

[31] Ps 18:2
[32] Jb 12:7-9
[33] Rom 2:14-15
[34] Ps 13:1
[35] Angelus Silesius, a German poet

# *LESSON 7*

## *God Cares for Us*

When the Israelites marched out of Egypt, God went before them in a pillar of fire, and showed them the way. He led them through the Red Sea, and saved them from the army of Pharao. Then, for many years, he led them through the desert. When they were to make camp, the pillar sank downward; when it was time to go on, the pillar rose up once more. God fed the Israelites with manna and gave them water from the very stones to drink. In this way he led them into the land he had promised long before to Abraham and to his descendants.[36]

Just as God cared for the Israelites during their journey into the land he had promised them, so he cares for us on our way to our heavenly home. He lights the way; he makes us holy; he protects us from the devil our enemy, and feeds us with the bread of heaven. God leads us lovingly and gives us everything we need on this journey to heaven.

God it is who gives us the things of this world—food, clothes, health, and talents. Everything is from our Father's hand. And so, even the things of this world are meant to help us toward our everlasting salvation.

We rest in God's hands. He has thought out beforehand the smallest details of each of our lives, and directs each event to our happiness. "God cares for each of us as if each alone were the only object of his love; and he cares for all of us as he does for each."[37] This care God takes of us is called God's "providence." God is good to all of his creatures. He does not think of anything as of little worth; he cares for each thing he has made, and shows kindness toward them all in countless ways. God is kind.

*Consider.* 1) How does God care for us on the way to heaven? 2) Explain the phrase "God's providence."

[36] Cf. Ex 13-17

[37] Augustine, *Confessions*, Bk. 3, Ch. 11

12. **Why do we say God is kind?**

We say that God is kind because he cares for all his creatures and gives them countless benefits.

13. **How does God care for us?**

God leads us lovingly, and gives us everything we need on the way to heaven.

*For my life.* I will trust myself each day to God's kindly guidance and look upon everything good which I find as God's gift.

*From holy scripture.* "Be not solicitous, therefore, saying, 'What shall we eat'; or, 'What shall we drink'; or, 'Wherewith shall we be clothed,' for after all these things do the heathens seek. For your Father knoweth that you have need of all these things. Seek ye therefore first the kingdom of God and his justice: and all these things shall be added unto you."[38] — "And still Lord my trust in thee is not shaken…my fate is in thy hand."[39] — "The Lord is my shepherd. How can I lack anything?"[40]

*Things to do.* 1) How did God care for Joseph in Egypt? 2) How did the heavenly Father care for the Child Jesus? 3) Make up a prayer thanking God for all the good things he has done for you. 4) Make up a prayer expressing your trust in God. 5) In which prayers and hymns do we ask especially for the things we need in this life? 6) In what prayers and hymns do we thank God for his gifts?

He is our shepherd true,
With watchful care unsleeping;
On us his erring sheep,
An eye of pity keeping.
He with a mighty arm
The bonds of sin doth break;
And to our burdened hearts
In words of peace doth speak.

[38] Mt 6:31-33
[39] Ps 30:15-16
[40] Ps 22:1

# *LESSON 8*

## *God Is Everywhere and Knows All Things*

When King Solomon had built the Temple at Jerusalem, he had the ark of the covenant brought into it with all ceremony. And as the priests carried the ark into the holy of holies a cloud filled the house of the Lord. Then Solomon fell down upon his knees and prayed: "Lord, my people's God, the skies cannot contain thee, how much less this house which I have built? Yet, O Lord, do not let this prayer go all unheeded...Listen to the cry of entreaty thy servant makes before thee this day." The Lord appeared to Solomon and said to him: "Never a day but my eyes and my heart are attentive here."[41]

God is not only in heaven; he is on earth, and in all places as well—God is near to us everywhere. "It is in him that we live and move and have our being."[42] God is all-present. In many places God is present in a special way. When we were baptized, the Holy Trinity came to dwell within us.

God fills the whole of his creation, and yet is not confined to any single place, and is not enclosed in any space. Heaven and earth cannot contain him. God is boundless.

God sees everything that happens, and hears everything that is said. He looks upon us human beings with a very special love, and hears our prayers. He sees not only our outward appearance but looks into our hearts as well. He has understanding not only for what we say, but for the most hidden cry our hearts may utter.

God knows everything: he knows the past, the present, and the future. He knows our most secret thoughts and wishes. "From him no creature can be hidden, everything lies bare, everything is brought face-to-face with him, this God to whom we must give our account."[43] God is all-knowing.

*Consider.* Where is God present in a special way?

[41] Cf. 3 Kgs 7:51-9:3
[42] Acts 17:28
[43] Heb 4:13

14. **Why do we say that God is everywhere?**
We say that God is everywhere because he is present in every place, in heaven, and upon the earth.

15. **Why do we say that God is boundless?**
We say that God is boundless because heaven and earth cannot contain him.

16. **Why do we say that God is all-knowing?**
We say that God is all-knowing because he knows everything: he knows the past, the present, the future, and even our most secret thoughts.

*For my life.* Wherever I am, whatever I do, I know God sees me through and through!

*From holy scripture.* "Where can I go then to take refuge from thy spirit, to hide from thy view? If I should climb up to heaven, thou art there; if I sink down to the world beneath, thou art present still. If I could wing my way eastward, or find a dwelling beyond the sea, still would I find thee beckoning to me, thy right hand upholding me."[44]—Jesus said to his disciples: "The very hairs of your head are numbered."[45]—"Your Father knoweth what is needful for you, before you ask him."[46]

*Things to do.* On what occasion especially should we remember that God knows and sees everything?

## LESSON 9

## God Is Holy and Just

When Isaias was called to be a prophet, he saw the glory of God. He wrote: "I saw the Lord sitting on a throne that towered above me, the skirts of his robe filling the temple. Above it rose the figures of the Seraphim, each of them six-winged…And ever the same cry passed between them: 'Holy,

[44] Ps 138:7-10
[45] Mt 10:30
[46] Mt 6:8

holy, holy is the Lord God of hosts.' The lintels over the door rang with the sound of that cry, and smoke went up, filling the temple courts.

"'Alas,' said I, 'that I must keep silence; my lips, and the lips of all my countrymen are polluted with sin; and yet these eyes have looked upon their King, the Lord of hosts.'"[47]

God is infinitely exalted above all created things. "His dwelling is in unapproachable light."[48] No creature can see him if he does not show himself; no one can come near to God unless God raises him up toward himself. God is holy. Therefore it is fitting and proper that angels and men should adore him.

God is infinitely exalted above everything that is evil. He loves always what is good in itself and perfect. He hates and detests all evil because it is the very opposite of what he is himself.

Since God is holy, he wants us to be holy too. That is why he bends down to us in graciousness, cleanses us from our sins, and fills us with his life of holiness. And that is why he demands of us that we should love what is good and hate what is evil. All holiness in heaven and upon earth comes from him.

On the last day, God will show his infinite holiness to the entire world. In the light of him, all good and evil will stand revealed. No man can escape his judgment. God will cast the wicked into hell forever; but the good will be allowed to see him face-to-face forever. God will reward each man or punish him according to his merits. "He will award to every man what his acts have deserved."[49] God is infinitely just.

Already in this world God rewards and punishes: to the good he gives inner peace and joy; he lets the evil feel the unrest of a bad conscience. God rewards also with outward good fortune and punishes with outward misfortune and suffering. Still it often happens in this world that the good have a bad time of it while the wicked prosper. Nonetheless, in this life no one who despises God is completely happy, and no good man is completely unhappy. However, God does not give to anyone a full reward or a full punishment until the next life.

[47] Is 6:1-5
[48] 1 Tm 6:16
[49] Rom 2:6

Only then shall we recognize how just God is.

*Consider.* 1) What does the sentence mean: "His dwelling is in unapproachable light"? 2) Why does God always love what is good? 3) Why does God hate all that is evil? 4) What does God do that we may also be holy? 5) What will happen when God shows his infinite holiness to the whole world on the last day? 6) In what way does God give rewards even in this world? 7) How does God punish even in this world? 8) When will men receive the full measure of their reward and punishment?

17. **Why do we say: "God is holy"?**

We say God is holy:

1. because he is infinitely exalted above all created things;
2. because he always loves what is good and detests what is evil.

18. **Why do we say: "God is just"?**

We say that God is just because he rewards the good and punishes the evil, according as each deserves.

*For my life.* Because God is holy and has made me holy too, I will love what God loves, and detest what he detests.

*From holy scripture.* "Who art thou, friend, to bandy words with God?"[50]—"Be ye holy because I, the Lord your God, am holy."[51]—"What God asks of you is that you should sanctify yourselves."[52]

*From the Church's life.* Each time we assist at Mass, we should join in the song of the angels: "Holy, holy, holy Lord God of hosts, thy glory fills all heaven and earth."

*Things to do.* 1) How do the priests and the faithful at Mass express their reverence for God's holiness? 2) What Bible stories tell us how God showed his holiness to men? 3) In what Bible stories do we read that God rewards the good? In which ones that he punishes evil? 4) In which petitions of the Our Father do we ask that God may be honored and his holy will fulfilled?

[50] Rom 9:20
[51] Lv 19:2
[52] 1 Thes 4:3

## *LESSON 10*

### *God Brings Good Out of Evil*

When the patriarch Jacob was dead, Joseph's brethren feared that he might take his revenge on them for the evil things they had once done to him. But Joseph said to them: "Do not be afraid; you thought to do me harm, but God turned it all to good account."[53]

God wills that our life should be a time of testing. Here on earth we are left free to decide for ourselves whether we will serve him. God encourages us to do what is good, and warns us against evil; he gives us the grace we need to undergo this time of testing. But because we do not yet see God, it is possible for us to abuse our freedom, and sin against him. God permits sin. It may seem to us that sin can interfere with God's plans, or even defeat them.

But in reality God knows how to turn evil to good. He rules the world in such a way that evil must serve his holy purposes. Even when God's Son died upon the cross, it looked as if the devil and sin had won a victory; really, however, the devil was overcome and the world was freed from sin and everlasting death. The mystery of sin remains something we cannot grasp so long as we live on earth. But on the last day, we shall be filled with astonishment when we see how all the evil in the world was made to serve the purposes of God.

*Consider.* 1) What does God do so that we may do what is good? 2) Why is it possible for us to sin on earth? 3) How is it that sin cannot interfere with or defeat God's plans? 4) How did the death of Christ on the cross show that God brings good out of evil?

19. **Why does God permit sin?**

God permits sin:

1. because he wants us to have freedom to decide whether we will serve him;
2. because he knows how to bring good out of evil.

[53] Cf. Gn 50:15-21

*For my life.* When I see evil in the world, I will not doubt God or become discouraged, but trust steadfastly that he will turn evil to good. Jesus won the victory over sin and the devil.

*From holy scripture.* "What means this turmoil among the nations? Why do the people cherish vain dreams? He who dwells in heaven is laughing at their threats, the Lord makes light of them."[54]

*Things to do.* How did God bring good out of the following evils: a) the injustice that Jacob's sons did against their brother Joseph; b) the stoning of St. Stephen; c) the persecution of the Christians in Jerusalem?

## *LESSON 11*

### *God Leads Us through Suffering to Salvation*

When the Israelites refused to listen to the warning of the prophets, God allowed heavy sufferings to come upon them. King Nabuchodonosor conquered Jerusalem, destroyed the city, burned the Temple, and took the people as captives to Babylon. During their Babylonian captivity, the Israelites came to themselves and did penance. Their faith in the one true God was strengthened, and their longing for the promised Redeemer was awakened anew. At the same time, the heathens among whom the Israelites were living learned from them of the true God and of the Savior who was to come into the world. In this way the punishment which God had sent became a blessing for Israelites and heathens alike.

God takes no pleasure in suffering and death. "Death was never of God's fashioning; not for his pleasure does life cease to be."[55] It is through sin that suffering and death came into the world. Our own sins too bring suffering upon ourselves and our fellow men.

God allows suffering to come upon us so that by this means he may lead us to salvation. God always has a holy purpose in everything he does, even though we do not understand it.

[54] Ps 2:1, 4
[55] Ws 1:13

God leads us through suffering to the lesson that we must turn aside from evil. Suffering can be a wholesome punishment through which we come to see our own fault. God also sends us suffering to purify us, just as one purifies gold in a fire. Through sickness, poverty, and other troubles, he wishes to cleanse us from faults and imperfections.

God also permits suffering to come upon us in order that we may remain good. Suffering is at the same time a testing: we are to show that even under suffering we fulfill the holy will of God. When we bear suffering as sent to us by God, we become like Christ. If we must suffer because we are Christians, we should think of the words of Christ: "Blessed are ye, when they revile you, and persecute you, and speak all that is evil against you untruly, for my sake; be glad and rejoice for your reward is very great in heaven."[56]

Through his suffering and death, Christ has made atonement for the sins of the world. Through suffering, God gives us the opportunity to atone with Christ.

If we suffer with Christ in this life, we shall also be glorified with him one day in heaven. Every pain which we have borne in obedience to God will earn for us a reward in heaven.

*Consider.* 1) Where do suffering and death come from? 2) Explain how God leads us through suffering to salvation. 3) How do we become like Christ by suffering? 4) What will God do if we bear suffering as coming from him?

20. **How did suffering and death come into the world?**
Suffering and death came into the world through sin.

21. **Why does God allow us to suffer?**
God permits us to suffer because through suffering he wants to lead us to salvation.

*For my life.* When I meet a difficulty in life, I shall pray as Jesus did: "Thy will be done." When I must suffer, I shall think of my crucified Savior.

[56] Mt 5:11-12

*From holy scripture.* "Meanwhile, we are well assured that everything helps to assure the good of those who love God."[57]—"Not that I count these present sufferings as the measure of that glory which is to be revealed in us."[58]

*Rule of life.* Don't ask: Why does God let me suffer? Ask instead: How can I best use this test?

*Things to do.* 1) Look for hymns and sayings which encourage us to bear suffering with patience. 2) Write a letter to comfort a man who has lost everything.

When you suffer, don't complain;
Jesus suffered far more pain!

## LESSON 12

### God Is All-Wise and All-Powerful

In his letter to the Romans, St. Paul tells how God marvelously carries out his holy plans. He continues: "How deep is the mine of God's wisdom, of his knowledge; how inscrutable are his jugdments, how undiscoverable are his ways! Who has ever understood the Lord's thoughts, or been his counselor? Who ever was the first to give, and so earned his favors? All things find in him their origin, their impulse, the center of their being; to him be glory throughout all ages. Amen."[59]

When God created the world, he gave it a wonderful order or design. But through the devil and through the sins of men, disorder has come into the world. Yet God knows how to order all things so that he achieves his holy purposes in spite of that. God is all-wise.

God directs the lives of men also according to his holy designs. It was through God's wise plans that Joseph was favored by Pharao, and the child Moses was preserved from death. We experience God's wisdom in its most

57 Rom 8:28
58 Rom 8:18
59 Rom 11:33-36

wonderful form in the way he leads us to heaven. As long as we are on earth, there will, of course, be many occasions when we cannot understand his plans. God says: "Not mine to think as you think, deal as you deal; by the full height of heaven above earth, my dealings are higher than your dealings, my thoughts than your thoughts."[60]

God carries his plans through by his own divine power. He made the world out of nothing by his own will. He holds the entire world in his hand, and guides each being powerfully and yet tenderly. We recognize God's supreme power most dearly in miracles, above all in the resurrection of his Son. The whole of his power will be revealed on the last day, when he makes the world anew. "Nothing can be impossible with God."[61] He can do everything that he wills. God is all-powerful. Nature shows us also how wise and powerful God is. The heaven with its stars, the creatures of the earth, the animals and plants, our own body with its marvelous structure and the play of its powers: these all declare that God is wise and powerful.

*Consider.* 1) How does God show his wisdom: a) in his ruling of the world; b) in the life of individuals? 2) In what ways does God show his power?

22. **Why do we say that God is all-wise?**

We say that God is all-wise because he knows how to order all things in such a way that his holy purposes are fulfilled.

23. **Why do we say that God is all-powerful?**

We say that God is all-powerful because he can do all that he wills.

*For my life.* God, who is all-wise and all-powerful, is my Father. How happy and carefree I should be!

*Proverb.* The sky, the earth and every flower
Show forth God's wisdom, love, and power.

[60] Is 55:8-9
[61] Lk 1:37

*From holy scripture.* "What diversity, Lord, in thy creatures! What wisdom has designed them all."[62]—"In heaven and on earth, in the sea and in the deep waters beneath us, the Lord accomplishes his will."[63]

## *LESSON 13*

## *God Has Mercy on Sinners*

One day, Jesus told the Pharisees a parable: There was a certain man who had two sons. And the younger of those said to his father, "Father, give me that portion of the estate which falls to me." So he divided his property between them. The younger son used up his portion of the inheritance and found himself in deep want. Thereupon he went back to his father. But while he was still a long way off, his father saw him, and took pity on him; running up, he threw his arms around his neck, and kissed him. Then he said to his servants: "Bring out the best robe, and clothe him in it; put a ring on his hand, and shoes on his feet. Then bring out the calf that has been fatted and kill it; let us eat and make merry; for my son here was dead, and has come to life again; was lost and is found."[64]

It is God's will that sinners be saved. "As I am the living God, the sinner's death is none of my contriving! I would have him leave his sin, and live on."[65] He sent his own Son into the world to "search out and save what was lost."[66]

God calls the sinner to do penance. He causes him to recognize his sin, and wakens within him the longing for the home of his heavenly Father.

God is patient with us weak men. For this reason, he often gives sinners a long time to repent and be sorry for their sins; God waits on the sinner, as the father does upon his lost son. God is patient.

[62] Ps 103:24
[63] Ps 134:6
[64] Cf. Lk 15:11-24
[65] Ez 33:11
[66] Lk 19:10

When the sinner repents, God forgives him. He bends down to him with great love, and takes him to himself again as his own child. No human being is of so merciful a heart, or can so generously forgive, as our heavenly Father. The worst sinners need not doubt him. God is merciful.

*Consider.* 1) How has God shown most clearly that he wills to save sinners? 2) What does God do to bring sinners to repent? 3) What does God do when a man does repent of his sins?

24. **Why do we say: "God is merciful"?**
We say that God is merciful because he calls the sinner to penance and gladly forgives him when he repents.

25. **Why do we say: "God is patient"?**
We say God is patient because he often gives the sinner a long time in which to repent.

*For my life.* Because God is merciful, I will be merciful too. Since God has had patience with me, I will have patience with others.

*From holy scripture.* "Bless the Lord, my soul, remembering all he has done for thee, how he pardons all thy sins, heals all thy mortal ills, rescues thy life from deadly peril, crowns thee with the blessings of his mercy...For his own worshippers the Lord has a father's pity."[67]—"Crimson-dyed be your guilt, it shall turn snow-white."[68]—"The Lord is not being dilatory over his promise, as some think; he is only giving you more time because his will is that all of you should attain repentance, not that some should be lost."[69]

*Things to do.* 1) Look in the Bible for examples of God's mercy and patience. 2) What does Christ teach us in the parable of the unmerciful servant?

[67] Ps 102:2-4, 13
[68] Is 1:18
[69] 2 Pt 3:9

# LESSON 14

## God Is Love

St. John writes: "What has revealed the love of God where we are concerned is that he has sent his only begotten Son into the world, so that we might have life through him...God is love; he who dwells in love dwells in God, and God in him."[70]

God has loved us from eternity; he always loved us before we were able to love him. "With unchanging love have I loved thee."[71] He has made us because of his love, he has redeemed us through his Son, and made us his children. Out of love he warns, punishes, and forgives. God is love.

Since God loves us, we may also love him. He wills that we should call him Father, and trust him with childlike confidence. We need not fear him as slaves would, but should love him as children do.

God's love has often taken the saints by storm. They saw that no one could satisfy their hearts' need save God alone. Therefore, they wanted nothing so much as to love God ever more and more. God showed them in turn the ever-greater riches of his love.

God longs to see each of us entirely united to him. He wills that we should come to him in heaven and live forever in love of him.

*Consider.* 1) How has God shown us his love? 2) How should we return God's love? 3) What has God's love spurred the saints to do?

26. **What does St. John say about the love of God?**
"God is love: he who dwells in love, dwells in God, and God in him."

*For my life.* Since God does everything out of love, I shall try to do everything out of love too.

[70] 1 Jn 4:9, 16
[71] Jer 31:3

*From holy scripture.* "God so loved the world that he gave up his only begotten Son, so that those who believe in him may not perish, but have eternal life."[72]

## *LESSON 15*

### *God Is Infinitely Perfect*

After the last supper, Jesus lifted up his eyes to heaven and prayed to his Father. And he said: "Now this is eternal life: that they may know thee, the only true God, and Jesus Christ whom thou hast sent."[73]

There is only one God. "The Lord alone is God, there can be no other."[74]

God is a "living God."[75] He is both life in himself, and the giver of all life. He allows us, his children, to have part in the life which he has in himself as God.

God's life is infinitely richer and higher than the life of created things. His intelligence masters the whole of what is, and his will holds and governs the universe. But God has no body as does a man, who can die. God is a Spirit. When holy scripture speaks about God's "eyes" and "hands," this means his knowledge and his power. Holy scripture speaks about God in pictures.

God is more glorious and holy than we could ever think or say: in him is all possible good. We creatures are imperfect, and we are limited. God has no limits, nor the least imperfection. He is infinitely perfect.

God has revealed to us the secret of his inner life. We know from his revelation that in the one God there are three Persons: the Father, the Son, and the Holy Spirit. God in the three Persons lives in boundless happiness forever and ever.

[72] Jn 3:16
[73] Jn 17:1-3
[74] 3 Kgs 8:60
[75] Jer 10:10

*Consider.* 1) Why do we call God "the living God"? 2) What does the Bible mean when it speaks of God's "eyes" and "hands"? 3) What is God's deepest secret?

27. **Why do we say that God is infinitely perfect?**
We say that God is infinitely perfect because he has every good quality without any limit whatever.

28. **Why do we call God a Spirit?**
We call God a Spirit because he has intelligence and will, but does not have a body.

*For my life.* God is a glorious mystery which I cannot fully understand. Therefore, I should think and speak of him only in a reverent way.

*From holy scripture.* "But the Lord God is in good earnest a God that lives, that has eternal dominion."[76]—"God is a spirit."[77] "Honor and glory through endless ages to the king of all the ages, the immortal, the invisible, who alone is God. Amen."[78]

*Things to do.* Write down all the qualities of God you can think of.

As with my hand I cannot span
The heavens or the earth below,
So God, who is ere time began,
My tiny mind can't fully know.

[76] Cf. Jer 10:10
[77] Jn 4:24
[78] 1 Tm 1:17

# Of the World's Creation, the Fall, and the Promise of Redemption

The first step in God's holy design was to create the world. With this great act of God, the history of the world and of mankind began.

## *LESSON 16*

## *God Created the World*

At the beginning of time, God created heaven and earth. He created light and the sky, the land and the sea, the stars of the heavens, and all the creatures upon the earth. And God saw everything that he had made and found it good.[79]

The world was not always there. It had a beginning. Nor did it come to be of its own accord: it came from God. It was God who made heaven and earth. God did not need any materials nor any tools to make the world, nor anyone to help him. He made the world out of nothing. "He spoke and they were made, he gave his command and their framework was fashioned."[80] By his almighty will alone he called everything into being. That is what we mean when we say that God created the world.

God did not have to make the world. Without it his life was infinitely full and happy.

God created the world in order to reveal his unbounded goodness and to share it with others. The universe was to reflect back his glory, and all created things were to receive something of his goodness. In addition, those creatures which had intelligence were to learn about him and come to love him, to serve him and glorify him, and thus to become happy and blessed forever. God made the world for his own glory and for the good

[79] Cf. Gn 1
[80] Ps 32:9

of his creatures. God loves the world which he has created. It is not his will that it should once more fall back to nothing. God sees to it that the world goes on existing; God keeps the world in being. God is always at work in his creation with his almighty power and wisdom and goodness. He determines the world's course, the history of its peoples, and the life of each individual person. He brings his creation surely to its eternal goal. God rules the world.

Since God has made everything, everything belongs to him. All beings and all things are at his disposal and are under his divine protection.

*Consider.* 1) What do we mean when we say God has "created the world"? 2) Why was it not necessary that God should create the world? 3) Why did God create the world? 4) Why does God sustain the world? 5) How does God rule the world? 6) What does it mean for us that God has created everything?

29. **Where does the world come from?**
The world comes from God; he created heaven and earth.

30. **For what purpose did God make heaven and earth?**
God made heaven and earth for his own glory and for the good of his creatures.

*Explanation.* The word *heaven* does not mean here God's heavenly kingdom where the angels and saints are, but the material heaven above us, containing the sun, moon, and stars.

*For my life.* Whenever I am enjoying God's beautiful world, I will not forget to thank him, for he made everything.

*From holy scripture.* "Our help is in the name of the Lord, who made heaven and earth."[81]

*The story of the creation in the Bible.* In this story, God wants to teach us what is important for our salvation: that he has made all things, that he has created man; that the laws which govern the universe and the lives of

[81] Ps 123:8

men are from him. These truths were expressed in such a way as to make them understandable to the people of the time when the Bible was written.

*Things to do.* 1) Pray the song of the three young men in the fiery furnace. 2) Pray Psalm 103. 3) What creatures and things are named in these two prayers?

## *LESSON 17*

### *God Has Created Angels*

"The Lord has set up his throne in heaven, rules with universal sway. Bless the Lord all you angels of his; angels of sovereign strength, that carry out his commandments, attentive to the word he utters; bless the Lord all you hosts of his, the servants that perform his will."[82]

God has created powerful beings who are wholly spirit, the angels. Angels have intelligence and free will, but no body. That is why we cannot see them.

God created the angels in his love, to look upon him and to live eternally with him. The angels could not do that by their own power; hence God gave them a share in his own divine life.

But before the angels were allowed to see God, they had first to be tested. Some of the angels failed the test and revolted against God. As punishment, they were thrown down into hell. They are called "evil spirits." Their leader is the devil (Satan, which means in Hebrew "the Enemy"). The evil spirits hate God and us, and seek to do us harm in soul and body.

The angels who remained true to God see God now, adore him and praise him in eternal happiness. They love God and serve him, fighting for his kingdom. They make known to us God's will, protect us in soul and body, and pray for us to God.

[82] Ps 102:19-21

The holy scriptures name different choirs of angels, such as cherubim and seraphim. We revere the archangel Michael as the leader of the angels in the war against Satan and the evil spirits.

God in his love has given to each of us an angel to be our companion. We call him our "guardian angel." The guardian angel loves us; he protects us in temptation and in danger, encourages us to do good, and helps us on the way to our heavenly home.

*Consider.* 1) Why did God create the angels? 2) What are the qualities of the angels? 3) What did God require from the angels before they might see him? 4) Why were some of the angels cast down into hell? 5) What do the angels who remained faithful to God do?

31. **What are angels?**
Angels are completely spiritual beings who adore God, love him, and carry out what he commands.

32. **What do the guardian angels do for us?**
The guardian angels protect us both in soul and body, pray for us, and encourage us to do good.

33. **What are the evil spirits?**
The evil spirits are fallen angels, who hate God and seek to ruin us in soul and body.

*For my life.* I will love my guardian angel, pray to him devoutly each day, follow his suggestions faithfully, and remember that he sees me everywhere.

*From holy scripture.* "He has given charge to his angels concerning thee, to watch over thee wheresoever thou goest; they will hold thee up with their hands lest thou shouldst chance to trip on a stone."[83]—Christ says: "See that you despise not one of these little ones; for I say to you, that their angels in heaven always see the face of my Father who is in

[83] Ps 90:11-12

heaven."[84]—Jesus calls Satan "the first murderer, a liar and the father of lies,"[85] "the prince of this world."[86]

*From the life of the Church.* The Church celebrates the feast of the archangel Gabriel on March 24th; that of the archangel Michael on September 29th; that of the Guardian Angels on October 2nd; and on October 24th the feast of the archangel Raphael.

*Things to do.* 1) Where do we read about angels in the Bible: a) in the old testament; b) in the new testament? 2) What is the meaning of the wings which angels usually have in pictures?

## *LESSON 18*

## *God Created Men*

"And God said: 'Let us make man, wearing our image and likeness...' So God made man in his own image, made him in the image of God... And now from the clay of the ground the Lord formed man, breathed into his nostrils the breath of life, and made of man a living person. God had planted a garden of delight, in which he now placed the man he had formed. Here, at the bidding of the Lord God, the soil produced all such trees as charm the eye and satisfy the taste; and here, in the middle of the garden grew the tree of life and the tree which brings knowledge of good and evil...So the Lord God took the man and put him into his garden of delight, to cultivate and tend it. And this was the command which the Lord God gave the man: 'Thou mayest eat thy fill of all the trees in the garden except the tree which brings knowledge of good and evil; if ever thou eatest of this, thy doom is death.'"[87]

God made the body of man out of earthly materials. He created the soul out of nothing. Through it he gave life to the body. The first human

[84] Mt 18:10
[85] Jn 8:44
[86] Jn 14:30
[87] Gn 1:26-2:15

beings were Adam and Eve; all men are descended from this original pair who are thus called our "first parents."

The soul of man is a spiritual thing. It has intelligence and can understand; it has a will and can make free choices. Because the soul is a spiritual being, it cannot die. In his soul, man is like God, the infinitely perfect Spirit, and is greater than all the other creatures in the world.

God made men in his love to see him and to live eternally with him; therefore, God gave them a share in his own inmost life. This great gift, which was in no way earned, we call "grace-life," or "sanctifying grace." By this gift of the life of grace, the first men became children of God and like God in a special way.

God also gave to our first parents some other wonderful gifts. They were allowed to live in paradise, where they were especially close to God. He illumined their understanding with a special light and strengthened their will with special power. Their longings and their strivings were all toward what was good. The first human beings were free from the inclination to do evil and lived happily in God's presence. Work was not tiresome for them; they were free from suffering, sickness, and all evil, and they were to be preserved from death. All these gifts we call the "special gifts of paradise." The graces which God gave to our first parents were to have been inherited by all men.

All men were to receive from Adam, along with their bodily life, the grace-life and the special gifts which Adam had had in paradise. All these gifts together we call "original grace."

Like the angels, the first men were to undergo a test. Therefore, God gave them a commandment. If they kept this commandment, they were to keep the grace-life and the special gifts of paradise for themselves and their descendants; if they disobeyed it, they were to lose these graces and gifts for themselves and for their children.

*Consider.* 1) What do we mean when we say: "God formed man out of the earth"? 2) By what means did God make man's body become alive? 3) What powers does man's soul possess? 4) Why cannot the soul of man die? 5) To whom is man like because of his soul? 6) In what special way were the first men like God? 7) What were the special gifts which man had in paradise? 8) How did God test the first men? 9) What was to happen if men passed the test? 10) What was to happen if men did not pass the test?

34. **How did God create man?**
God formed man from the dust of the earth, and then breathed into him the breath of life.

35. **What was the most precious gift which God gave to the first of mankind?**
The most precious gift which God gave to the first of mankind was the grace-life.

36. **What were men supposed to inherit from Adam besides the life of their bodies?**
Besides their bodily life, all men were to inherit from Adam the grace-life and the special gifts of paradise.

*For my life.* I shall show reverence to every person, because he bears the likeness of God.

*Things to do.* 1) How is man different from the beasts? 2) How is the soul different from the body? 3) How is the soul like to God? 4) How is the soul different from God?

## *LESSON 19*

### *Our First Parents Committed Sin*

"The serpent said to the woman: 'What is this command God has given you not to eat the fruit of any tree in the garden?' To which the woman answered: 'We can eat the fruit of any tree in the garden except the tree in the middle of it; it is this God has forbidden us to eat or even to touch, on pain of death.' And the serpent said to her: 'What is this talk of death? God knows well that as soon as you eat this fruit, your eyes will be opened, and you yourselves will be like God, knowing good and evil.' And with this, the woman, who saw that the fruit was good to eat, saw too how pleasant it was to look at, and charmed the eye, took some fruit from the tree and ate it; she gave some to her husband, and he ate with her."[88]

In the hour of their trial our first parents did not listen to God, but rather followed the devil and ate of the fruit; they wanted to be as God was. Adam and Eve knew clearly that they were disobeying God's command, and yet they did so of their own free will. They sinned seriously against God. This sin of Adam and Eve we call the "first sin" or "original sin."

By this sin committed in paradise, our first parents ceased to be the children of God; they lost the life of grace and were no longer fit to enter heaven. That was the worst result of their sin.

By their sin, they also lost the special gifts of paradise. They might no longer live in special nearness to God, and had to leave paradise. Their intelligence was darkened and their power of will was made weaker; they now had an inclination toward evil. They had many things to suffer, and had to earn daily food with much wearisome labor; and at the end of it all, they had to die. Through the sin of our first parents, the devil won power over mankind.

Although the first of the human race had sinned so grievously, God took pity on them. Because of the Savior who was to come, he gave them grace to recognize that they had sinned, and to be sorry. God forgave them their sin. But they had to endure as a penance the hardships of life in this world.

*Consider.* 1) Why was the original sin such a serious one? 2) What was the worst result of the original sin for our first parents? 3) What did our first parents lose along with the grace-life? 4) How did God take pity on our first parents?

37. **What sin did our first parents commit?**
Our first parents wanted to be like God, and therefore ate the forbidden fruit.

38. **What did our first parents lose by original sin?**
Through original sin, our first parents lost the life of grace and the special gifts of the state of paradise.

[88] Gn 3:1-6

*For my life.* The sin of Adam shows me that mortal sin is the greatest misfortune. I will be ready to lose anything rather than commit a mortal sin.

## *LESSON 20*

### *The Results of Original Sin for All Men*

"It was through one man that guilt came into the world; and since death came owing to guilt, death was handed on to all mankind by one man."[89]

Because Adam, who was the head of all mankind, committed sin, the guilt of his sin has been inherited by all his descendants. This is called "original sin," or "the heritage of guilt." Because of Adam's sin, we are born without the grace-life, which, according to God's plan, we were to inherit from Adam. Only God's Mother remained free of the heritage of guilt by a special privilege of grace.

In addition, the evil results of the original sin have descended on all men; that is why we have an inclination to sin, which is called "concupiscence." This shows itself in an unreasonable desire for the things of this world, for example, pleasure, possessions, honor, and fame. Moreover, men have to live among many troubles and sufferings and must finally die. Through original sin, the devil obtained power over the world.

If God had not shown pity to sinful men, no one would have been able to reach his eternal goal, for no one can redeem himself.

*Consider.* 1) Why is the guilt of Adam's sin inherited by all men? 2) What do we mean by "the heritage of guilt"? 3) Who was the only person to remain free from this heritage of guilt? 4) What were the results of the heritage of guilt?

39. **What misfortune did Adam's sin bring upon all mankind?**
All men have inherited the guilt of Adam's sin and its evil consequences.

[89] Rom 5:12

40. **What does the heritage of guilt consist of?**
The heritage of guilt consists of this: that, because of Adam's sin, we come into the world without the grace-life which, according to God's plan, we should have inherited from Adam.

*For my life.* How much unhappiness the single sin of Adam has brought upon all men! From this I can see what a terrible evil sin is.

*From holy scripture.* "Man has all the thoughts and imaginations of his heart, even in youth, so bent toward evil."[90]—St. John the apostle says of concupiscence: "What does the world offer? Only gratification of corrupt nature, gratification of the eye, the empty pomp of living; these things take their being from the world, not from the Father."[91]

*Our evil inclinations.* There are seven chief evil inclinations: pride, covetousness, impurity, envy, gluttony, anger, and sloth. They are called the "seven capital sins," or the "root vices," because many other sins have their beginning in these seven.

*What would you answer?* Many persons say: "There isn't any heritage of guilt or original sin. We don't see it anywhere." We would reply: "Of course we cannot see the inherited guilt itself, but we do see its results. They are the evil inclinations we feel within us. We do not easily remain faithful to God; in spite of all our good resolutions, we sin over and over again. We see the results of original sin in the disorder of the world outside us, too. Despite all the efforts of good people, there are always injustice, war, and other evils." Many say: "God is unjust because he lets others suffer on account of Adam's sin." Our answer is that God is just; he owed the grace-life to no one, nor the special gifts of paradise. But God is also merciful; what Adam lost, all men can regain through Christ, and the suffering we undergo will be richly rewarded by God.

[90] Gn 8:21
[91] 1 Jn 2:16

# LESSON 21

## God Promised the Redemption

"And the Lord God said to the serpent: 'I will establish a feud between thee and the woman, between thy offspring and hers; she is to crush thy head, while thou dost lie in ambush at her heels.'"[92]

After the first sin, God made a promise to Adam: "The devil will one day be defeated. A Savior will be born of human stock; he will save mankind from sin and its evil results."

Later on, through the patriarchs and prophets, God foretold many things about this Redeemer. He is to be born in Bethlehem of a Virgin Mother. He will be a great prophet, and will do marvelous things. He will be a priest, and he will suffer for his people, and die for all mankind.

Finally, he will be exalted to be King and judge of all peoples.—Priests and kings under the old covenant were anointed with oil, and hence they were called "the anointed ones." Because the promised Redeemer was to be both a priest and king, he was called "the anointed one." In Hebrew, this is *Messias*, and in Greek *Christos*, from which our word *Christ* comes.

The last messenger from God under the old covenant was John the Baptist. He was called the "Forerunner of the Savior."

Much of what God had promised under the old covenant was brought to fulfillment in Christ. Much is being fulfilled all the time in his Church. On the last day, everything that God has ever promised will be fulfilled.

*Consider.* 1) What did God promise after the fall into sin? 2) Through whom did God foretell more details about the salvation which was to come? 3) What did God cause to be proclaimed about the Savior who was to come? 4) What does the word *Messias* mean? 5) Why was the coming Savior called the "Messias"? 6) What was the task of John the Baptist? 7) What do you know about the fulfillment of God's promises?

[92] Gn 3:15

41. **In what words did God promise redemption to our first parents?**
"The Lord God said to the serpent: 'I will establish a feud between thee and the woman, between thy offspring and hers; she is to crush thy head, while thou dost lie in ambush at her heels.'"

*For my life.* God did not reject men forever, as he did the sinful angels. Instead, he took pity on them. For this I shall be grateful to him.

*God's word.* 1) Prophecies about the salvation to come: "Rejoice heaven, and let earth be glad; let the sea and all the sea contains give thunderous applause. The fields and all the burden they bear, full of expectancy; no tree in the forest but will rejoice to greet its Lord's coming. He comes to rule the earth, brings the world justice, to every race of men its promised award."[93]—"A time is coming, the Lord says, when I mean to ratify a new covenant with the people of Israel and with the people of Juda…I will be their God, and they will be my people."[94]—"The furthest dwellers on earth will bethink themselves of the Lord and come back to him; all races of the heathen will worship before him; to the Lord royalty belongs, the whole world's image is his due."[95]

2) Prophecies about the Redeemer: "Juda shall not want a branch from his stem, a prince drawn from his stock, until the day when he comes who is to be sent to us, he the hope of the nations."[96]—"From the stock of Jesse a scion shall burgeon yet; out of his roots a flower shall spring."[97]—"Sign you ask none, but sign the Lord will give you. Maid shall be with child, and shall bear a son, that shall be called Emmanuel (which means 'God with us.')"[98]—"Bethlehem-Ephrate! least do they reckon thee: among all the clans of Juda? Nay, it is from thee I look to find a prince that shall rule over Israel."[99]—"For our sakes a child is born, to our race a son is given, whose shoulder will bear the sceptre of princely power. What name shall

[93] Ps 95:11-13
[94] Jer 31:31-33
[95] Ps 21:28-29
[96] Gn 49:10
[97] Is 11:1
[98] Is 7:14; Mt 1:23
[99] Mi 5:2; Mt 2:6

be given him? Peerless among counselors, the mighty God, Father of the world to come, the Prince of Peace."[100]—"The Lord has anointed me, on me his spirit has fallen; he has sent me to bring good news to men that are humbled, to heal broken hearts, promising the release of captives, the opening of prison doors, proclaiming the year of the Lord's pardon, the day when he, our God, will give us redress."[101] "Take courage and have no fear: see where your Lord is bringing redress for your wrongs. God himself, coming to deliver you! Then the eye of the blind shall be opened, and deaf ears unsealed; the lame man, then, shall leap as the deer leap, the speechless tongue cry aloud."[102]—"Thou art a priest for ever in the line of Melchisedech."[103]—"A victim? Yet he himself bows to the stroke; no word comes from him. Sheep led away to the slaughterhouse, lamb that stands dumb while it is shorn, no word from him."[104]—"Then I saw in my dream, how one came riding on the clouds of heaven, that was yet a Son of man; came to where the Judge sat, crowned with age, and was ushered into his presence. With that, power was given him, and glory, and sovereignty; obey him as all must, men of every race and tribe and tongue; such a reign as his lasts for ever, such power as his the ages cannot diminish."[105]

*Things to do.* 1) What do the prophets say: a) about the ancestry of the Redeemer; b) about his task and his deeds; c) about his sufferings; d) about his kingdom? 2) Which promises have already been fulfilled? 3) Why do we celebrate Advent each year, although the Savior has already come?

[100] Is 9:6
[101] Is 61:1-2; Cf. Lk 4:18-19
[102] Is 35:4-6; Cf. Mt 11:5
[103] Ps 109:4; Heb 5:6
[104] Is 53:7; Cf. Acts 2:27
[105] Dn 7:13-14; Cf. Mt 26:64

# Of Jesus Christ Our Lord

"And in Jesus Christ, his only Son, our Lord."
(2nd Article of the Creed.)

While John was performing baptisms at the river Jordan, the promised Redeemer came up, Jesus Christ, God's only Son, our Lord. We must believe in him, if we are to enter the kingdom of God.

## *LESSON 22*

### *Jesus Christ Has Proclaimed the Kingdom of God*

After his baptism in the Jordan, Jesus went out into the desert, where he fasted for forty days and nights. Then he returned to Galilee, and preached the gospel of God's kingdom. "The appointed time has come," he said, "and the kingdom of God is near at hand. Repent and believe the gospel."[106]

Jesus went throughout the whole country as a messenger of his heavenly Father and announced the wonderful news: God's kingdom is near. The prophets had promised God's kingdom, good men had lived in longing for it, the scribes and the Pharisees had talked about it. Jesus, however, announced it. "Now is the time; God's kingdom is coming."

Jesus proved by great miracles that God's kingdom was at hand. He healed those who were ill, drove out evil spirits, recalled the dead to life, and in a most marvelous way gave a great crowd of people food in a desert. He pointed out: "If I, by the Spirit of God cast out devils, then is the kingdom of God come among you."[107] The crowds cried out: "God has visited his people."[108]

Both by his words and his great deeds, Jesus showed at the same time that he was the Messias who had been promised so long before by God.

[106] Cf. Mk 1:12-15
[107] Mt 12:28
[108] Lk 7:16

When John the Baptist sent his disciples to ask Jesus: "Is it thy coming that was foretold or are we yet waiting for some other?" Jesus answered: "Go and relate to John what you have heard and seen. The blind see, the lame walk, the lepers are cleansed, the deaf hear, the dead rise again, the poor have the gospel preached to them. Blessed is he that shall not be scandalized in me."[109]

*Consider.* 1) Who gave Jesus the task of proclaiming the joyful news of God's kingdom? 2) How was his preaching different from that of the prophets? 3) How did Jesus show that the kingdom of God was near? 4) What were men able to learn about Jesus himself from his words and works?

42. **What did Jesus announce after his baptism in the Jordan?**
After his baptism in the Jordan, Jesus announced: "The time is accomplished and the kingdom of heaven is at hand; repent, and believe the good tidings."

*For my life.* I shall do what I can so that others may learn the good news of Jesus, and live according to it.

*From holy scripture.* "Seek ye first the kingdom of God and his justice, and all these things shall be added to you."[110]—"The works that I do in the name of my Father, they give testimony of me."[111]

*Things to do.* 1) What miracles of Christ do you find mentioned in the gospels? 2) What can you do so that others may learn the good news announced by Jesus?

## *LESSON 23*

### *Jesus Christ Taught Men*

Jesus, seeing how great the crowd was, went up onto the mountain, and sat down, and the disciples came around him. And he began speaking to

[109] Mt 11:3-6
[110] Mt 6:33
[111] Jn 10:25

them. Afterward, the multitudes found themselves amazed at his teaching. For he spoke as one who had power, not as the scribes and Pharisees.[112]

Jesus taught the people everywhere: in the Temple and in the synagogues, in the cities, in the villages, on the mountains, in deserts, and on the shores of the Lake of Genesareth.

Jesus taught with an authority that was not to be contradicted. He had no need to ask any other man. He knew his Father, and the way to him, because he had come from the Father. Jesus knew men and he found the right word to say to all. When he was preaching to ordinary people, he used parables, but he gave his close followers a deeper insight into his meaning. He spoke kindly to the sick, and to sinners; he denounced the hypocrisy of the Pharisees in the strongest words.

Jesus Christ is the teacher of all peoples and of all centuries. He teaches men through the medium of his Church, and he enlightens them by the Holy Spirit. His word holds good for all eternity. He said: "Heaven and earth shall pass, but my words shall not pass."[113]

*Consider.* 1) Where did Jesus teach? 2) Why could he teach with absolute authority? 3) How did Jesus show that he had the right word for each individual person? 4) By what channel does Jesus now speak to us?

43. **What does Jesus say about his teaching?**
Jesus says: "Heaven and earth shall pass, but my words shall not pass."

*For my life.* When the gospel is being read, I should stand, and pay attention. Jesus is speaking to me!

*From holy scripture.* "One is your master, Christ."[114]—"Everyone, therefore, that heareth these my words, and doth them, shall be likened to a wise man that built his house upon a rock. And everyone that heareth these words, and doth them not, shall be like a foolish man that built his house upon the sand."[115]

[112] Cf. Mt 5:1-2; 7:28-29
[113] Mt 24:35
[114] Mt 23:10
[115] Mt 7:24, 26

*Things to do.* 1) Name some truths which Jesus has taught us. 2) Name some places where Jesus taught. 3) Name some people with whom Jesus spoke as individuals.

## *LESSON 24*

## *Jesus Christ Lived Entirely for His Father*

One day, Jesus, being tired from a long walk, sat down by Jacob's well, near the city of Sichar in Samaria. His disciples had gone into the city to buy something to eat. While they were gone, a Samaritan woman came by, and Jesus spoke to her about the redemption which was to come. When the disciples came back, they said to him: "Master, eat!" And Jesus said to them: "My meat is to do the will of him who sent me."[116]

Jesus was always thinking of his Father, whether he was looking at the beautiful lilies in the fields, or at the birds flying across the sky, whether he was among the people, with his disciples, or with wicked men.

Jesus loved his Father in heaven more than anyone else; his whole life was influenced by this love. No other human being has ever loved the Father so much.

It was because of this great love that Jesus prayed to his Father. Often he left the crowds and went where he might have quiet so that he could speak to his Father. Often he would pray throughout the night. Prayer with him was like a burning fire within his heart.

Jesus' love for his Father showed itself especially in that he always did his Father's will. He carried out obediently whatever the Father commanded him; he bore with patience whatever the Father let come to him. Untiringly he worked for the honor of his Father. The saying, "Zeal for thy house has eaten me up,"[117] was a description of the way he lived.

Jesus was always obedient to the Father. The devil could not lead Jesus astray, although he used all his power against him. Jesus was absolutely without sin. He is the holiest of all men.

[116] Cf. Jn 4:5-34
[117] Jn 2:17

*Consider.* By what can we see that Jesus lived entirely for his Father?

44. **What did Jesus say about his obedience to the Father's will?**
Jesus said: "My meat is to do the will of him that sent me."

*For my life.* Jesus is my master from whom I must learn how to live. I must follow his example, and love the Father, speak to him with the confidence of a child, and do what he wishes with joy.

*Things to do.* 1) What places in the holy scripture tell us that Jesus prayed? 2) Set down briefly some prayers of Jesus which we find in the gospels.

## *LESSON 25*

## *Jesus Christ Had Mercy on Mankind*

As Jesus was passing through Jericho, he saw the tax collector Zachaeus to the side of the road sitting in a fig tree. And so he said: "Zachaeus, come down quickly; I am to lodge today at your house." So Zachaeus climbed down quickly and received him with joy. When they all saw it, they murmured, saying: "He has gone to lodge at the house of one who is a sinner." But Jesus replied: "The Son of man is come to seek and to save that which was lost."[118]

Jesus took pity on men because he deeply loves them. "I am moved with pity for the multitude," he said.[119]

He did not think of his own comfort, but of the mission which the Father had given him to perform. "The Son of man is not come to be ministered unto, but to minister."[120]

With great tenderness Jesus was drawn to all those who were despised or who were in some need. He wanted the children to come to him; he healed the sick, fed those who were hungry, and preached his gospel to

[118] Cf. Lk 19:1-10
[119] Mt 15:32
[120] Mk 10:45

the poor. He said: "Come to me, all you that labor and are burdened, and I will refresh you."[121]

Jesus received sinners with special loving-kindness. He went after them, like a shepherd after his lost sheep, begged them to repent, and forgave them their sins. Even when he threatened them with judgment, he did so from love. He wept over Jerusalem that would not do penance. It was love which drove him even to give up his life for sinners.

*Consider.* 1) How did Jesus show his love for men? 2) How did Jesus receive the humble folk, and those who were in suffering? 3) How did Jesus show his love for sinners?

45. **With what words does Jesus invite all men to come to him?**
Jesus says: "Come to me, all you that labor and are burdened and I will refresh you."

*For my life.* I shall follow the word of St. Paul: "You must befriend one another, as Christ has befriended you, for God's honor."[122]

*From holy scripture.* Jesus said: "I came, not to judge the world, but to save the world."[123]—"He went about doing good."[124]—After he had washed the feet of his disciples, Jesus said: "I have given you an example that as I have done to you, so you do also."[125]

*From the Church's life.* The Church honors the most Sacred Heart of Jesus. She considers how Jesus loved his Father and loved men, and calls upon us to make reparation for our sins. On the second Friday after Corpus Christi, she celebrates the feast of the most Sacred Heart of Jesus. There is also devotion to the most Sacred Heart of Jesus on the first Friday of each month.

*Things to do.* 1) Think over which people you yourself could help. 2) How can you help them?

121 Mt 11:28
122 Rom 15:7
123 Jn 12:47
124 Acts 10:38
125 Jn 13:15

## LESSON 26

### *Jesus Christ Is the Son of God and Is True God*

At the feast of the Dedication of the Temple, Jesus said: "My Father and I are one." At this the Jews took up stones to cast at him. They accused him of blaspheming against God. They said: "Thou, being a man, makest thyself God." Jesus answered: "How can you say: Thou blasphemest, because I have said: I am the Son of God? Believe the works that I do; then you will know that the Father is in me and I am in the Father."[126]

The heavenly Father has revealed that Jesus is the Son of God. At his baptism in the river Jordan, the Father's voice spoke from heaven: "This is my beloved Son in whom I am well pleased."[127] The Father spoke the same words at Christ's transfiguration on the mountain.

Jesus has himself said that he is the Son of God. He calls himself "the Son";[128] he said: "I and the Father are one."[129] He is the only begotten Son of God.—Jesus once asked his apostles: "Whom do you say I am?" Peter answered: "Thou art the Christ, the Son of the living God." Jesus approved this confession with the words: "Blessed art thou, Simon Bar-Jona: because flesh and blood hath not revealed it to thee, but my Father who is in heaven."[130]—The high priest said to Jesus: "I adjure thee by the living God, that thou tell us if thou be the Christ the Son of God." Jesus answered: "I am."[131]—Jesus has given power of conviction to his words, both by his miracles and his holy life, and went to his death for this conviction.

The apostles have also given witness that Jesus is the Son of God, and gave up their lives for this belief. Paul writes: "God did not even spare his own Son, but gave him up for us all."[132] John says: "What has revealed the

[126] Cf. Jn 10:22-38
[127] Mt 3:17
[128] Mt 11:27
[129] Jn 10:30
[130] Cf. Mt 16:15-17
[131] Cf. Mt 26:63-64
[132] Rom 8:32

love of God, where we are concerned, is that he has sent his only begotten Son into the world, so that we might have life through him."[133]

Because Jesus is the only begotten Son of God, he is God, just as the Father is. Thomas exclaimed: "My Lord and my God!"[134] John writes: "He is true God."[135] Paul speaks of Jesus as Christ, who rules as "God over all things, blessed for ever. Amen."[136] Jesus has the same divine being as his Father; he is, in the words of the Creed in the Mass, "God of God, light of light, true God of true God, of one substance with the Father."

In everything he works together with the Father. He receives the same adoration and glory as the Father.

Ever since the time of the apostles, the whole Church has taught and recognized that Jesus Christ is God's Son and true God. She has defended this truth against the teachers of error and the unbelievers. Innumerable martyrs have sealed this belief with their blood. The popes and bishops, priests and faithful, learned and unlearned men, our parents and ancestors, lived and died in this faith.

*Consider.* 1) On what occasions did the heavenly Father testify that Jesus was his Son? 2) What words did Jesus use to say that he was the Son of God? 3) What did Peter say to Jesus' question: "Whom do men say that I am?" 4) What did Jesus answer to the high priest? 5) By what means did Jesus bear witness to the truth of his words? 6) In what words have the apostles given testimony that Jesus Christ is the Son of God and true God? 7) In what ways is Jesus equal to the Father?

### 46. Who gives us testimony that Jesus Christ is the Son of God and himself true God?

Testimony that Jesus Christ is the Son of God and himself true God comes to us: a) from the heavenly Father; b) from Jesus Christ himself; c) from the apostles and the whole Church.

[133] 1 Jn 4:9
[134] Jn 20:28
[135] 1 Jn 5:20
[136] Rom 9:5

*For my life.* I shall firmly and fearlessly believe and testify before men that Jesus Christ is the Son of God.

*From holy scripture.* "He that believeth in the Son of God is not judged. But he that doth not believe is already judged; because he believeth not in the name of the only begotten Son of God."[137]

# Our Savior Became Man, Suffered, and Was Glorified

In order that we may know our Savior and his work better, we will now consider how he became man, suffered, rose from the dead, returned to heaven, and how he will come back on the last day. In all this we shall see how he loved us, how much he had to endure for our sakes, and how wonderfully his Father glorified him on the completion of his task.

## *LESSON 27*

### *The Son of God Became Man*

"Conceived by the Holy Ghost, born of the Virgin Mary."
(3rd Article of the Creed.)

God sent the angel Gabriel to a city of Galilee called Nazareth, where a virgin dwelt. The name of the virgin was Mary. The angel said to her: "Behold, thou shalt conceive in thy womb, and shalt bear a son, and shalt call him Jesus. He will be great, and shall be called the Son of the Most High."[138]

[137] Jn 3:18
[138] Cf. Lk 1:26-38

The Son of God lived from all eternity with the Father and the Holy Ghost in divine glory and infinite love. For this reason, Jesus could say: "Amen, amen, I say to you, before Abraham was made, I am."[139]

The Son of God is born of the Father from all eternity. That is why we say in the Creed at Mass: "He was born of the Father before all time." He comes from the Father, somewhat as a thought or a word comes from a man's mind: that is why the Son of God is also called "the Word."

At the appointed time, the angel of the Lord brought the message to Mary, and the Holy Ghost came down upon her. At this moment, the Son of God took flesh from Mary, and was made man. We think of this mystery which we cannot fully grasp when we pronounce the words: "The Word was made flesh, and dwelt among us."[140]

The Son of God became a real man, with flesh and blood, body and soul. He was sensitive as we are, to hunger and thirst; he was joyful and sad, suffered and feared the approach of death. He was like us in everything except sin.[141] Even in his present glorified state, he remains a man, and will forever remain a man.

Jesus is at one and the same time God and man; God from all eternity, and man from a certain moment in time. He has divine nature and also human nature; he is the God-man.

The Son of God became man in order to carry out the great design of his Father: he was to announce the joyful news of the kingdom of God, and to show us by his word and example the way to the Father; he was to free us from sin, and make us once more the children of God.

*Consider.* 1) Where did the Son of God live from all eternity? 2) What do we mean by the words: "He was born of the Father before all time"? 3) Why is the Son of God also called "the Word"? 4) How do we know that the Son of God beome a real man?

### 47. Who is Jesus Christ?

Jesus Christ is the only begotten Son of God, who became man for our sakes.

[139] Jn 8:58
[140] Jn 1:14
[141] Cf. Heb 4:15

48. **Why did the Son of God become man?**
The Son of God became man,
1. to proclaim to us God's kingdom and show us the way to the Father;
2. to save us from our sins, and to make us once more the children of God.

*For my life.* When I hear the bell ring for the *Angelus*, I shall recall that the Son of God became man for my sake, and I shall pray the *Angelus* attentively.

*From the life of the Church.* On the 25th of March, the Church celebrates the feast of the Annunciation. On the 25th of December, the Church celebrates the feast of the Birth of Christ (Christmas). The letters *IHS* are a shortened form of the word *Jesus* in Greek. The letters *XP* are the first two letters of the word *Christ* written in Greek. These two things are usually put together in the symbol ☧ or ⳨.

*Things to do.* 1) How do you say the *Angelus?* 2) What hymns or carols do you know for Christmas? 3) What words do we find in the Masses of Christmas and Advent mentioning that the Son of God became man? 4) Collect some pictures of the annunciation and of the birth of our Lord. 5) How should we as Christians prepare ourselves for the feast of Christmas? 6) How should we celebrate the night of Christmas Eve? 7) What is the meaning of the Christmas tree? 8) What is the meaning of giving presents at Christmas time? 9) Build a Christmas crib.

## *LESSON 28*

## *The Mother of Our Redeemer Is the Blessed Virgin Mary*

When Jesus was born, wise men came from the East to Bethlehem. Going into the dwelling, they found the child with his mother Mary, and fell down to worship him.[142]

The Mother of the Redeemer is the most Blessed Virgin Mary. From all eternity God had chosen her to be the Mother of his Son. Because her

[142] Cf. Mt 2:1-11

Son is truly God, she is the Mother of God. By this fact, Mary has a dignity which exceeds that of all angels and men.

Although she became a Mother, Mary remained a Virgin. Joseph was not the physical father of Jesus, but cared for him and protected him while he was a child. He was told in a dream by an angel that Mary would be with child by the action of the Holy Spirit, in order to become the Mother of the Redeemer.

Because Mary was chosen to be the Mother of the Son of God, she was not to live a single instant of her life under the influence of sin; hence God preserved her from the guilt of original sin, and gave her the grace-life in the very first instant of her life. As her mother conceived her, she was free of the slightest taint of sin, and full of grace. Therefore, we call Mary the "Immaculate Conception." This grace too Jesus merited like all other graces by his death on the cross.

God made Mary so rich in graces that she always did the will of God. She was kept free also from any sin of her own. Mary is the purest and the most holy of all women.

*Consider.* 1) Who is St. Joseph? 2) Why do we say that Mary was immaculately conceived? 3) Why did God keep Mary free from the guilt of original sin? 4) Why is Mary the purest and holiest of all women?

### 49. What are God's special gifts to Mary?

Mary is:

1. free from the guilt of original sin and from any sin of her own;
2. Mother of God and at the same time a most pure Virgin.

### 50. Why do we call Mary the Mother of God?

We call Mary the Mother of God because her Son is truly God.

*For my life.* Let no day go by without a Hail Mary.

*From the life of the Church.* The Church celebrates on the 8th of December the feast of the Immaculate Conception of Our Lady. On this date of the year 1854, her special privilege of grace was defined by Pope Pius IX as an article of faith.

Since St. Joseph protected the Child Jesus and his Mother on earth, the Church has declared him to be her own protector. She celebrates his feast on the 19th of March, and on the 1st of May the feast of St. Joseph the Workman.

The Sunday after the Epiphany of Our Lord is the feast of the Holy Family.

*Things to do.* 1) Name the five joyful mysteries of the rosary. 2) Turn back to Lesson 21 and look up what the prophets said about the Mother of the Redeemer.

Daily, daily, sing to Mary
Sing, my soul, her praises due;
All her feasts, her actions, worship
With the heart's devotion true.
Lost in wond'ring contemplation
Be her majesty confessed:
Call her Mother, call her Virgin,
Happy Mother, Virgin blest.

## *LESSON 29*

### *The Son of God Was Rejected by the Leaders of the Chosen People*

When Jesus had solemnly declared before the council that he was the Son of God, and that he would one day come again on the clouds of heaven, the high priest rent his garments and said: "He has blasphemed, what need have we of further witnesses? Mark well, you have heard the blasphemy for yourselves. What is your finding?" And they answered: "The penalty is death." Then they fell to spitting upon his face, and buffeting him, and smiting him on the cheek, saying as they did so: "Show thyself a prophet, Christ; tell us who it is that smote thee."[143]

[143] Cf. Mt 26:63-67

The chosen people had heard the words of Jesus and had seen the miracles he performed, and the holy way he lived. And yet many of them would not listen to the message which he had come to give. Their leaders stirred the people up against him, and condemned the Son of God to death. Many of his disciples left him too, and Judas, one of the twelve apostles, betrayed him. St. John said: "He came unto his own, and his own received him not."[144]

It was the devil who had led men into all these sins. He now saw that his power would be brought to an end if men were to believe in Jesus, and follow him. Therefore, he used all his power to see that men should reject the good news which Jesus brought, and should put him to death.

That men should have rejected the Son of God is a deep and terrible mystery. All the sinfulness and weakness of man can be seen in this rejection. It shows us what frightful ruin sin has worked in the hearts of men.

*Consider.* 1) Explain the words: "He came unto his own, and his own received him not." 2) How did the apostles behave toward Jesus in the night before his suffering began? 3) Why did the devil do all he could to deceive men, so that they would reject the message of Jesus, and kill him? 4) What do we learn from the fact that men have rejected the Son of God?

51. **In what words does St. John say that men have rejected the Son of God?**
St. John says: "He came unto his own, and his own received him not."

*For my life.* I shall not take my sins lightly, for they have also added to the pains Christ had to undergo.

*From holy scripture.* Jesus complained about Jerusalem, a city that would not do penance: "Jerusalem, Jerusalem, thou that killest the prophets, and stonest them that are sent unto thee, how often would I have gathered together thy children, as the hen doth gather her chickens under her wings, and thou wouldst not?"[145]—In the epistle to the Hebrews, St. Paul says of

[144] Jn 1:11
[145] Mt 23:37

sinners: "Would they crucify the Son of God a second time, hold him up to mockery a second time, for their own ends?"[146]

*From the life of the Church.* On Good Friday, the Church sings the Savior's song of complaint for the ingratitude of people and of all mankind. It begins: "My people, what have I done, how have I given you pain? Answer me: I led you out of the land of Egypt, but you have prepared a cross for your Redeemer."

*Things to do.* How in the passion of Jesus did the sinfulness and weakness of men show itself: a) among the leaders of the people; b) among the people; c) in Pontius Pilate; d) in Judas; e) in Peter; f) in the other apostles?

## LESSON 30

## Jesus Christ Chose to Die upon the Cross

"Suffered under Pontius Pilate, was crucified, died, and was buried."
(4th Article of the Creed.)

After Jesus had been condemned to death, they led him out to be crucified. Jesus himself bore the cross and went up to the place which was called "The Place of the Skull," in Hebrew, "Golgotha." There they crucified him. Jesus said: "Father, forgive them, for they know not what they do." About the ninth hour he said: "It is finished," and then in a loud voice, he cried out: "Father, into thy hands I commend my spirit." Then he bowed his head and yielded up his spirit.[147]

Jesus knew that his enemies would condemn and crucify him; but he also knew that, in accordance with his Father's will, he was to undergo this suffering and death to redeem men. Jesus accepted the death on the cross of his own free will. He said: "No man taketh my life away from me; but I lay it down of myself. I have power to lay it down, and I have power to take it up again."[148]

[146] Heb 6:3
[147] Cf. Mt 27:31ff; Mk 15:20ff; Lk 23:26ff; Jn 19:16ff
[148] Jn 10:18

Jesus carried out his Father's will to death; his feelings might well draw back from the bitterness of suffering and death, but Jesus "accepted an obedience which brought him to death, death on a cross."[149] He said: "That the world may know that I love the Father; and as the Father hath given me commandment, so do I."[150]

Jesus loved us men so much that he died for us. "He was ill spoken of, and spoke no evil in return, suffered and did not threaten vengeance."[151] He even prayed on the cross for his enemies. Jesus gave his life out of love for us sinful men.

*Consider.* 1) What did Jesus know about the way he was to end his life on earth? 2) Why was it hard even for Jesus to fulfill the will of his Father? 3) For whom did Jesus give his life?

52. **In what spirit did Jesus give up his life?**
Jesus gave up his life in obedience to his Father in heaven, and for love of us sinful men.

*For my life.* I will think with love and sympathy of our Lord in his passion; I will ask him to help me always to do God's will.

*From holy scripture.* On the Mount of Olives, Jesus prayed, saying: "Father, if thou wilt, remove this chalice from me; but yet not my will, but thine be done."[152] — "Greater love than this no man hath, that a man lay down his life for his friends."[153]

*From the life of the Church.* We bring to mind the sufferings of our Lord especially during Holy Week, above all on Good Friday. The other Fridays of the year are also dedicated to the sufferings of our Lord. That is why we abstain from meat on Fridays. In some places, the bells are rung on Thursday evening in remembrance of his agony in the garden, and on Friday in remembrance of the hour when he died.

149 Phil 2:8
150 Jn 14:31
151 1 Pt 2:23
152 Lk 22:42
153 Jn 15:13

We do honor to the sufferings of our Lord when we make the stations of the cross, say the sorrowful mysteries of the rosary, or the devotion to the five wounds, or take part in the Good Friday service. On many a wayside-cross in the countries where they are found, we read the words: "I did this for you; what are you doing for me?"

*Things to do.* 1) What were the words in which Jesus foretold that he would suffer? 2) Write out the words which Jesus said: a) in the Garden of Olives; b) before his judges; c) on his way to the place where he was crucified; d) on the cross. 3) Look up some hymns about the sufferings of Jesus. 4) Name the fourteen stations of the cross. 5) Name the five sorrowful mysteries of the rosary. 6) At what moment of life is it especially important to think of the sufferings and death of Christ? 7) Where are the crosses in our parish church? Where are other representations of the sufferings of our Lord? 8) Collect pictures of the passion of Christ.

## *LESSON 31*

## *Jesus Christ Has Saved Us by His Death*

"God has rescued us from the power of darkness, and transferred us to the kingdom of his beloved Son. In the Son of God, in his blood, we find the redemption that sets us free from our sins."[154]

By his obedience even to death, our Lord made up for the disobedience of Adam and his descendants. By his most bitter sufferings, Jesus freed us from the guilt of original sin, from our own sins, and from everlasting damnation. The death and sufferings of Jesus were of infinite value, because he is the Son of God.

By his death on the cross, Jesus has triumphed over the devil. He has broken Satan's power, and freed us from his domination. "There is no judgment now against those who live in Jesus Christ."[155]

By means of his death, Jesus won back for us eternal life. He went on ahead of us to the Father; we are to follow him there, and to live forever

[154] Col 1:13-14
[155] Rom 8:1

with him and the Father. He has won for us by his death all the glory of the life to come.

Jesus has also won all the graces we need. We owe it to our Redeemer's love for us that we can live as children of God. All that is holy, the life that fills the Church, streams out of the Heart of our Savior and Redeemer.

*Consider.* 1) For what has Jesus made reparation by his death? 2) How has Jesus freed us from the rule of Satan? 3) What graces has Jesus earned for us?

53. **From what has Jesus set us free?**
Jesus has set us free from sin and eternal damnation.

54. **What has Jesus earned for us?**
Jesus has earned for us the grace of God and everlasting life.

*For my life.* When I pass a cross, I shall greet my Savior in this way: "We adore thee, O Christ, and we bless thee, because by thy holy cross thou has redeemed the world." There should be a cross in every Christian home in a place of honor.

*From holy scripture.* "The Son of man has not come to be ministered unto, but to minister, and to give his life a redemption for many."[156]—"A leper, so we thought of him, a man God had smitten and brought low; and all the while it was for our sins he was wounded, it was guilt of ours crushed him down; on him the punishment fell that brought us peace, by his bruises we were healed."[157]—"A multitude will become acceptable to God through one man's obedience, just as a multitude through one man's disobedience became guilty."[158]

*From the life of the Church.* Before the Communion at Mass we pray: "Lamb of God, who takest away the sins of the world, have mercy on us."

[156] Mk 10:45
[157] Is 53:4-5
[158] Rom 5:19

On Holy Thursday, the introit verse of the Mass says: "Let us glory in the cross of our Lord Jesus Christ. In him is salvation, life, and resurrection, for us. In him we are saved and delivered."

On Good Friday, the priest uncovers the cross and sings three times: "Behold the wood of the cross upon which hung the salvation of the world." Then all kneel down and reply: "Come let us adore."

## LESSON 32

### *Jesus Offered a Sacrifice of Infinite Worth upon the Cross*

"Christ gave himself up on our behalf, a sacrifice breathing out fragrance as he offered it to God."[159]

Men have made offerings since time began. With prayer they have made ready visible offerings to show honor to God as the Lord of all. By these offerings, men have expressed the inward desire to give themselves to God, to thank God for good things received, and to beg his good pleasure, or to make reparation for their sin. In old testament days, such sacrifices were ordered by God himself.

The sacrifices which were made under the old covenant were brought to the full measure of perfection in the sacrifice of the cross. In this offering, Jesus presented himself to the Father for our sakes. His sacrifice was the sacrifice of the new covenant.

The passion and death of Jesus was a sacrifice of infinite value. In this sacrifice, the Son of God made man was at the same time the sacrificing priest and the sacrificial gift. He offered himself to his Father in a spirit of perfect love and utter self-giving.

Christ is the high priest for all mankind. He offered his sacrifice for all men and for all ages. For this reason, there is under the new covenant only one sacrifice: the sacrifice of our Lord Jesus Christ which is made present in every Mass we celebrate.

[159] Eph 5:2

Consider: 1) Why does the sacrifice of Jesus have infinite worth? 2) Why did Jesus Christ offer himself? 3) For whom did Jesus Christ offer himself? 4) Why is there only one sacrifice in the new covenant? 5) When is the sacrifice of the cross made present?

55. **What does *sacrifice* mean?**
*To sacrifice* means to offer to God a visible gift to do him honor as the Lord of all creation.

56. **What is the sacrifice of the new covenant?**
The sacrifice of the new covenant is the sacrifice of Jesus Christ on the cross, which is made present in every Mass.

57. **Why was the death of Jesus Christ on the cross a sacrifice?**
The death of Jesus Christ on the cross was a sacrifice because Jesus offered himself on the cross to the Father for our sakes.

*For my life.* At each Mass, I shall unite myself with the offering of Jesus and give myself wholly to the Father.

*From holy scripture.* At the last supper, our Lord said: "For them do I sanctify myself: that they also may be sanctified in truth."[160]—"Rid yourselves of the leaven which remains over, so that you may be a new mixture, still uncontaminated as you are. Has not Christ been sacrificed for us, our paschal victim?"[161]—"He sits for ever at the right hand of God, offering for our sins a sacrifice which is never repeated; by a single offering he has completed his work for all time in those whom he sanctifies."[162]

*From the life of the Church.* The cross on the altar reminds us that it is upon the altar that the sacrifice of Christ is made present.

[160] Jn 17:19
[161] 1 Cor 5:7
[162] Heb 10:12, 14

# LESSON 33

## *Jesus Christ Went Down to the Dead*

"He descended into hell."
(5th Article of the Creed.)

When Jesus was dead, Joseph of Arimathea went to Pilate, and asked for the body of Jesus. He then took it, wrapped it in a clean shroud, and laid it in a new tomb which he had hewn out of the rock. He rolled a great stone to the door of the tomb and went away. The high priest and the Pharisees put a seal on the stone and secured the tomb with a guard of soldiers.[163]

When Jesus died, his soul departed from his body. But his Godhead remained united both to his soul and to his body.

The soul of Jesus went down to the souls of the good men who had died, and who were waiting for their redemption. Among these were the souls of Adam and Eve, of the patriarchs and prophets, and of John the Baptist. They had not as yet gone to heaven, because heaven was not open since Adam's sin. Now Jesus proclaimed that they were saved.

The place where the souls of the good were is called "hell" in the Creed. This is because, long ago, the word *hell* meant the "kingdom of the dead." This is not the same as the "hell of the damned," so it has also another name and is called "limbo."

The body of Jesus lay cold and motionless in the grave until the third day; but it was preserved from corruption. The prophecy was fulfilled: "Thou wilt not allow thy faithful servant to see corruption."[164]

*Consider.* 1) Who was in limbo? 2) Why could no one go into heaven before the death of Jesus? 3) What did Jesus announce to the souls of the good men who had died? 4) From what was the body of Jesus preserved?

[163] Cf. Mt 27:57-66
[164] Ps 15:10

58. **Where did the soul of Jesus go after his death?**
The soul of Jesus went after his death to limbo, to the souls of the good men who had died.

*For my life.* Every grave should make me remember that we all must die someday; but also that we shall all rise again.

## *LESSON 34*

### *Jesus Christ Rose from the Dead*

"The third day he rose again from the dead."
(5th Article of the Creed.)

At the hour of dawn on the first day of the week, an angel of the Lord came from heaven, rolled the stone back from the tomb, and sat upon it. He said to the women: "Fear not you: for I know that you seek Jesus who was crucified. He is not here, for he is risen, as he said."[165]

On the morning of the third day, Jesus rose in glory from the dead. His body and soul were now forever united, and filled with heavenly glory. His body was glorified; his soul was filled with unbounded joy. He appeared to his apostles, but he did not remain with them, as he had done formerly when he was still subject to death.

Jesus rose from the dead by his own power; for he is the Son of God, and has the power of God. But he is also a real man. Therefore, the holy scripture says in many passages that he was "awakened" from the dead.

By his resurrection, Jesus broke the power of death. He now suffers and dies no more. "Death has no more power over him."[166] Christ has overcome death.

By his resurrection, Jesus has been glorified. His enemies had rejected him, and put him to death as a blasphemer. But the resurrection proves that he was indeed the Redeemer who had been promised, and the Son of God.

[165] Cf. Mt 28:1-6
[166] Rom 6:9

"Christ has risen from the dead, the firstfruits of those who have fallen asleep."[167] His resurrection also gives the certainty that we shall rise. "He will form this humbled body of ours anew, molding it into the image of his glorified body, so effective is his power to make all things obey him."[168] His resurrection is the beginning of the new creation.

In baptism, Christ, our risen Lord, wakens us from the death of sin, and gives us part in his life as God. This life is, of course, still hidden in us, but it will one day be revealed when he comes again.

*Consider.* 1) What was Jesus like after he rose? 2) Why could Jesus rise from the dead by his own power? 3) Why can we nonetheless say that Jesus was awakened? 4) Why can we say that Jesus has overcome death? 5) What does the expression mean, "firstfruits of those who have fallen asleep"? 6) How does Christ give us a share in his life as God?

59. **What miracle did Jesus do on the third day after his death?**
On the third day after his death, Jesus united his soul again with his body and gloriously rose from the dead.

60. **What does the resurrection of Jesus teach us?**
The resurrection of Jesus teaches us,
1. that Jesus is truly the Son of God;
2. that we also shall rise again.

*For my life.* When I was baptized, I was brought from death to life, came out of the night into the light of day. Now I shall live as a child of the light.

*From holy scripture.* "A man had brought us death, and a man was to bring us resurrection from the dead; just as all have died with Adam, so with Christ, all will be brought to life."[169]—"He who has raised Jesus from the dead will raise us too."[170]

[167] 1 Cor 15:20
[168] Phil 3:21
[169] 1 Cor 15:21-22
[170] 2 Cor 4:14

*From the life of the Church.* The Church celebrates the resurrection of our Lord at Easter. The celebration of the night in which he rose—Holy Saturday to Easter morn—is the most solemn service of the Church's entire year. The service held during this night is called the "Paschal Vigil"; it is filled with the greatest joy over the resurrection of Christ, and our resurrection with him in baptism. The paschal candle burns as a symbol of the risen Lord, and the candles of the faithful are lit from it as a sign that we have received the new life from Christ. Each Sunday is a day kept in memory of the resurrection—a "little Easter."

*Things to do.* 1) Make a prayer of your own to the risen Lord. 2) Why is water for baptism blessed on Holy Saturday night? 3) Why do we renew the vows of baptism during the Paschal Vigil? 4) What hymns for Eastertide do you know? 5) Why is food blessed on Easter day?

By his death he has destroyed our death,
and by rising he has won for us new life.[171]

## *LESSON 35*

### *We Have Sure Proof of the Resurrection of Jesus*

Thomas, one of the twelve apostles, had not believed that Jesus was risen, and appeared to the other apostles. Eight days after the resurrection, the disciples were once again all together, and Thomas with them. Then Jesus came and stood in their midst, although the doors were shut, and said to them: "Peace be to you." Then he said to Thomas: "Put your finger here, and see my hands! Bring your hand here and put it into my side, and be not unbelieving, but believing." Then Thomas said to him: "My Lord and my God." Jesus said to him: "Because you have seen me you have believed. Blessed are they that have not seen, and yet have believed."[172]

[171] From the Easter preface.
[172] Cf. Jn 20:24-29

Jesus showed himself after his resurrection, "not to the people at large, but to the witnesses whom God had appointed beforehand,"[173] the apostles and disciples. They saw him often, touched him, spoke and ate with him. Later still, Jesus also appeared to Saul, who was to become an apostle.

The enemies of Jesus could not deny his resurrection. But in order to deceive the people, they bribed the soldiers to say that "his disciples came in the night and stole his body away while we slept."[174] That was a lie: men who were asleep could not see what had happened while they slept.

The apostles preached the resurrection of Jesus everywhere as the most important truth of the faith. St. Paul says: "If Christ has not risen, then our preaching is groundless, and your faith, too is groundless."[175] The apostles were "witnesses of the resurrection,"[176] and went to their deaths as witnesses for it.

Jesus confirmed the testimony of his apostles by miracles and has confirmed it again and again by his powerful action in the Church. It is his doing that the Church never fails but is always growing and bearing fruit. From this we can know that Christ is not dead, but is living and reigning now.

*Consider.* 1) To whom did Jesus show himself after he had risen? 2) What did the enemies of Jesus do when the soldiers came back from the empty tomb? 3) Why did the apostles preach the resurrection of Jesus everywhere? 4) How did Jesus confirm what the apostles were saying? 5) How do we recognize that Jesus lives and rules?

61. **How could the apostles bear sure testimony that Jesus had risen?**
The apostles had seen the risen Jesus with their own eyes, had touched him and talked with him.

[173] Acts 10:41
[174] Cf. Mt 28:11-15
[175] 1 Cor 15:14
[176] Acts 1:22

62. **How did the apostles give testimony that Jesus had risen?**
The apostles preached the resurrection of Jesus everywhere, and went to their deaths as witnesses for it.

*For my life.* I shall believe joyfully in the risen Lord.

*The appearances of Jesus after he had risen.* To Mary Magdalene;[177] to the devoted women on the road;[178] to Peter;[179] to the two disciples at Emmaus;[180] at Jerusalem in Thomas' absence;[181] eight days later, when Thomas was there;[182] to the disciples as they were fishing on the Lake of Tiberius;[183] to more than five hundred of the disciples together;[184] to the apostle James;[185] to all the apostles before his ascension;[186] last of all to Saul.[187]

## *LESSON 36*

## *Jesus Christ Ascended to Heaven*

"He ascended into heaven."
(6th Article of the Creed.)

After his resurrection, Jesus remained for forty days on earth. During this time, he instructed the apostles about the kingdom of God. On the fortieth day, he led them out to the Mount of Olives, where he raised his hands and blessed them. While he was blessing them, he was raised up before their eyes and a cloud took him out of their sight.[188]

177 Cf. Mk 16:9; Jn 20:16
178 Cf. Mt 28:9
179 Cf. Lk 24:34; 1 Cor 15:5
180 Cf. Lk 24:3-32
181 Cf. Lk 24:36-43; Jn 20:19-23
182 Cf. Jn 20:26-29
183 Cf. Jn 21:1-23
184 Cf. 1 Cor 15:6
185 Cf. 1 Cor 15:7
186 Cf. Mk 16:19; Acts 1:9
187 Cf. Acts 9:1-6; 1 Cor 15:8
188 Cf. Lk 24:50-53; Acts 1:3-9

On the fortieth day after he had risen, Christ went up to heaven by his own power. He left "his own who were in the world,"[189] and returned to his Father in the glory of heaven. From thence he will come back again in order to complete his redemptive work.

The ascension of our Lord was a triumphal procession. Victoriously he rose into the heavens above all his enemies. In triumph he led with him the hosts of the redeemed whom he had brought out of limbo.

In heaven, Jesus took his place on the throne at his Father's right hand. Now as man he took possession of the power and glory which he had actually possessed from all eternity as Son of the Father.

Jesus was King from the time of his birth, because he was the Son of God. But he had also earned the right to his kingdom, because he gave his life for us.

Jesus has gone before us into the heavenly kingdom. He says: "In my Father's house there are many mansions...I go to prepare a place for you...I will come again, and will take you to myself, that where I am, you also may be."[190]

*Consider.* 1) Why was the ascension of Jesus a triumphal procession? 2) What do we mean when we say that "Jesus took his place on the throne at his Father's right hand"? 3) What two facts make Jesus King? 4) Why has Christ prepared a place for us to live in heaven?

**63. What did Jesus do on the fortieth day after his resurrection?**
On the fortieth day after his resurrection, Jesus ascended into heaven by his own power.

**64. With what words did Jesus comfort the apostles as he left them?**
Jesus said to the apostles as he left them: "In my Father's house there are many mansions...I go to prepare a place for you...I will come again, and will take you to myself, that where I am, you also may be."

[189] Jn 13:1
[190] Jn 14:2-3

*For my life.* I will do everything in my power to win the place which Christ has prepared for me in heaven.

*From holy scripture.* "Risen, then, with Christ, you must lift your thoughts above, where Christ now sits at the right hand of God."[191] — "And then he lowered his own dignity, accepted an obedience which brought him to death, death on a cross. That is why God has raised him to such a height, given him that name which is greater than any other name."[192]

*From the life of the Church.* Forty days after Easter, the Church celebrates the ascension of Christ. On this day, the paschal candle is put out after the reading of the day's gospel, signifying that since his ascension, Christ is no longer visible to us on earth.

## *LESSON 37*

### *Jesus Christ Is Our Lord*

"He sitteth at the right hand of God the Father Almighty."
(6th Article of the Creed.)

"Everything in heaven and on earth and under the earth must bend the knee before the name of Jesus, and every tongue must confess Jesus Christ as the Lord, dwelling in the glory of God the Father."[193]

Since Jesus went up to heaven, he rules with the Father over us. Jesus Christ is our Lord. Even as man he shares in the power and the glory of the heavenly Father. We confess to that in the Creed when we say the words, "sitteth at the right hand of God the Father Almighty." From heaven Christ carries on with divine power the work of the redemption which he began on earth.

Christ our Lord teaches us even now in his Church. He calls men to his service and sends them out to preach his word. His message is spread throughout the whole world. He is our greatest teacher.

[191] Col 3:1
[192] Phil 2:8-9
[193] Phil 2:10-11

Christ our Lord offers himself in the Mass, acts upon us in the sacraments, brings our prayers into the Father's hearing, and is always interceding for us. All graces are given us through the power of Christ's sufferings and death. He is our high priest.

Christ our Lord leads us on with infinite wisdom and deepest love toward our goal in eternity. He directs us through the successors of the apostles, and guides our souls through the Holy Spirit. He is at work in the lives of all men. He is the shepherd and King of all men, but especially of his own faithful.

*Consider.* 1) Why do we call Christ "Lord"? 2) What does Christ do as our heavenly teacher? 3) What does Christ do as our high priest? 4) How does Christ direct our lives from heaven?

65. **What do we confess with the words, "sitteth at the right hand of God the Father Almighty"?**
We confess that Jesus Christ even as man shares in the power and glory of our Father in heaven.

66. **What are the three offices which Christ our Lord holds?**
Christ our Lord is our supreme teacher, our high priest, and our chief shepherd.

*For my life.* Christ should be Lord over my life. Each morning I shall offer the work of the whole day to him.

*From the life of the Church.* In the *Gloria* of the Mass we sing to Christ: "Thou alone art Lord." It is through Christ that the Church prays to the heavenly Father. She usually closes her prayers with the words: "Through our Lord Jesus Christ thy Son who is God living and reigning with thee in the unity of the Holy Spirit forever and ever. Amen."

The Church honors Christ as King, for example, in the procession on Palm Sunday, and in the adoration of the cross on Good Friday. On the last Sunday in October, she celebrates the feast of Christ the King.

*Christian Customs.* It is a Christian custom to carry a cross or a medal of Christ on one's person. In the United States, some Catholics mount a small statue of Christ on their automobiles. In many countries, families enthrone the Sacred Heart of Jesus by having a statue or picture of our Lord in their homes. Youth organizations often carry banners which represent the sign of the cross. In Europe, one may often see crosses by the roadside or on hilltops or in marketplaces, put there to remind people that Christ is the Lord of creation.

*Things to do.* 1) How is Christ at work in our lives: a) as teacher; b) as high priest; c) as shepherd? 2) Write a litany of Christ, including all the names and titles of his that you can remember; for example, Savior, Master, Risen Lord. 3) What hymns to Christ do you know? 4) What does the preface for the feast of Christ the King say about Christ our Lord? 5) Collect pictures which show our Lord risen from the dead and in glory.

Hail Redeemer, King divine,
Priest and Lamb the throne is thine;
King whose reign shall never cease
Prince of everlasting peace!

## *LESSON 38*

### *Jesus Christ Will Come Again*

"From thence he shall come to judge the living and the dead."
(7th Article of the Creed.)

And as they strained their eyes toward heaven, to watch his journey, all at once, two men in white garments were standing at their side. "Men of Galilee," they said, "why do you stand here looking heavenward? He who has been taken from you into heaven, this same Jesus will come back in the same fashion, just as you have watched him going into heaven."[194]

On the last day, Jesus will come again, in great majesty and glory, surrounded by his angels.

[194] Cf. Acts 1:10-11

At his return, Christ will call all men before him, good and bad, living and dead. The dead will rise from their graves, and all will follow his voice.

Then Christ will judge all men. Those who have lived the life of grace may now remain eternally with him. Those who have rejected his grace will be eternally separated from him.

After the judgment, Christ will deprive the devil of the last vestige of his power, banish suffering and death from the world, and fill the whole universe with his glory.

Then Christ will have finished the saving work which he began in his earthly life. All will be subject to him, and he will rule openly as the King of all creation. When all has been subjected to Christ's power, he will then hand over the new, redeemed creation to his Father, and the heavenly Father will rule over it in measureless glory forever.

*Consider.* 1) When will Christ come again? 2) Whom will Christ then call into his presence? 3) What will the judgment of Christ be about? 4) What will Christ do after the judgment? 5) What will Christ do when he has completed the work of redemption?

67. **Why will Jesus come back on the last day?**

Jesus will come back on the last day to judge all men and to complete the work of salvation.

*For my life.* Christ is to come again: I must live in such a way that I may always think of that day with joy.

*From holy scripture.* "Christ is your life, and when he is made manifest, you too will be made manifest in glory with him."[195]—"All of us have a scrutiny to undergo before God's judgment seat, for each to reap what his mortal life has earned, good or ill according to his deeds."[196]—"Full completion comes after that, when he places his kingship in the hands of God,

[195] Col 3:4
[196] 2 Cor 5:10

his Father, having first dispossessed every other sort of rule, authority, and power."[197] — "Come Lord Jesus."[198]

*From the life of the Church.* Often, especially on the last Sundays of the Church's year, and in Advent, the Church calls to mind the return of Christ and warns us to make ready for his coming.

Sober, just, and devoted, let us live in this world
and await in blessed hope the appearance
of our great God and Savior, Jesus Christ in glory.[199]

## Of the Holy Ghost and His Action

"I believe in the Holy Ghost."
(8th Article of the Creed.)

When Christ our Lord went up to the glory of his Father, he did not want to leave us behind in loneliness. Therefore, he sent to us from his Father the Holy Ghost, to be with us throughout all time.

### *LESSON 39*

### *The Holy Ghost Came Down upon the Apostles*

On the day of Pentecost, the apostles were gathered together with Mary the Mother of Jesus and the other disciples in the upper room in Jerusalem. Suddenly there came a sound from heaven like that of a strong wind blowing, and it filled the whole house where they were. And there appeared to

[197] 1 Cor 15:24
[198] Apoc 22:20
[199] From a prayer of the Church's office during Advent.

them what seemed to be tongues of fire which parted and came to rest on each of them. And they were all filled with the Holy Ghost.[200]

The apostles and disciples were enlightened by the Holy Ghost. He taught them everything, and recalled to their minds everything which Jesus had said to them; he gave them the right words with which to proclaim the message of their Lord to both the Jews and the pagans.

The apostles and disciples received a new inflow of strength from the Holy Ghost. He drove out of them their timidity and fear of men, comforted them when they were being persecuted, and gave them the patience to suffer bravely. He gave them the strength even to give up their lives for the faith.

The apostles and disciples were made holy by the Holy Ghost. He entered into them with his gifts and graces, and remained in them ever afterward.

Already in the old testament, the Holy Spirit had come upon the patriarchs and the prophets. But on this day of Pentecost (Whitsunday), the fullness of what the Holy Ghost could give was poured out over the apostles and disciples. Now what the prophet had said was fulfilled: "I will pour out my spirit on all mankind."[201]

*Consider.* 1) How was it made clear that the Holy Ghost enlightened the apostles and disciples? 2) How was it made clear that he strengthened them? 3) How did he make them holy? 4) What had God foretold in the old testament about the coming of the Holy Spirit?

68. **What did the Holy Ghost do to the apostles?**
The Holy Ghost enlightened, strengthened, and sanctified the apostles.

*For my life.* The Holy Spirit who once filled the apostles and disciples lives in me, too. I ought therefore to be an apostle of Christ also.

*From the life of the Church.* We celebrate the descent of the Holy Ghost upon the apostles and the Church on the fiftieth day after Easter, and ten

[200] Cf. Acts 2:1-4
[201] Jl 2:28; Acts 2:17

days after the ascension of Christ, on what is called Pentecost (or Whit) Sunday.

*Things to do.* 1) What do the following symbols tell us about the Holy Ghost: a) the strong wind; b) the fire; c) the tongues? 2) What color are the Mass vestments in Masses of the Holy Ghost? 3) What does this color remind us of?

## *LESSON 40*

### *The Holy Ghost Is Truly God like the Father and the Son*

Before Jesus left his disciples, he said to them: "And I will ask the Father, and he shall give you another Paraclete that he may abide with you forever...The Paraclete, the Holy Ghost, whom the Father will send in my name will teach you all things and bring all things to your mind whatsoever I shall have said to you."[202]

The Holy Ghost, who came down upon the apostles and disciples on Pentecost day, is truly God like the Father and the Son. Therefore, he is to be glorified and adored just as they are.

The Holy Ghost proceeds from the Father and the Son through all eternity: he is the third Person of the Godhead. Father and Son love one another in an infinite love; the Holy Ghost is the living flame of this love between Father and Son. The Father and the Son have sent the Holy Spirit to bind us together with the Father and the Son and to set us alight with the fire of their own love.

*Consider.* 1) Why do we adore the Holy Ghost? 2) From whom does the Holy Ghost proceed? 3) Why do we call the Holy Ghost the "living flame of love between the Father and the Son"?

69. **Who is the Holy Ghost?**
The Holy Ghost is the third Person of the Godhead; he is true God, like the Father and the Son.

[202] Jn 14:16, 26

70. **What do we acknowledge about the Holy Ghost in the Creed which we say during Mass?**
We acknowledge: "I believe in the Holy Ghost, the Lord and giver of life, who proceeds from the Father and the Son; he is adored and glorified with the Father and the Son, he has spoken by the prophets."

*For my life.* I will often pray: "Come Holy Spirit, fill the hearts of thy faithful, and kindle in them the fire of thy love."

*Things to do.* 1) On what occasions ought we to pray to the Holy Ghost? 2) In your prayer book, see what prayers and hymns you can find in honor of the Holy Ghost.

## *LESSON 41*

## *The Holy Ghost Works in the Church in Various Ways*

"Let us rejoice in honor of the Holy Spirit, who makes the entire Catholic Church holy, and fills each soul; who breathes forth faith, who teaches wisdom, who is the source of love, the protector of chastity, and the author of all good actions."[203]

The Holy Ghost remains continuously with the Church and works in her. He enlightens her, so that she can never err; he makes her holy by constantly filling her with grace. He leads her through all persecutions and dangers to her destination in eternity.

Each one of us has received the gifts and the graces of the Holy Ghost. He makes us to be children of God, and helps us to live as such; he pours the love of God into our hearts, and gives us his seven gifts: wisdom and understanding, counsel and fortitude, knowledge and piety, and the gift of the fear of the Lord.[204]

The Holy Ghost gives special gifts for special tasks. To the bishops and teachers in the Church he gives whatever powers they need to perform their office. He gives strength to the martyrs and confessors to stand up

[203] Leo the Great, *Sermon 75*, Ch. 5
[204] Cf. Is 11:2

bravely for their faith. He fills with his love all those who devote themselves to work for the sick or who have care of souls. Often the Holy Spirit gives extraordinary gifts, such as the gift of being able to know what is on the conscience of other people, or the power to work miracles.

Every gift which goes beyond what nature can perform, and which is to further our salvation, is called "grace." Christ has earned all graces for us; they are given us through the Holy Ghost.

Without grace we could not be saved. No created thing could see God by its own unaided power, nor could it do anything at all to approach the sight of him. Grace is necessary to us that we may come to believe, live as children of God, and make the journey to heaven.

*Consider.* 1) What does the Holy Ghost do within the Church? 2) What does the Holy Ghost do within us? 3) What do we call the seven gifts of the Holy Ghost? 4) Name some of the tasks for which the Holy Ghost gives special graces.

71. **What do we mean by *grace*?**

By *grace*, we mean every interior gift which goes beyond what unaided nature could perform, and which God gives us to further our salvation.

72. **Why do we need God's grace?**

We need God's grace because, without it, we could not do the least thing toward our salvation.

*For my life.* How rich the Church is through the Holy Spirit! I shall thank God for all the treasures which the Church has ready to give to me.

*From holy scripture.* "And yet there are different kinds of gifts, though it is the same Spirit who gives them."[205]—"The spirit yields a harvest of love, joy, peace, patience, kindness, generosity, forbearance, gentleness, faith, courtesy, temperateness, purity."[206]

[205] 1 Cor 12:4
[206] Gal 5:22-23

*Things to do.* 1) Read slowly to yourself: a) the sequence of Pentecost (Whitsunday); b) the hymn "Come, Holy Ghost, Creator come." 2) Look for the names which are given to the Holy Spirit in the prayers and hymns of the Church. 3) Write out what these hymns say about the action of the Holy Ghost.

## LESSON 42

### We Are Enlightened and Strengthened by the Holy Ghost

In the Acts of the Apostles, we are told about the beginning of St. Paul's mission in Philippi: "On the Sabbath day, we went out beyond the city gates, by the river side, a meeting place, we were told, for prayer; and we sat down and preached to the women who had assembled there. One of those who were listening was a woman called Lydia, a purple-seller from the city of Thyatira, and a worshipper of the true God; and the Lord opened her heart, so that she was attentive to Paul's preaching."[207]

The Holy Ghost enlightens us. He opens our minds and hearts that we may believe God's truth, and see what is God's will.

We are also strengthened by the Holy Ghost. He moves us to live according to our faith, and to do the will of God. He gives us the inclination and the power to do what is good; he strengthens us in temptation, and fills us with loathing for what is evil; he comforts us in suffering, and helps us to remain true until death.

By these graces, God helps us to reach the end of our journey in eternity. And so, we call such graces "helping," or "actual graces." Without them we could not do the least thing to set out on the way of salvation, to follow it, much less to reach the end of it. "Both the will to do it and the accomplishment of that will are something which God accomplishes in you, to carry out his loving purpose."[208] We should therefore pray often for the grace of God.

[207] Acts 16:13-14
[208] Phil 2:13

God gives each man at least enough grace to make it possible for him to reach heaven. "It is his will that all men should be saved."[209] No one is lost other than by his own fault.

God does not, however, give all men the same graces. He brings us along different roads to the same eternal goal. God does not give all men the same number of graces, either. God will give more grace if we pray often, receive the sacraments, and let ourselves follow his holy inspirations. And when we are in greater need, God gives his graces more richly.

The grace of God only brings us to salvation when we make use of it. We ought to follow the suggestions of God's grace readily even in small things.

God does not force us to do anything by his grace. It is therefore possible for us to resist his grace. If we do that, it is our own fault that grace does not bring us to salvation. St. Paul says: "We entreat you not to offer God's grace an ineffectual welcome."[210]

*Consider.* 1) Why does the Holy Ghost enlighten us? 2) Why does the Holy Ghost strengthen us? 3) What do we call the graces by which the Holy Ghost enlightens and strengthens us? 4) Why should we often pray for God's grace? 5) When does God give his grace most plentifully?

73. **What does God do in us by his helping grace?**
God enlightens and strengthens us, that we may live and die as his children.

74. **How much grace does each man receive from God?**
Each man receives from God at least enough grace for him to be saved.

75. **What must we do when God gives us grace?**
We must make use of the grace of God and not dare to resist it.

*For my life.* I will often ask the Holy Ghost to enlighten me, especially when I examine my conscience, or when I have something very important to decide.

[209] 1 Tm 2:4
[210] 2 Cor 6:1

*From holy scripture.* Jesus said: "No man can come to me, except the Father, who hath sent me, draw him."[211]—"I am the vine; you the branches: he that abideth in me and I in him, the same beareth much fruit: for without me you can do nothing."[212]—"Those who follow the lead of God's Spirit are all God's sons."[213]

## LESSON 43

### We Are Made Holy by the Holy Spirit

St. Paul writes in the letter to the Galatians: "...when the appointed time came, then God sent his Son on a mission to us. He took birth from a woman, took birth as a subject of the law, so as to ransom those who were subjects of the law, and make us sons by adoption. To prove that you are sons, God has sent out the Spirit of his Son into our hearts, crying out in us, 'Abba, Father.' No longer, then, art thou a slave, thou art a son; and because thou art a son, thou hast the son's right of inheritance."[214]

Through the Holy Spirit, we share in the life of God, who is infinitely holy. We are therefore children of God, brothers and sisters of Jesus Christ, and heirs of everlasting life. This wonderful gift is called the "grace-life." This grace-life is far greater than our natural life; that is why it is also called "supernatural life."

The Holy Spirit lives in those who are God's children. He is the breath of the life of God in us, the pledge that we shall one day live eternally with the Father. With the Holy Spirit, there dwell in us the Father and the Son, too. Christ said, "We shall come and make our abode with him."[215] For this reason, St. Paul warns us: "Do you not understand that you are God's temple, and that God's Spirit has his dwelling in you."[216]

[211] Jn 6:44
[212] Jn 15:5
[213] Rom 8:14
[214] Cf. Gal 4:4-7
[215] Jn 14:23
[216] 1 Cor 3:16

By this grace-life, we are intimately bound and joined to God, who is the source of all grace, and thereby we are made holy. For this reason, we call the grace-life "the grace which makes holy," or "sanctifying grace." "Since we live by the Spirit, let the Spirit be our rule of life."[217] If we are the children of God, then we ought to live as children should: we should love God, and give him glory, receive the holy sacraments, and do his will. If we do all this, we shall increase in grace and bring forth much fruit for the life to come.

*Consider.* 1) What life does the Holy Spirit give us? 2) Why do we call the grace-life "supernatural life"? 3) Who lives in the children of God? 4) Why do we call the grace-life "sanctifying grace"? 5) What should we do because we are God's children?

76. **What does the grace-life do to us?**

The grace-life makes us the children of God, brothers of Christ, and heirs to eternal life.

*For my life.* The most precious thing I have on earth is the grace-life. Only one thing is really important: to live as a child of God. Only one thing is really terrible: to be separated from God, to die without his grace and so to be forever lost.

*From holy scripture.* "See how the Father has shown his love for us; that we should be counted as God's sons, should be his sons."[218]

Christian, be conscious of your dignity![219]

[217] Gal 5:25
[218] 1 Jn 3:1
[219] Leo the Great, *Sermon 21*, Ch. 3

# Of the Mystery of the Holy Trinity

When we think about the work of our redemption, we come to know what the Father, the Son, and the Holy Spirit have done for us. We may now take a glance into the deepest mystery of our faith, the mystery of the one God in three Persons.

## *LESSON 44*

### *The All-Holy Trinity*

Before Jesus went up to heaven, he said to his apostles: "All power is given to me in heaven and in earth. Going therefore teach ye all nations; baptizing them in the name of the Father, and of the Son, and of the Holy Ghost. Teaching them to observe all things whatsoever I have commanded you."[220]

The Father, the Son, and the Holy Ghost are three Persons. Already at Jesus' baptism, they had made themselves known. The Father has sent the Son into the world; the Son became man, and saved us; the Holy Ghost came down upon the Church, and is at work making us holy. We receive baptism in the name of the Father, the Son, and the Holy Ghost.

Each of the three divine Persons is truly God, for each has the divine nature.

The Son and the Holy Spirit are just as infinitely holy and perfect, all-knowing, all-powerful, and eternal as the Father. They are therefore worthy to be adored and glorified equally with the Father.

But these three Persons are only one God. They possess one divine knowledge, one divine will, and one divine life in immeasurable happiness. We call the one God in three Persons the "Blessed Trinity."

The truth of the three Persons in the one Godhead is the greatest and most mysterious truth of our faith. We cannot grasp it: we should need God's own power of understanding to do that. We would never have been

[220] Mt 28:18-20

able to know that there are three Persons in one God if Christ had not revealed it to us.

All that we have, all that we are, is received from the Holy Trinity. Therefore, we must give thanks and praise continuously to the Holy Trinity. We should give special thanks to the Father, because he has made us out of nothing, and called us to an eternal life; to the Son, because he has redeemed us; and to the Holy Spirit, because he has made us holy.

*Consider.* 1) When did the three divine Persons make themselves known? 2) Why are the three divine Persons to be adored and glorified equally? 3) In what are the three divine Persons one? 4) What name do we give to the God who is three-in-one? 5) Why can we not grasp the truth of the one God in three Persons?

77. **What does our faith teach us about the Blessed Trinity?**
There are three Persons in God: God the Father, God the Son, and God the Holy Ghost, and these three Persons are but one God.

78. **For what favors do we thank the three Persons?**
God the Father has made us from nothing; God the Son has redeemed us; and God the Holy Ghost has made us holy.

*For my life.* When I make the sign of the cross and speak the words, "In the name of the Father and of the Son and of the Holy Ghost," I will remember: I belong to the Holy Trinity.

*From holy scripture.* "The grace of our Lord Jesus Christ, and the love of God, and the imparting of the Holy Spirit be with you all."[221]

*From the teaching of the saints.* "My God, how small would you have to be for me to be able to understand you."[222]—"To wish to fathom this mystery is boldness; to believe it is happiness; to realize it is everlasting life."[223]

*From the Church's life.* On the First Sunday after Pentecost, the Church celebrates the feast of the Most Holy Trinity.

221 2 Cor 13:13
222 Francis de Sales
223 Bernard of Clairvaux

*A prayer.* "Glory be to the Father, and to the Son, and to the Holy Ghost. As it was in the beginning, is now, and ever shall be, world without end. Amen."

*Things to do.* 1) In what Bible stories do you find all three divine Persons named? 2) What hymns to the Holy Trinity are in the hymnbook? 3) What representations and symbols of the Holy Trinity do you know?

Blessed be the Holy and undivided Trinity!

## *SECTION II*

# Of the Church and the Sacraments

## How Christ Founded and Equipped the Church

"The holy Catholic Church, the communion of saints."
(9th Article of the Creed.)

In God's eternal kingdom, men from every nation and from all ages are to be brought together before him. God will be their King forever, and they will be his people. In order to make for himself a people even here on earth, God, through his Son Jesus Christ, founded the Church.

### *LESSON 45*

### *Jesus Christ Began to Lay the Foundation of His Church during His Public Life*

In the year 1943, Pope Pius XII issued an encyclical letter concerning the Church as the mystical body of Christ. In this letter, he writes: "The divine Savior began the building of his mysterious temple, the Church, even while he was still preaching and proclaiming his commandments...He chose the apostles, sending them as he had been sent by the Father, that is to say, as teachers, rulers, and sanctifiers of the community of believers.

He designated him who was to be their chief, and his own vicar on earth; and he made known to them all the things which he had heard from the Father."[224]

When Jesus proclaimed the news of the kingdom of God which was to come, many came to believe in him, and were made his followers. In this way, Jesus gathered around him the people with which God desired to make his new alliance.

From this crowd of disciples, Jesus chose twelve men who were to be always in his company. They were to be the foundation-members of the new people. Because they were to be sent out on his business, he called them the apostles; in Greek, that is what the word means: "those who are sent."

Simon, the son of Jonas, was chosen by Jesus to be the chief among the apostles, and to hold his place on earth. Jesus said to him: "And I say to thee: That thou art Peter; and upon this rock I will build my Church, and the gates of hell shall not prevail against it. And I will give to thee the keys of the kingdom of heaven. And whatsoever thou shalt bind upon earth, it shall be bound also in heaven: and whatsoever thou shalt loose on earth, it shall be loosed also in heaven."[225]

*Consider.* 1) How did Jesus gather around him the people with which God desired to make his new alliance? 2) For what purpose did Jesus choose his apostles? 3) What does the word *apostle* mean? 4) To what office did Jesus appoint Simon, the Son of Jonas?

79. **How did Jesus set about founding his Church?**
Jesus gathered followers about him, chose from them the twelve apostles, and appointed Peter his vicar on earth.

80. **In what words did Jesus appoint Peter to hold his place on earth?**
Jesus said to Peter: "Thou art Peter (the Rock), and upon this rock I will build my Church, and the gates of hell shall not prevail against it. And I will give to thee the keys of the kingdom of heaven: whatsoever thou shalt

[224] Pius XII, *Mystici Corporis*, n. 26-27
[225] Mt 16:18-19

bind upon earth, it shall be bound also in heaven; and whatsoever thou shalt loose on earth, it shall be loosed also in heaven."

*For my life.* I have the great good fortune to belong to the people of God. In the community of the believers, I shall be happy to serve the King of heaven.

*Things to do.* 1) Where in the Bible do we learn: a) that men gathered about Jesus; b) that Jesus called certain men to be his disciples; c) that Jesus sent his disciples out on a mission? 2) On what occasion during Jesus' preaching did Peter appear as the first of the apostles?

## *LESSON 46*

### *By His Death, Jesus Christ Won Life for His Church*

As Jesus hung on the cross, he completed the building of the mysterious temple, his Church. By the blood which he had shed on the cross, he removed the obstacle of the divine wrath and enabled all the heavenly gifts, particularly the sacraments of the new and eternal testament, to flow forth from the fountains of the Savior for the salvation of men. It was on the tree of the cross that he purchased his Church, that is, all the members of his mystical body.[226]

God's people of the old alliance for the most part did not believe in Jesus, and their leaders condemned him to death; they had broken their pact with God. But Jesus' disciples, who believed in him, were weak and imperfect too; all men were tainted with sin, and were unworthy to be God's people.

Jesus offered his life for his disciples, for the people that had been untrue to him, and for all men, in order to set them free from sin, and make them into a holy people of God: "He gave himself for us, to ransom us from our guilt, a people set apart for himself, ambitious of noble deeds."[227] God has made a new and eternal alliance with us in the blood of Jesus. He

[226] Cf. Pius XII, *Mystici Corporis*, n. 26, 30

[227] Ti 2:14

made the small band of disciples into a holy people of God by means of the Holy Ghost: this is our holy mother the Church. In her the eternal people of God is ever growing, a people which God is gathering for himself from every nation and every age.

When the old alliance (or covenant) was made, it was sealed by the sacrifice of animals. The new and eternal alliance was sealed with the sacrifice of our Lord Jesus Christ on the cross. His blood is the blood of the "new and eternal covenant."

Eve, who was the mother of sinful mankind, had once been formed out of the side of Adam. The Church, mother of redeemed mankind, came forth from the side of the dying Savior.

Jesus' death won life for her.

*Consider.* 1) Why was mankind unworthy to become God's people? 2) What did Jesus do to make mankind into a holy people of God? 3) What has God done to us on account of the blood of Jesus? 4) Compare the creation of Eve with the birth of the Church.

81. **What did Jesus do for his Church by his death on the cross?**
By his death on the cross, Jesus won life for his Church.

*For my life.* Christ bought the Church with his blood. Therefore, I will always be thankful that I belong to her.

*From holy scripture.* "Christ showed love to the Church when he gave himself up on its behalf. He would hallow it, purify it in the water to which his word gave life."[228]—"Thou wast slain in sacrifice; out of every tribe, every language, every people, every nation thou hast ransomed us with thy blood and given us to God."[229]

*Things to do.* 1) Read how God made his first covenant with his people on Sinai. 2) Take a piece of paper, and write on the upper left-hand side, "old covenant," and on the upper right, "new covenant." Then write out in the proper column the answer for each the following questions: a) Where

[228] Eph 5:25-26
[229] Apoc 5:9-10

did God make the covenant? b) With whom? c) Through what agent? d) What was sacrificed to seal the covenant? 3) What is the rite in which we take part in the sacrifice of the new alliance?

## *LESSON 47*

### *After His Resurrection, Jesus Completed the Founding of His Church*

After he had risen, Jesus appeared to his apostles and disciples during forty days, and spoke to them about the kingdom of God. He commanded them not to leave Jerusalem, but to wait for the events promised by the Father. He said: "The Holy Spirit will come upon you, and you will receive strength from him. You are to be my witnesses in Jerusalem, and throughout Judea, in Samaria, yes, to the ends of the earth."[230]

After he had risen, Jesus said to his apostles: "As the Father hath sent me, so also I send you."[231] He handed over to them the task which he had received from the Father. The Church was to give glory to God, and to lead men to eternal happiness.

Before Jesus went up to heaven, he said to the apostles: "All power is given to me in heaven and in earth. Going therefore teach ye all nations; baptizing them in the name of the Father, and of the Son, and of the Holy Ghost. Teaching them to observe all things whatsoever I have commanded you: and behold I am with you all days, even to the consummation of the world."[232] By these words, Jesus solemnly entrusted to his apostles and their successors the duty to teach all men, to sanctify and to guide them; he handed over to his Church the offices of teacher, priest, and shepherd.

To Peter, Jesus said: "Feed my lambs; feed my sheep."[233] In these words, he made Peter his vicar on earth and the visible head of the Church; he gave to him and to his successors full power to preside over his flock until he himself should return.

230 Cf. Acts 1:3-8
231 Jn 20:21
232 Mt 28:18-20
233 Jn 21:15-17

Since he went up to heaven, Christ sits at the right hand of God the Father as Lord of his Church. Until his return on the last day, he will act in heaven as teacher, high priest, and shepherd of his people. Christ is the invisible head of the Church.

On Pentecost Sunday, Christ sent the Holy Ghost down upon his Church from his Father. Through the Holy Spirit, he filled the Church with his own divine life and gave to her the power to carry out the tasks which he had entrusted to her.

*Consider.* 1) From whom had Christ received the task which he entrusted to his Church? 2) Whom did Jesus make the visible head of the Church? 3) Who is the invisible head of the Church? 4) What did Christ do for his Church on Pentecost?

82. **Why did Christ found his Church?**
Jesus founded his Church to give God glory and to lead men to eternal happiness.

83. **With what words did Jesus send his apostles out into the world?**
Jesus said to the apostles: "All power is given to me in heaven and in earth. Going therefore teach ye all nations; baptizing them in the name of the Father, and of the Son, and of the Holy Ghost. Teaching them to observe all things whatsoever I have commanded you: and behold I am with you all days, even to the consummation of the world."

84. **What threefold office has Christ delegated to his Church?**
Jesus has delegated to his Church the offices of teacher, priest, and shepherd.

85. **In what words did Jesus make Peter the chief shepherd of the Church?**
Jesus said to Peter: "Feed my lambs; feed my sheep."

86. **How did Jesus complete the founding of his Church?**
Jesus completed the founding of his Church by sending the Holy Ghost.

*For my life.* The community assembled for the worship of God is itself holy; for it is God's people, Christ is in the midst of it, and it is filled with the Holy Ghost.

*From the holy scripture.* "Where there are two or three gathered together in my name, there I am in the midst of them."[234]

*Things to do.* 1) Which apostle was no longer alive at Pentecost? 2) Who was chosen in his place? 3) Which apostle was added even later to the others? 4) How did Peter take the lead as head of the Church: a) at the election of Matthias; b) at Pentecost; c) at the council of the apostles in Jerusalem? 5) What do we read in the Bible about the life of the first Christians? 6) Name some of the special gifts and graces which the Holy Ghost gave to the first Christians.

## *LESSON 48*

### *The Church Is the Mystical Body of Christ*

St. Paul writes: "Each of us has one body, with many different parts, and not all these parts have the same function; just so we, though many in number, form one body in Christ, and each acts as the counterpart of another."[235]

The members of the Church are united with one another like the members of a body; that is why St. Paul calls the Church a body.

The head of this body is Christ, our Lord in heaven. He holds the whole body together, directs it, and makes it alive. That is why St. Paul calls the Church the "body of Christ."

The life's breath of this body is the Holy Spirit. He flows forth from Christ, the head, into the members. He binds the members together with the head, and with one another. The Holy Ghost is, then, the soul of the Church.

The members of this body are the faithful. All are to love Christ as their head, and their fellow Christians as his members, and be united with both

[234] Mt 18:20

[235] Cf. Rom 12:4-5

head and members in prayer and sacrifice. Each member must also strive to know his own special task, and to do it faithfully.

When we were baptized, we were engrafted into the mystical body of Christ. It is by baptism that one is made a member of the Church.

*Consider.* 1) Why do we call the Church a body? 2) Why do we call Christ the head of the body? 3) Why do we call the Holy Spirit the soul of the body? 4) What do the members of the body of Christ have to do? 5) How are we engrafted into the mystical body of Christ?

87. **What does St. Paul teach about the Church?**
St. Paul teaches that the Church is the body of Christ: Christ is its head, and we are its members.

*For my life.* I shall live not for myself alone, but for all members of Christ's body.

*From holy scripture.* "Christ is our head. On him all the body depends; it is organized and unified by each contact with the source that supplies it."[236]

*From the life of the Church.* In the year 1943, Pope Pius XII wrote a letter to the whole Church about the mystical body of Christ.

*Things to do.* 1) How do the members of the body of Christ act together with their head: a) in the celebration of the Mass; b) in the conversion of the unbelievers? 2) What persons in the parish have special duties? 3) Make up a prayer of petition and one of thanks from what you have read in this lesson.

## *LESSON 49*

## *The Holy Constitution of the Church*

After the feast of Pentecost, the apostles went out and preached the joyful news, and founded communities of Christians. They chose out suitable men, laid hands upon them, and made them bishops. In this way, Timothy

[236] Eph 4:15-16

was placed by St. Paul as bishop in Ephesus, Titus as bishop in Crete.[237] Peter came in the course of his preaching to Rome, and became the first bishop of that city. He died as a martyr there about the year 67. The huge church of St. Peter is built on the site of his grave.

In Christ's mystical body, not everyone has the same task: there are some who command and others who obey. The first rulers of the Church were Peter and the other apostles.

Christ willed that his Church should last until the end of the world. For this reason, the offices which he gave to Peter and the other apostles have to be carried on until the end of the world. Christ has willed that his Church should always have rulers to be in charge.

The authorities of the Church are the pope and the bishops of the Catholic Church; they are the successors of the apostles. They act as teachers, priests, and shepherds in the name of Christ. When the bishops of the whole world meet together under the leadership of the pope to discuss and decide important questions, their meeting is called a "general" or an "ecumenical council."

The pope is the visible head of the whole Church. He is the successor of St. Peter in the highest office of teacher and shepherd. This office is called the "primacy." Because Peter died as bishop of Rome, it is the bishop of Rome who is his proper successor. All bishops, priests, and faithful are under his guidance.

The bishop governs a part of the Church. This part is called his "diocese." Dioceses are divided into parishes, and over each parish the bishop places a pastor who is the parish priest. The parish priest is the spiritual father of everyone within his parish. He is also called the "pastor," a Latin word which means "shepherd."

Lay people, too, are to take part in the work of the Church under the leadership of those whom God has appointed to rule it. In their families and in their sphere of daily work and their public lives, they are to do all in their power for the honor of God and the salvation of other men (Catholic Action).

[237] Cf. 1 Tm 1:3; Ti 1:5

*Consider.* 1) Why is the Church governed by rulers? 2) Who are the rulers of the Church? 3) What is a general council? 4) What is a diocese or bishopric? 5) Who is the head of a parish? 6) How should the laity help in the tasks of the Church?

88. **Who are the rulers of the Church?**
The rulers of the Church are the pope and the bishops.

89. **What position does the pope hold?**
The pope is the successor of St. Peter, the vicar of Christ on earth, and the visible head of the Church.

90. **What are the bishops of the Catholic Church?**
The bishops of the Catholic Church are the successors of the apostles.

*For my life.* I shall love and revere the pope as the one who holds the place of Christ on earth; I will pray for him, and always be faithful to him.

*From holy scripture.* "Obey those who have charge of you, and yield to their will; they are keeping unwearied watch over your souls, because they know they will have an account to give."[238]

*An explanation.* The Church is called "Roman" Catholic because its chief ruler is the lawful bishop of Rome. The word *pope* means "father." The pope is also called the "holy father," because it is his holy office to rule the Church with a father's care. The word *catholic* means "universal," or "extending all over the world."

*Other offices in the Church.* The cardinals help the pope to govern the whole Church. They elect a new pope after the previous one has died. The vicar general and the members of the cathedral chapter, sometimes called "canons," and in the United States "consultors," help the bishop to govern his diocese.

[238] Heb 13:17

In many dioceses, there are auxiliary bishops who ordain and confirm on behalf of the bishop of the diocese. The assistant priests, sometimes called "curates," help the parish priest to administer his parish.

Several parishes are formed together into a deanery, which is presided over by a priest who is called the "dean" or "archpriest." Several dioceses are put together into a province. The principal bishop of a province is called an "archbishop."

*Things to do.* 1) What is the name of our present pope? 2) Where does he live? 3) What is our bishop's name? 4) Where does he live? 5) What is the cathedral church of our diocese? 6) What is our parish priest's name? 7) What other priests are there in our parish? 8) Who else besides the assistant priests help the parish priest in his work for the parish? 9) What are the parishes near us? 10) To what deanery does our parish belong? 11) Draw the mitre, the staff (crozier), the ring, and the pectoral cross of the bishop. 12) What color is worn by: a) the pope; b) the cardinals; c) the bishops; d) the priests? 13) Make a drawing which shows the constitution of the Church.

# The Church at Work in the World

The Church does the work of Christ in the whole world. She carries out the teaching office, proclaiming the joyful news of Christ. She fulfills the priestly office, glorifying God in the celebration of the liturgy and distributing God's graces. She acts as shepherd, leading us to heaven.

## *LESSON 50*

### *The Church Proclaims and Teaches*

While he was on a journey preaching, St. Peter was called to the house of Cornelius, an officer, who was a devout man. He went to Cornelius' house, and preached to everyone there how Christ had been crucified, rose from the dead, and would come again as judge. While Peter was still speaking, the Holy Spirit came down upon everyone who was hearing him, and Peter had them all baptized in the name of Jesus Christ.[239]

The Church proclaims the good news of Christ everywhere, and teaches us. She instructs us by sermons and lessons, and, by what is sung or read in the holy liturgy, she leads us ever deeper into mysteries of the faith.

It is Christ who speaks to us through the Church. It is his word that she proclaims, his teaching that she imparts, and by his Holy Spirit that she is enlightened.

The teaching office in the Church belongs to the pope and to the bishops who are united with him. It is their duty to preserve the doctrine of Christ free from error, and to make it known without letting it be corrupted. When the pope and the bishops in agreement proclaim something to be a teaching of faith, they cannot be wrong, because Christ and his Holy Spirit protect the Church from error. At a general council, the bishops decide whether a teaching is, or is not, contained in some truth that has been revealed by God; and, if not, whether it is true or false.

The supreme teacher of the Church is the pope. Without him a council cannot make an infallible, that is to say, an unerring decision. Yet the pope himself can make an infallible decision, even alone. He is infallible, that is to say he cannot make an error, when he defines a decision for the whole Church about faith or about how Christians should behave, and commands the whole Church to accept it. Christ said to Peter: "I have prayed for thee that thy faith fail thee not: and thou being once converted, confirm thy brethren."[240]

The bishop teaches the faithful of his diocese, chiefly by means of the catechism which he orders to be used in his diocese, by preaching, and by letters which he writes to his people (called "pastoral letters"). Other priests preach and teach with authority from him.

The faithful have the duty to help by their word and example that their fellow men should come to know the true faith and should grow in this knowledge. Parents, teachers, and catechists have this duty in especial measure.

[239] Cf. Acts 10
[240] Lk 22:32

*Consider.* 1) By what means does the Church instruct us? 2) Why can we say that when the Church is teaching us, it is Christ who speaks? 3) What is the proof that the pope is the supreme teacher of the Church? 4) In what ways does the bishop teach us? 5) What persons of the faithful are especially called to instruct others in the faith?

91. **Why is the Church infallible?**
The Church is infallible because through his Holy Spirit Christ preserves her from error.

92. **Who are the teachers in the Church?**
The teachers in the Church are the pope and bishops who are in communion with him.

93. **What is the purpose of the Church's teaching office?**
The purpose of the Church's teaching office is to preserve the teaching of Christ and to proclaim it without error.

94. **In what case is the pope infallible?**
The pope is infallible when he defines a doctrine concerning a teaching of faith or Christian behavior, and commands the whole Church to accept it.

*For my life.* I shall listen to the pope and the bishops with reverence, especially when they speak to us by an encyclical or a pastoral letter. Their voice is the voice of Christ.

*From holy scripture.* Jesus said to his apostles: "He that heareth you, heareth me: and he that despiseth you, despiseth me. And he that despiseth me, despiseth him that sent me."[241] Before he left them, Jesus said: "I will ask the Father and he shall give you another Paraclete, the spirit of truth, that he may abide with you for ever...He will teach you all things, and bring all

[241] Lk 10:16

things to your mind, whatsoever I shall have said to you."[242] Paul calls the Church "the pillar and foundation upon which truth rests."[243]

*The life of the Church.* Until now, there have been twenty general councils. The last two councils were those at Trent (1545-63) and the Vatican (1869-70). At the Vatican Council, the doctrine of the infallibility of the pope was solemnly proclaimed as an article of faith.

*The words of a convert.* "Only in the Catholic Church do I find clearness and decisiveness in the most important question in life. For that reason, I became a Catholic."[244]

*What would you say?* Many say: "The pope cannot be infallible because any man can sin and make mistakes." We reply: "Of course the pope can sin; he can also be in error when he expresses his private opinions. But when he speaks as the supreme teacher of the Church, and makes a binding decision about what we must believe or how we must behave, then he cannot be wrong because the Holy Ghost preserves him from error."

*Things to do.* 1) What means does the Church use to proclaim the faith? 2) What is done to proclaim the faith: a) in church; b) in the school; c) in the family; d) in parish organizations? 3) What can I do to help others to learn about the Catholic faith?

## LESSON 51

### The Church Draws Her Teaching from Holy Scripture and from Oral Tradition

The holy apostle Paul warns the faithful: "Stand firm, brethren, and hold fast by the traditions you have learned, in word or in writing, from us."[245]

What the Church teaches us comes from God who is the source of all truth; she hands on to us what God has revealed, and what was taught and believed from the very beginning of the Church. St. Paul says: "I have

[242] Jn 14:16-17, 26
[243] 1 Tm 3:15
[244] Chesterton, G. K.
[245] 2 Thes 2:14

handed on to you the message that was handed on to me."[246] In the course of time, the Church, under the guidance of the Holy Ghost, has explained some of these truths in a more exact manner, especially at times when these truths were attacked. For Christ had promised to her: "The truth-giving spirit will guide you into all truth."[247]

Many of the things which God has revealed, he caused to be written down in sacred books. Through the Holy Ghost, he prompted the authors to write these books; and while they were writing, he helped them in such a way that they did in fact put down accurately all those things which God desired to tell us through their means. These writings are called "holy scripture" or "the Bible" (which means "the Book"). Because holy scripture was inspired by God, it has God for its author. It is "the word of God."

Those parts of holy scripture that were written before Christ came are called the "old testament"; those parts which were written after Christ had come are called the "new testament."

The Church preserves holy scripture as a very precious treasure. Under the guidance of the Holy Spirit, she presents holy scripture to us, and explains it. The Church wishes us to listen eagerly to the word of God, and we should love to read it for ourselves. That is why there ought to be a Bible, or at least a new testament, in every Catholic home. But we ought to read only those translations of holy scripture which have been approved by the Church.

Not all the truths which God has revealed are written down in holy scripture. Many of them were only preached by the apostles, and were then handed on by the Church as precious traditions. We call these truths "oral tradition" because they were handed on by word of mouth. Very soon after the apostles' time, most of these truths were written down by learned and holy men whom we call "the Fathers of the Church."

The holy scripture and oral tradition are the two sources of our faith. With the help of the Holy Ghost, the Church preserves both of them without error, and draws upon them for what she teaches us.

[246] 1 Cor 15:3
[247] Jn 16:13

*Consider.* 1) From where does the Church draw her teaching? 2) Why is holy scripture called "the word of God"? 3) Why is it not enough if we believe only what is in holy scripture? 4) What do we call those truths which were only preached by the apostles but were not written down by them?

95. **Whence does the Church draw her teaching?**
The Church draws her teaching from holy scripture and from oral tradition.

96. **What sort of books are in the old testament?**
The old testament contains historical books, teaching books, and prophetic books.

97. **What sort of books are in the new testament?**
The new testament contains the four gospels, the Acts of the Apostles, the epistles, and the Apocalypse (or "Revelations") of St. John.

98. **What are the names of the four evangelists?**
The four evangelists are called Matthew, Mark, Luke, and John.

*For my life.* I will handle the books of holy scripture with great reverence; before reading them, I will pray to God that he will help me to understand and obey his word properly. I will buy myself a Bible, or at least a new testament, to be a treasure for my whole life. If I cannot buy one, I will try to get somebody to give me one.

*From the teaching of the saints.* "When you pray, you are talking to God. When you read holy scripture, God is talking to you."[248]—"He who does not know holy scripture does not know Christ."[249]

*Imprimatur.* We can know that an edition of the Bible, or of any other book about religion, has the approval of the Church when we see in it the Church's permission that it be printed: *Imprimatur.*

[248] Augustine
[249] Jerome, *Commentary on Isaiah*, "Prologue"

*What would you say?* Some people say: "The Bible alone is enough." But we answer: "Firstly, the Bible does not contain everything that God has revealed. St. John tells us: 'There is much else besides that Jesus did; if all of it were put in writing, I do not think the world itself would contain the books that would have to be written.'[250] And St. Paul wrote: 'Hold fast by the traditions you have learned, in word or in writing, from us.'[251] Secondly, the Bible does not itself tell us which books belong to it; we can know which they are only by tradition."

*The books of the old testament.* 1) Historical books: the most important are the five books written by Moses, the book of Josue, the book of Judges, the books of Kings, and the books of the Machabees. 2) Teaching books: the most important are the book of Job, the Psalms, and the book of Wisdom. 3) Prophetic books: the most important are the books of the four great prophets Isaias, Jeremias, Ezechiel, and Daniel.

*The books of the new testament.* 1) The four gospels. 2) The Acts of the Apostles, which St. Luke wrote. 3) The fourteen epistles of St. Paul, and the seven epistles of the other apostles (Saints James, Peter, John, and Jude). 4) The Apocalypse (or "Revelations") of St. John.

A complete list of all the books of the Bible is on page 329 of this catechism.

## *LESSON 52*

### *The Church's Mission to Preach Everywhere*

Before he went up to heaven, Jesus said to his disciples: "Go into the whole world and preach the gospel to every creature! He that believeth and is baptized shall be saved: but he that believeth not shall be condemned."[252]

The missions are one of the most important tasks of the Church. There are still millions who are waiting to hear the joyful news of Christ. Moreover, there is a spirit of unwillingness to believe which is spreading

[250] Jn 21:25
[251] 2 Thes 2:14
[252] Mk 16:15-16

nowadays even into the most distant lands and is robbing men even of the little that they do know about God. If we love Christ, we shall do all within our power to help pagans to learn about the truth and so come to faith in Christ.

In the missionary lands, there are at work priests, brothers, sisters, catechists, teachers, doctors, and others who help. Many of the missionaries come from Christian countries, but some are from the mission lands themselves. They strive by preaching and instruction, by prayer and the celebration of the worship of God, by teaching children and by caring for the sick, to win men for Christ.

We must all help those who are carrying out our Lord's missionary command. Missionaries and new converts wait for our help. Most important is the help we give by our prayers and sacrifices; without grace, no man can come to Christ. We can and ought also to give aid to the work of the missions, by money and other gifts, by distributing the missionary papers, by making collections for the missions. The money we give or collect serves to build churches, schools, and hospitals, to give the missionaries the things they need to live, and to set up new mission stations.

Anyone who wants to work in the missions must feel a great desire to take part in the spreading of the kingdom of Christ. He must also be of good health and sufficient intelligence. It is a great grace to be called by God to be a missionary. Whoever feels that God is calling him to work in the missions should follow this call with great joy.

*Consider.* 1) Why are the missions one of the most important of the Church's tasks? 2) Who work in the missions? 3) How do the missionaries seek to lead men to Christ? 4) What is done with the money that is collected for the missions? 5) What qualities must anyone have if he wants to go and work in the missions?

99. **How can all Christians help those who are spreading the faith?**
All Christians can help those who spread the faith in the missions by prayer, by gifts, and by working to make the missions known.

*For my life.* How ashamed I ought to be if I neglect giving help to the missionaries! I will pray each day for them, and help them regularly by my offerings.

*From the life of the Church.* On the second last Sunday in October is held World Mission Sunday; the feast of the Holy Innocents, or the Sunday after it, is World Mission Day for children.

The patron saints of the missions are St. Francis Xavier and St. Theresa of the Child Jesus.

*Some figures about the missions.* More than two-thirds of the world are not yet Christian; about fifty-seven million children who come into the world each year are not baptized. In 1950, there were in the missions: twenty-six thousand priests, nine thousand brothers, sixty-one thousand nuns. About half of these are natives of the mission countries. Two and a half million catechumens were being instructed for baptism.

*The Pontifical Mission Aid Societies.* To help the missions, there are many associations or societies. The most important are those headed by the pope, called the Pontifical Aid Societies: they are the Association for the Propagation of the Faith, the Society of St. Peter, Apostle, for the training of priests in missionary countries; the Society of the Holy Childhood. The holy father wishes all Catholic children to be members of the Society of the Holy Childhood. Members say a Hail Mary every day and add to it, "Holy Mary, Mother of God, pray for us and for all poor pagan children." Also, once a month they give a small contribution for the missions. The slogan of this society is: "All the world's children should be God's children."

*Things to do.* 1) Name some great missionaries to the pagans. 2) In what countries did they preach? 3) What missionaries worked in our own country? 4) What missionary magazines do you know? 5) What missionary orders do you know? 6) What can our class do for the missions?

# LESSON 53

## The Church Celebrates the Worship of God

In the Acts of the Apostles, we read about the life of the first Christians: "They persevered with one accord, day by day, in the temple worship, and, as they broke bread in this house or that, took their share of food with gladness and simplicity of heart, praising God and winning favor with the people."[253]

The service of common worship is the most holy task which the Church has to perform. In her common worship, the Church praises and glorifies God, thanks him for his goodness, makes reparation for sins, and begs him for his gifts. The summit and center of the Church's service of worship is the celebration of the Holy Eucharist.

When we come together for the Church's worship, Christ is present in our midst. He is our high priest: the priest at the altar is only his representative. Because Jesus is our high priest, we pray and offer "through Jesus Christ our Lord."

When we take part in the Church's worship, we are filled with heavenly grace. In the worship of the Church, we also pray for light and grace for those who do not belong to her.

The faithful ought to celebrate with the Church, by praying along with the priest and offering with him. By their baptism, they are both enabled and appointed to do this. The more fully each person takes part in worship, the more God is glorified, and the more grace everyone will receive from him.

*Consider.* 1) What does the Church do in her services of worship? 2) How should the faithful act at the Church's services? 3) Through whom does the Church pray to God? 4) What is given to us in the worship of the Church?

100. **What is the Church's holiest duty?**
The holiest duty of the Church is to celebrate the worship of God.

[253] Acts 2:46-47

*For my life.* I will take my part eagerly in the worship in our parish church. I will take a prayer book with me to every service.

*From holy scripture.* "You are a chosen race, a royal priesthood, a consecrated nation, a people God means to have for himself; it is yours to proclaim the exploits of God who has called you out of darkness into his marvelous light."[254]

*The pope teaches.* "It is most important that, when the faithful assist at sacred ceremonies, they should not be detached and silent spectators, but, filled with a deep sense of the beauty of the liturgy, they should raise their voices in answer to the priest or choir."[255]

*Processions and pilgrimages.* On certain days, such as Corpus Christi, and the Ember days, in some countries Catholics go in procession through the streets and the fields to give common praise to God, and to make open profession of their faith, and to ask God's blessing. From the most ancient times, the faithful have made journeys to visit holy places, such as Rome or Jerusalem or other places where God has shown in some way that he is especially attentive to their prayers. Such journeys are called pilgrimages.

*Things to do.* 1) What different kinds of Church service do you know? 2) What part do the following persons take in the Mass: a) the priest; b) the servers; c) the prayer-leader; d) the choir; e) the organist; f) the faithful? 3) What should the faithful do: a) at the gospel; b) at the *Dominus vobiscum*; c) when there are community prayers; d) when there is singing; e) when the priest sings the preface or the Our Father? 4) Make drawings of the sacred vessels, the vestments, and other things which are used in the worship of the Church.

## *LESSON 54*

### *The Church Administers the Holy Sacraments*

At Ephesus, St. Paul met disciples who had not yet heard of the Holy Ghost. He asked them: "What baptism did you receive?" And they said: "John's baptism"; so Paul told them: "John baptized to bring men to

[254] 1 Pt 2:9

[255] Pius XI, *Divini Cultus*

repentance; but he bade the people have faith in one who was to come after him, that is in Jesus." On hearing this, they received baptism in the name of the Lord Jesus; and when Paul laid his hands upon them, the Holy Spirit came down upon them.[256]

The Church gives us the seven holy sacraments in order that we may have life, and have its fullness. She baptizes us to set us free from sin, and to make us the children of God. She confirms us that we may receive the strength of the Holy Spirit. She feeds us with living bread in the Holy Eucharist. In the sacrament of penance, she looses us from our sins. To those who are very ill she gives the sacrament of holy anointing (extreme unction) to strengthen them both in body and soul. In the sacrament of ordination, she gives the powers of the priesthood and the graces needed for priestly life and work. In the sacrament of marriage (matrimony) she joins the bride and bridegroom together in a sacred union of lives.

Every sacrament has an outward or visible sign; for instance, in baptism, the washing with water and the words which are spoken as this is done. By this outward sign, a definite inward grace is signified, and at the same time given. These holy grace-giving signs are instituted by Christ.

In the sacraments, it is Christ our high priest who is at work. The persons who administer the sacraments are only his instruments. Christ distributes to us through the sacraments the graces which he has won for us on the cross.

Some sacraments imprint on the soul a kind of mark or quality which can never be lost. It is called the "character." In baptism, we take on the character of a follower of Christ; in confirmation, that of a soldier of Christ; in the sacrament of holy order, that of a priest of Christ. Therefore, these sacraments can only be received once.

We must receive the sacraments worthily. Anyone who desires to receive the sacraments of baptism or of penance must be sorry for his sins. The other sacraments may be received only by one who already has the grace-life. When anyone receives a sacrament unworthily, he does not receive the spiritual grace, but rather commits a mortal sin, a crime against

[256] Cf. Acts 19:1-7

God which is called a "sacrilege." But whoever receives the sacraments worthily draws everlasting life from the fountain who is our Savior. The more we love him, the more grace we receive.

*Consider.* 1) What particular graces do we receive in each sacrament? 2) Who acts in the sacraments? 3) What do the outward signs mean? 4) Which sacraments can be received only once? 5) Why can these be received only once? 6) What is required to receive baptism and penance? 7) What is necessary if we are to receive the other sacraments?

101. **Which are the seven sacraments?**

The seven sacraments are: 1) baptism, 2) confirmation, 3) the Holy Eucharist, 4) penance, 5) the anointing of the sick, 6) holy order, 7) matrimony.

102. **What things are needed to make a sacrament?**

The things needed to make a sacrament are: 1) the outward sign; 2) the inward grace; 3) the institution by Jesus Christ.

*For my life.* Christ offers me his sacraments with so much love; I will not wound his love by not caring about them; instead, I will receive them gratefully.

*The ceremonies.* To the signs which were chosen for use by Christ, the Church has added other signs full of meaning; for example, the giving of a white garment and a burning candle in baptism. These ceremonies should make the meaning of the sacrament still clearer to us, and increase our regard for them.

*Things to do.* 1) Which three sacraments were all given on the same day to converts in ancient times? 2) Which two sacraments are meant for special states in life? 3) Draw symbols for the different sacraments.

# LESSON 55

## The Church Blesses and Consecrates

Once, some mothers brought their children to Jesus, that he might lay his hands on them and pray over them. But the disciples rebuked them. Then Jesus said to them: "Suffer little children and forbid them not to come to me: for the kingdom of heaven is for such." And embracing them and laying his hands upon them, he blessed them.[257]

According to the mind of Jesus, the Church calls down God's blessing upon us and upon the things that we use. She blesses children, mothers, the sick, the bride at her wedding, and the faithful at the end of the Mass. She blesses our houses, our food and drink, fields and meadows, the beasts and their stables, the workshop and the tools, the streets and bridges, the railways, cars, and airplanes.

Some persons and things are set apart wholly for the service of the Church by a special blessing: this is called "consecration." By such a blessing, for example, the Church consecrates abbots, monks, and certain nuns. She consecrates the church building, the altar, the chalice and paten used in Mass, and blesses the cloths for the altar and the church vestments, water and candles, crosses and pictures, medals and rosaries, organs and bells, and the graves of the faithful. We must treat consecrated things and persons with reverence. The Church often uses exorcisms over persons or things; an exorcism is a solemn appeal to God that he will remove these persons or things from the influence of the devil. Examples are persons who are being baptized, and those who are possessed by evil spirits. Exorcisms are also used for water which is to be blessed, or used in baptism.

When the Church blesses and consecrates, she makes the sign of the cross; it is the sign of our redemption. Holy water is also very often used in blessings.

[257] Cf. Mt 19:13-15; Mk 10:16

The blessings and consecrations are similar to the sacraments; for this reason, they are called "sacramentals." They are not however instituted by Christ, as the sacraments were; instead, they were instituted by the Church.

They do not have effect by their own God-given power, as do the sacraments; whatever power they have comes from the Church's prayer.

When the Church blesses and consecrates, she usually asks from God some benefit for soul or body, or protection against the devil. The sacramentals are to help us live holy lives in this world, and to use the things of this world for God's honor and for our salvation.

When we receive a blessing or use blessed things, we should put our confidence in God's goodness and in the prayer of the Church. If we imagine that we shall receive help not from God but from the outward sign alone, we commit the sin of superstition. The more devoutly we receive the blessings of the Church or use the things consecrated to holy use, the more grace we receive from God. The faithful too can give some blessings. Parents bless their children. It is also a Christian custom to make the sign of the cross over various things, for instance, in some places over bread before it is cut to eat. We bless ourselves when we make the sign of the cross.

*Consider.* 1) From whom has the Church authority to consecrate, to bless, and to exorcise? 2) What things does the Church bless? 3) What things does the Church consecrate? 4) Why does the Church pronounce exorcisms? 5) What is usually done when something is blessed? 6) What name do we give to blessings and consecrations, because of their likeness to the sacraments? 7) How are they different from the sacraments?

103. **What does the Church beg of God when she blesses and consecrates?**
When she blesses and consecrates, the Church begs of God the well-being of soul and body and protection against evil spirits.

*For my life.* In the morning when I get up, and in the evening when I go to sleep, I shall make the sign of the cross and use holy water.

*From the life of the Church.* "When we come and go, when we dress, eat, go to sleep, before all that we do, we make upon our foreheads the sign of the cross."[258]

*Things to do.* 1) What blessed things are found in a Christian house? 2) What does the Church bless and consecrate: a) on Ash Wednesday; b) on Palm Sunday; c) on the Vigil night of Easter; d) on Candlemas; e) on the Assumption of Our Lady? 3) When are houses blessed? 4) What is the blessing of St. Blaise for? 5) What is holy water used for? 6) Keep a vessel with holy water in your room. 7) See that there are blessed candles in your house.

## *LESSON 56*

## *The Pastoral Task of the Church*

When St. Paul had returned from his third missionary journey, he invited those in charge of the Church at Ephesus to meet him in Miletus, to say farewell to them. And he said to them: "Keep watch then over yourselves, and over God's Church, in which the Holy Spirit has made you bishops; you are to be the shepherds of that flock which he won for himself at the price of his own blood."[259]

The Church has the pastoral charge to urge the faithful to lead a Christian life. She warns and encourages us to what is good and protects us from dangers which threaten our eternal salvation; she commands and makes laws. For some very serious sins, she has ordained penalties, to frighten men from sin, and to bring sinners to take thought of themselves. The most serious penalty is excommunication: when a person is excommunicated, he is shut off from many graces and privileges, especially from receiving the sacraments and from Christian burial.

It is a part of the Church's pastoral charge also to look after those who are in need. She therefore seeks with special love to help all who are in distress of soul or body.

[258] Tertullian, *De Corona Militis*, Ch. 3
[259] Cf. Acts 20:17-38

The pope and the bishops are the shepherds of the Church. They have authority to make laws and to inflict Church penalties. Christ gave them this authority when he said to the apostles: "Whatsoever you shall bind upon earth shall be bound also in heaven: and whatsoever you shall loose upon earth shall be loosed in heaven."[260] The chief shepherd of the Church is the pope. He is the successor of St. Peter to whom Jesus said: "Feed my lambs, feed my sheep."[261] It is Christ, our heavenly shepherd, who rules us through the pope and the bishops.

Each parish is ruled by its pastor (parish priest, rector), who is appointed by the bishop. The faithful are to follow their shepherd, and help him in his work of ministry.

*Consider.* 1) How does the Church lead us to live a Christian life? 2) Why has the Church set punishments for certain sins? 3) What is the gravest punishment of the Church? 4) Whom does the Church particularly wish to help? 5) Who are the shepherds of the Church? 6) In what words did Christ make his apostles and their successors the shepherds of the Church?

104. **How does the Church perform her office as shepherd?**
The Church leads us to live a Christian life.

*For my life.* The Church is my mother; I will always be led by her, whether she seems to me strict or mild.

*From holy scripture.* "Teach them to observe all things, whatsoever I have commanded you."[262]—"We have treated every one of you as a father treats his children, encouraging you, comforting you, imploring you to lead a life worthy of the God who now invites you to the glory of his kingdom."[263]

*From the teaching of the saints.* "No one can have God for his father who does not have the Church for his mother."[264]

*A principle.* In no parish should anyone be completely neglected.

[260] Mt 18:18
[261] Jn 21:15-17
[262] Mt 28:20
[263] 1 Thes 2:11-12
[264] Cyprian, *On the Unity of the Church*, n. 6

*From the life of the Church.* In parish life, the pastoral care of the Church is shown in these and other ways: encouragements or warnings in sermons, instructions, and in the confessional; regulations, visits, circular letters, parish magazines, lists showing what films are good or bad; the lay apostolate, parish meetings, youth works; visits to the sick, help for the poor. Those in any kind of trouble can go for help to the various charitable organizations of the parish.

*Some ways of doing good in the parish.* Tell newcomers to the parish where the Church is and what time the services are. Tell the parish priest when new Catholics move in. Make friends with their children and take them to childrens' services or youth clubs. Help to distribute Catholic papers. Speak out against bad talk. Help to make up parcels for those in need. Give help in youth organizations.

## LESSON 57

## *The Church's Care for Scattered Christians*

St. Paul often told the Christian communities which he had founded that they ought to help other communities. In a letter to the Corinthians, he holds up to them the example of the community in Macedonia: "And now, brethren, we must tell you about the Church in Macedonia, how well they have stood the test of distress, how abundantly they have rejoiced over it, how abject is their poverty, and how the crown of all this has been a rich measure of generosity in them." Then he appeals to the Corinthians: "Give them proof of your charity."[265]

In parts of our country, Catholics are very few and have to live among other people who are not of our faith. There are often not enough priests or nuns or teachers or churches for these scattered Catholics. Perhaps they can have Mass only occasionally, and it must be in a room or hall or other place which is not a church. They have to go a long way to get to Mass at all. There are no Catholic schools for their children who get little or no

[265] Cf. 2 Cor 8:2-24

instruction in the faith. When they grow up, these children may not be able to find a fellow Catholic to marry; they marry someone who is not a Catholic and often lose their faith on account of this. Some of them die without the sacraments because the priest is not called or cannot get to them in time.

The Church has the duty of helping these scattered Catholics who have such great difficulties. She must strengthen them that they may remain true to their faith, support one another, and win converts. The Church has to found new parishes, build new churches, send priests and nuns; chalices and Mass vestments, altars and missals have to be provided, and often motor cars are needed since without them the priests cannot reach the scattered people.

Those Catholics who are in well-established parishes should do all they can to help this work for their scattered brethren. They should pray for them, and they should give money to those funds which bishops devote to such purposes.

Every Catholic must realize that a time might come when he himself might have to live in some part of the country where there are almost no Catholics. Therefore he must fit himself to stand alone and remain true to his faith even in such circumstances; he should be able to instruct others who are ignorant and weak, to help the priest in his mission to scattered Catholics. Every young Catholic should prepare for tasks like this.

*Consider.* 1) What are the chief difficulties facing Catholics who live in non-Catholic parts of the country? 2) What must the Church do for such scattered Catholics? 3) What can we do to help the Church in this task? 4) For what tasks must every Catholic who lives in such a district be ready?

*For my life.* These scattered Catholics are my brothers and sisters; I will help them with my prayers and contributions.

*From holy scripture.* "If one member suffers, all the rest suffer with it."[266]

[266] 1 Cor 12:26

# LESSON 58

## The One True Church

St. Paul wrote in his letter to the Ephesians: "You are no longer exiles or aliens; the saints are your fellow citizens; you belong to God's household. Apostles and prophets are the foundation on which you were built. And the chief cornerstone of it is Jesus Christ himself; in him the whole fabric is bound together, as it grows into a temple, dedicated to the Lord; in him you too are being built in with the rest, so that God may find in you a dwelling place for his Spirit."[267]

Christ has founded only one Church. He said: "On this rock I will build my Church."[268] So there is only one true Church.

We can recognize the true Church from certain qualities which Christ gave to it. The Church of Christ has to be one in faith, one in sacraments, and under one head. It must be holy because Christ makes it holy; it must be catholic (that is universal, for everybody) because Christ founded it for all nations and for all ages. And it must be apostolic: that is, those in authority over it must be lawful successors of the apostles.

Only the Catholic ("Roman Catholic") Church has all these four qualities. For she is one: having the same faith throughout, and the same sacraments under one visible head, the pope. She is holy: we see that from the holiness of her teaching and of her works, and especially from her saints, of whom God has glorified so many by means of miracles. She is catholic: for she preserves the entire faith and all the sacraments, has been in existence through all times since the time of Christ himself, and has spread throughout the whole world. She is apostolic: because she goes back to the apostles; her bishops are the lawful successors of the apostles, and the pope is the lawful successor of St. Peter. It is this which shows most clearly of all that she is the true Church of Christ.

There are indeed other Christian communities named "churches," but not one of them has all these four qualities. Above all, they are not

[267] Eph 2:19-22
[268] Mt 16:18

apostolic, for they did not begin to exist until long after the time of the apostles. Those who lead them are not the lawful successors of the apostles, and are not in communion with the successor of St. Peter. So none of these other communities can be the true Church of Christ.

It is the Catholic Church alone which has received Christ's authority, and been equipped by him with the means to lead men to everlasting happiness. She alone has the authority to proclaim God's word, to offer the holy sacrifice, to administer the sacraments, and to guide men in the Christian way of life.

Those Christians who belong to a non-Catholic body for the most part do not know that the Catholic Church is really their true home. They do not possess the full truth and are subject to many errors and miss many graces. But Christ died for them too, and the Church prays for them and offers sacrifice for them too. So it is possible for them to reach everlasting happiness if only they do the will of God as well as they know how.

*Consider.* 1) From what words of Jesus do we know that he intended to found only one Church? 2) What does the word *catholic* mean? 3) What does the word *apostolic* mean? 4) Why must the true Church be: a) one; b) holy; c) catholic; d) apostolic? 5) What things show that the Catholic ("Roman Catholic") Church is in fact: a) one; b) holy; c) catholic; d) apostolic? 6) What shows most clearly of all that the Catholic ("Roman Catholic") Church is the true Church of Christ? 7) Why can no other Christian community or "church" be the true Church of Christ? 8) Why is the Catholic Church called "the only way to salvation"? 9) How is it that even those who are not Catholics can be saved? 10) What must we do to help them also to be saved?

105. **Why is there only one true Church?**
There is only one true Church because Christ founded only one Church.

106. **What qualities must the true Church have?**
The true Church must be one, holy, catholic, and apostolic.

107. **Which Church has these four qualities of the true Church?**
Only the Catholic Church has these four qualities of the true Church.

108. **Why is the Catholic Church called "the only way to salvation"?**
The Catholic Church is called "the only way to salvation" because she alone has received from Christ both the commission and the means to lead men to salvation.

*For my life.* I will thank God with all my heart that I am so fortunate as to live in the one true Church. I will always acknowledge her joyfully and fearlessly. I will also pray that the separated Christians may find their way home into the community of the one true Church.

*From holy scripture.* After the last supper, Jesus prayed: "That they all may be one as thou, Father, in me and I in thee; that they also may be one in us; that the world may believe that thou hast sent me."[269]

*From the life of the Church.* From the 18th to the 25th of January, Christians of all communities pray for unity of faith. This is called "The Church Unity Octave."

At the present time, the Church has rather more than four hundred million members.

*Different rites within the Catholic Church.* Most Catholics celebrate Mass and other services of the Church in Latin, but not all of them do so. There are some who have their services in Greek or in Russian or in other languages, but they are true Catholics just as much as we are because they have the same faith and the same sacraments; their bishops are lawful successors of the apostles and they are in communion with the pope, the successor of St. Peter. They are called "Catholics of the Eastern rites" because all of them have existed in the East since the times of the apostles. But there are quite a lot of them now in various cities of the United States and Canada. These Eastern Catholics have their own church law which is rather different from the church law of the West; for instance, they may have married priests, and may receive Holy Communion in the forms both of bread and of wine, whereas we of the Latin rites have only unmarried priest and receive Holy Communion under the form of bread alone.

[269] Jn 17:21

*Christian communities outside the Catholic Church.* In the eleventh century, many of the Eastern Catholics separated themselves from the pope and refused to acknowledge him as the vicar of Christ. They called themselves "Orthodox," and have split into many national churches, and number about 150 million all told. One of the most important of these is the Russian Orthodox Church in which a great many of the Russians believe, even though their country is ruled by Communists who do not believe in God at all. These Orthodox Christians have nearly all of the true faith, and have true sacraments with real bishops and priests; if only they would acknowledge the pope as Christ's vicar on earth, they would be Catholics again.

In the sixteenth century, there were other Catholics, this time of the Latin rite, who refused to obey the pope and cut themselves off from the Catholic Church. These lost the true faith as well, and began to believe errors taught to them by Luther, Calvin, Zwingli, and others. Thus there are various protestant churches, such as the Lutheran Church which has many members in the United States. In England, the most important church is the Church of England which was started only about four hundred years ago. Up till then, England was a Catholic country, and Westminster Abbey, York Minster, and the very old cathedrals and parish churches now held by the Church of England were built by Catholics. But King Henry VIII quarreled with the pope and cut England off from the Catholic Church. Many people in the Church of England call themselves "Anglo-Catholics," believe many Catholic doctrines, and have services which look like the Mass; the same is true of many in the Episcopalian Church of America. But they do not possess the real Mass or the real priesthood. It is very sad that they should be separated from us because most of them are good people who serve God as well as they know how; and we should often pray for them that they may find their way into the true Church.

## LESSON 59

### The Communion of Saints

During the Holy Sacrifice of the Mass, the Church thinks of all those who are united with her. During the Canon of the Mass, she prays for all the faithful, especially for those who are present. Then she thinks of all the saints in heaven and asks God to hear their prayers for us and grant us help and protection. After the consecration, she prays for the dead, that God may grant them eternal rest with him.

The faithful on earth form a holy community whose head is Christ. They pray and offer sacrifice for each other, especially when they meet to worship together. They have a share in the prayers and sacrifices of the Church and in all the prayers and good works of each one, especially in those which they purposely offer for each other.

The faithful on earth are in communion with the saints in heaven. All the saints are our brothers and sisters in Christ. We celebrate their memory, ask for their prayers, and try to follow their example. They praise God with us and pray to him for us.

And through Christ we are united also with the souls in purgatory. We help them by our prayers and good works, by gaining indulgences for them, and above all by means of the Holy Mass. They are grateful to us, and pray for us to God.

The faithful on earth have still got to fight in order to win their eternal salvation; and so they are called the "Church militant." The saints in heaven have already won the victory, and so are called the "Church triumphant." The souls in purgatory must still suffer in order to be purified from the effects of their sins, so they are called the "Church suffering."

The faithful on earth, the saints in heaven, and the souls in purgatory form all together one great holy community; they are all sanctified by the Holy Ghost and united to each other through him. This great united community is called the "communion of saints."

On the last day, Christ will bring the Church militant and the Church suffering to join the Church triumphant. The whole great family will then be assembled together with God the Father. Then the communion of saints will be complete.

*Consider.* 1) How does the communion of the faithful on earth show itself: a) with one another; b) with the saints in heaven; c) with the souls in purgatory? 2) What do we call the community of the faithful on earth? 3) What do we call the community of the saints in heaven? 4) What do we call the community of the souls in purgatory? 5) Why do we call these three communities, taken together, the "communion of saints"? 6) How will Christ bring the communion of saints to completion?

109. **Who belong to the communion of saints?**

To the communion of saints there belong:

1. the faithful on earth;
2. the saints in heaven;
3. the souls in purgatory.

*For my life.* Whatever good I do helps the entire Church, and whatever evil I do harms the whole Church; what a great responsibility I have! Among the saints in heaven and among the faithful on earth are many unknown friends of mine; I will remember gratefully that I receive many favors through their prayers.

*From holy scripture.* St. Paul wrote: "I am glad of my sufferings on your behalf, as, in this mortal frame of mine, I help to pay off the debt which the afflictions of Christ still leave to be paid, for the sake of his body, the Church."[270]—"A holy and wholesome thought it is to pray for the dead."[271]

*From the life of the Church.* Almost every day the Church celebrates the feast of some saint. November 1st is the feast of All Saints, and November 2nd is the commemoration of All Souls.

*Things to do.* 1) For which of the faithful should we pray most of all? 2) Which of the saints are especially near to us? 3) For which of the souls

[270] Col 1:24

[271] 2 Mc 12:46

in purgatory should we pray most? 4) In the Canon of the Mass, find the places which mention: a) the living; b) the saints in heaven; c) the dead.

## *LESSON 60*

### *Mary Is Our Mother and Our Queen*

"Hail, holy Queen, Mother of mercy, hail our life, our sweetness, and our hope. To thee do we cry, poor banished children of Eve; to thee do we send up our sighs, mourning and weeping in this vale of tears. Turn, then, most gracious advocate, thine eyes of mercy toward us; and after this our exile, show unto us the blessed fruit of thy womb, Jesus. O clement, O loving, O sweet Virgin Mary!"

Among all the saints, the most Holy Virgin Mary stands in the first place. It was her privilege to give her help to God at the incarnation of his Son. She is the Mother of our Savior; and because Jesus is our brother, she is our Mother too.

As Jesus was offering himself for us on the cross, Mary stood near him and took part in his sacrifice. The sword of sorrow pierced her very soul. She is the Mother of Sorrows, the Refuge of Sinners, the Comforter of the Afflicted.

After our Lord had gone up into heaven, Mary remained with the group of the disciples, prayed with them in the upper room in Jerusalem, and on Pentecost received with them the outpouring of the Holy Spirit. Both in joy and in sorrow she took part in the life of the infant Church. She is the Mother of Christians.

Because Mary was so closely bound up with her Son in his passion and death, she was to be like him also in his heavenly glory. Her body was preserved from corruption because she remained always free from sin. She was taken up body and soul into heaven. This is called the "assumption."

And now she is reigning in heaven as Queen over all the angels and saints. She reigns with Christ, her Son, over all the earth. With a merciful Mother's love, she embraces all the brothers and sisters of her Son. She is our Lady, our heavenly Mother; she prays for us and obtains graces for us.

*Consider.* 1) Why does Mary stand in the first place before all the saints? 2) Why is Mary our Mother? 3) Why do we call her "the Mother of Sorrows"? 4) What part did Mary take in the life of the infant Church? 5) Why was Mary taken, body and soul, up to heaven? 6) What does Mary do for us now in heaven?

110. **How was Mary glorified at the end of her life on earth?**
At the end of her life on earth, Mary was glorified by being taken up body and soul into heaven.

*For my life.* Because I love Jesus, I love also his holy Mother. I will honor her as my Queen, pray to her as my Mother, and trust myself to her care.

*From the life of the Church.* The Church celebrates the feast of the Assumption of Mary into heaven on August 15th. The truth that Mary was taken up bodily into heaven has always been believed by the Church; but it was defined as an article of faith by Pope Pius XII on November 1st, 1950. On November 1st, 1954, Pope Pius XII proclaimed a feast of the Queenship of Mary, to be celebrated on May 31st.

*Things to do.* 1) Collect some pictures which represent events in our Lady's life, especially the annunciation, Mary standing under the cross, receiving the Holy Ghost at Pentecost, being taken up into heaven, and reigning as Queen of heaven. 2) In which new testament stories is Mary mentioned? 3) What words of Mary are preserved in the new testament? 4) Make a comparison between Eve and Mary; in what ways are they alike, and in what ways are they different?

# We Are Made Holy in Baptism

"The forgiveness of sins."
(10th Article of the Creed.)

Some day we are to be eternally happy in God's kingdom. Therefore, we must believe in God, be baptized, and live as God's children.

## *LESSON 61*

### *Conversion to God*

When the crowd which had assembled at Pentecost heard that Christ, whom they had rejected, had risen from the dead and been enthroned at God's right hand, their consciences were stung. And they said to Peter and the other apostles: "Brethren, what must we do?" Peter said to them: "Repent, and be baptized, every one of you, in the name of Jesus Christ; to have your sins forgiven; then you will receive the gift of the Holy Spirit."[272]

God causes the good tidings to be preached by the Church, and enlightens the hearts of men that they may hear the message. He opens their eyes that they may know him, the only true God, and Jesus Christ whom he has sent.[273]

Anyone who has heard the good tidings must turn away from his own gods and idols, from his errors and sins; with all his heart he must turn toward God, our heavenly Father, and Christ our Savior and Lord. He must "turn away from idolatry to the worship of God, so as to serve a living God, a God who really exists, and to wait for the appearing of his Son from heaven, Jesus, whom he raised from the dead, our Savior from the vengeance to come."[274]

[272] Cf. Acts 2:37-38
[273] Cf. Jn 17:3
[274] 1 Thes 1:9-10

This turning toward God, or conversion, is sealed by baptism. This is by the command of Jesus who said: "All power is given to me in heaven and on earth. Going therefore teach ye all nations; baptizing them in the name of the Father, and of the Son, and of the Holy Ghost. He who believes and is baptized shall be saved."[275] Therefore, everyone who is converted to God must be baptized.

*Consider.* 1) What does God do in order that men may be converted? 2) What does a man do when he has been converted? 3) By what is this conversion sealed?

111. **What did Jesus say when he commanded baptism?**

Jesus commanded baptism with the words: "All power is given to me in heaven and on earth. Go therefore and make disciples of all peoples, baptizing them in the name of the Father, and of the Son, and of the Holy Ghost."

*For my life.* Many men have not yet heard the good tidings of God's kingdom. I will pray every day that they may be converted and that thus God may be ever more glorified.

*From the life of the Church.* In early Christian times, practically everybody who was baptized was already grown up. But it was not long before children also were allowed to be baptized. Later on, it became a duty to have children baptized. So now Christian parents bring their children for baptism soon after they have been born. Parents have the duty of instructing their children in the faith and of leading them to the practices of the Christian life.

*Things to do.* 1) What stories in the Bible tell us about people being converted to believe in God? 2) Read the story of how St. Augustine was converted. (His feast is on August 28th.) 3) Make up a prayer asking for the conversion of pagans.

[275] Mt 28:18-19; Mk 16:16

# LESSON 62

## *The Rite of Baptism*

On the road from Jerusalem to Gaza, the deacon Philip told the court official of the queen of Ethiopia the good news about Jesus. And as they were driving along the road, they came to a stream. And the official said: "See, there is water here; why may I not be baptized?" Philip answered: "If thou dost believe with all thy heart, thou mayest." And he answered: "I believe that Jesus Christ is the Son of God." So he had the chariot stopped, and both went down into the water, and Philip baptized him there.[276]

Before anyone is baptized, he renounces Satan and his own sins; he declares his belief in Christ and his divine teaching; and he vows to live and die as a Christian. We call these promises the "baptismal vows." At the baptism of children, the godfather or godmother (or both) makes these promises in the name of the child.

Then the priest pours water over the head of the person and says at the same time the words: "I baptize thee in the name of the Father, and of the Son, and of the Holy Ghost." It is lawful also to baptize by plunging a person completely under the water, as used to be done in the early Church.

This pouring of water or plunging into water shows that baptism is a bath by which we are washed free from our sins. The words show that in baptism we are consecrated to the Blessed Trinity—to the Father who created us, to the Son who redeemed us, and to the Holy Ghost who sanctifies us.

Baptism ought to be given by the parish priest or his representative, whenever possible in the church. But if the person to be baptized is in danger of death, and no priest could get to him in time, then someone else who is present should baptize at once. Anyone can give valid baptism, provided that he has the right intention and does it in the manner prescribed by the Church.

[276] Cf. Acts 8:26-38

*Consider.* 1) What does the pouring of water in baptism mean? 2) What is meant by the words used in baptism? 3) Who should usually give baptism? 4) Where should baptism usually take place? 5) In what circumstance can and ought anyone whatever to give baptism? 6) How does one give baptism in case of need?

112. **What does a person about to be baptized have to promise?**
A person about to be baptized has to renounce Satan, profess faith in Jesus Christ, and promise to live and die as a Christian.

113. **How is baptism given?**
The one who baptizes pours water on the head of the candidate and at the same time says the words: "I baptize thee in the name of the Father, and of the Son, and of the Holy Ghost."

114. **Who can baptize validly?**
Everyone can baptize validly.

*For my life.* When I take holy water, I will think gratefully of my baptism and I will say devoutly, "My Almighty God, Father, Son, and Holy Ghost, bless me."

*From the life of the Church.* On Sundays, at the beginning of the principal Mass, the priest sprinkles the people with holy water. This reminds us to be sorry for our sins and to think of the dignity we were given in baptism.

*Godparents* have a holy duty to carry out. They should help in the Christian education of their godchild, especially if the parents of the child should die early, or not fulfill their duties of giving a Christian upbringing. This is why godfathers and godmothers must be Catholics, and fulfill their own duties as Catholics. Parents cannot be sponsors to their own children.

*The baptismal name.* Parents should give to their children the name of some saint. This saint is then the child's patron, model, and advocate.

*Christian custom.* It is good that every child of a Catholic family should have his or her own baptismal candle which can be lighted on the child's feast day or baptismal anniversary.

*Things to do.* 1) Where do we read in the Acts of the Apostles that new converts were baptized? 2) Draw all the things that are used in baptism. 3) Describe the font in our parish church. 4) Draw this font. 5) When is the baptismal water blessed? 6) What should you do if an unbaptized child were in danger of death and no priest could come in time? 7) What is the feast day of the saint you are called after? 8) On what date were you baptized?

## *The Solemn Baptism of Children*

### At the Entrance of the Church

1. *The first questions.* Priest: "Peace be with you. What is your name?" The sponsors tell him what the child's name is to be. Priest: "What do you ask of the Church of God?" Sponsors: "Faith." Priest: "What does faith offer you?" Sponsors: "Life everlasting."
2. *Exorcism.* Ever since our first parents sinned, the devil has power over men. So now the priest blows three times on the face of the child, commanding the devil to depart and give place to the Holy Ghost.
3. *Signing with the cross.* The priest makes the sign of the cross on the forehead and breast of the child.
4. *The laying on of hands.* The priest puts his hand on the child's head, thus claiming it for Christ.
5. *The giving of salt.* The priest gives the child a taste of blessed salt. As salt protects things from corruption, so faith should protect the child from sin.
6. *Exorcism.* Again, the priest commands Satan to depart, and he makes the sign of the cross on the child's forehead, commanding Satan never to violate this seal of Christ.
7. *Entrance into the Church.* The priest puts the end of his stole on the child and leads it into God's house saying, "Enter the temple of God, so that you may take part with Christ in everlasting life."

### Outside the Baptistery

1. *The Creed and the Our Father.* All who are present say together the Apostles' Creed and the Our Father.
2. *Exorcism.* The priest commands Satan yet again to go away from this child that it may become a living temple of God.
3. *Opening of the senses.* The priest touches the ears and nose of the child and says: "Ephphetha," which means, "Be opened." The child's senses are to be opened to perceive God.
4. *Renouncing the devil.* Priest: "Do you renounce Satan?" "And all his works?" "And all his display?" Each time the sponsors answer: "I do renounce."
5. *Anointing with baptismal oil.* The priest anoints the child with holy oil on the breast and between the shoulders. The child is to be strengthened for the fight against Satan.

### Inside the Baptistery

1. *Profession of faith.* By the font, the priest makes the sponsors once more profess the faith.
2. *The baptism.* Now the priest pours water three times in the form of a cross on the head of the child, and at the same time says the baptismal words.
3. *Anointing with chrism.* The priest anoints the newly-baptized child with chrism on the crown of the head. This anointing shows that the child is now a Christian and has a share in the royal dignity and the priesthood of Christ.
4. *The white garment.* The priest gives the child a white garment with the words: "Receive this white robe and carry it unstained to the judgment seat of our Lord Jesus Christ, so that you may have everlasting life."
5. *The burning candle.* The priest gives to the child a burning candle with the words: "Receive this lighted candle, and keep your baptism above reproach. Keep the commandments of God; so that when the Lord comes to his marriage feast, you may meet him in the halls of heaven

with all his saints, and may live with him forever." Then he says to the child: "Go in peace; may the Lord be with you."

### *How Baptism Is Given in Emergency*

If an unbaptized child (or a person under instruction for baptism) is in danger of death, the priest should be sent for at once. But if there is any fear that the child might die before the priest comes, anyone able to do so must give baptism at once. It would be very wrong to delay the baptism. For baptism in an emergency, ordinary water will do. Pour the water over the head of the child and say at the same time: "I baptize thee in the name of the Father, and of the Son, and of the Holy Ghost."

A baptism done like this must be reported to the parish priest so that he may enter it in the baptismal book. If the child does not die after all, the other ceremonies for solemn baptism are to be supplied later on.

## *LESSON 63*

### *Baptism Is the Source of New Life*

One of the rulers of the Jews, whose name was Nicodemus, came by night to Jesus to ask him about the kingdom of God. Jesus said to him: "Amen, amen, I say to thee, unless a man be born again, he cannot see the kingdom of God." Nicodemus said to him: "How can a man be born again when he is old? Can he enter a second time into his mother's womb and be born again?" Jesus answered: "Amen, amen, I say to thee, unless a man be born again of water and the Holy Ghost, he cannot enter into the kingdom of God."[277]

In baptism, Christ cleanses us from the inherited guilt of original sin, from our own personal sins if we have any, and from all punishment due to these sins. Though we have done nothing to deserve it, all our guilt is forgiven because Christ died on the cross for us.

In baptism, Christ gives to us a new kind of life — the grace-life. By this grace-life, we become children of God, brothers and sisters of Christ, and

[277] Cf. Jn 3:1-5

heirs to everlasting life. It is because we begin a new life in baptism that it is called the sacrament of "new birth."

In baptism, the Father, Son, and Holy Ghost come to dwell in us; so one who has been baptized is a "temple of God."

One who has become a child of God in baptism ought to live as a child of God. To make this possible, God gives new and permanent powers, above all, the divine virtues of faith, hope, and charity. Besides this, God takes the baptized under his special care and gives him many actual graces throughout his whole life.

In baptism, Christ stamps upon our soul a mark that can never be lost; it is called the "character." That is why we can be baptized only once. Through this character, we are marked forever as disciples of Jesus Christ, who belong to him always and have a part in the work he came to do. We become members of his mystical body and are received into the community of the Church. We become "christened," that is, Christians. By our baptism, we obtain the right to take part in the celebration of the Holy Eucharist and to receive other sacraments.

Before baptism, we cannot receive any other sacrament; for baptism is the first of the sacraments.

It is also the necessary sacrament. Christ said: "Unless a man be born again of water and the Holy Ghost, he cannot enter the kingdom of God."[278] That is why the Church gives an order: "Children must be baptized as soon as possible."[279]

*Consider.* 1) What do we become by baptism? 2) Why is baptism called the "sacrament of new birth"? 3) Who comes to dwell in us when we are baptized? 4) What powers has God given us in baptism? 5) Why can we receive baptism only once? 6) Into what community are we received when we are baptized? 7) What is the Church's law about baptism of children?

[278] Jn 3:5
[279] *Codex Juris Canonici*, Can. 770

115. **What does Christ bring about in baptism?**
In baptism, Christ takes away from us all sins and the punishment due for them; and he gives us the grace-life and many other graces.

116. **In what words did Jesus say that baptism is the necessary sacrament?**
Jesus said: "Unless a man is born again of water and of the Holy Ghost, he cannot enter the kingdom of God."

*For my life.* "Through the sacrament of baptism, you became a temple of the Holy Ghost. Never drive from your heart so great a guest by committing a serious sin."[280]

*From holy scripture.* "In our baptism, we have been buried with Christ, died like him, that so, just as Christ was raised up by his Father's power from the dead, we too might live and move in a new kind of existence."[281] "He has proved his love for us by washing us clean from our sins in his own blood, and made us a royal race of priests, to serve God his Father."[282]

*From the life of the saints.* St. Louis, king of France, often used to say: "The little chapel in the palace where I was baptized means more to me than the Cathedral at Reims where I was crowned king. For in baptism, I was made God's son; and that is better than being made a king."

*Can the unbaptized ever go to heaven?* If anyone by his own fault keeps putting his baptism off until he dies without it, then he will not be able to go to heaven. But if anyone dies as a martyr before he could be baptized, he is, as it were, baptized in his own blood, sanctified by that, and receives the martyr's crown in heaven. This is called "baptism of blood." If anyone is sorry for his sins through love of God and wants to be baptized, yet dies before anyone can baptize him, he goes to heaven. He is saved by what we call "baptism of desire." If anyone does not know that Christ commanded men to be baptized, it is possible for him to reach heaven if he is sorry for his sins through love of God, and is willing to do whatever God wants of him; for this willingness to do what God wants really includes (without his

[280] Leo the Great, *Sermon 21*, Ch. 3
[281] Rom 6:4
[282] Apoc 1:5-6

knowing it) a desire for baptism. All the unbaptized people who are saved are in fact saved only by the grace of Christ.

*Things to do.* 1) What do the scripture readings in the Paschal Vigil tell us about baptism? 2) What rights have we got when we are baptized? 3) What duties have we got when we are baptized? 4) Draw the little shell or cruet which the priest uses when he baptizes; also a baptismal robe and a baptismal candle. 5) Collect a contribution for the baptism of pagan children.

## *LESSON 64*

### *Faith*

When Jesus revealed to the Jews that he was going to give them his flesh to eat and his blood to drink, many of his disciples left him and would follow him no more. Then Jesus said to the twelve apostles: "Will you also go away?" Simon Peter answered: "Lord, to whom shall we go? Thou hast the words of eternal life. We have believed and have known that thou art the Christ, the Son of God."[283]

Our heavenly Father has revealed to us his divine secrets. Everything that he says is true; for he is himself eternal truth; he can never make a mistake and never tell a lie. Therefore, we must obediently accept everything that God has revealed, hold to it as true, and build our lives on it; we must believe—that is, have faith in—God.

God has revealed himself most of all through his Son Jesus Christ. Only those who know him can know the Father. Therefore, we must hear the word of Christ, and must think deeply about his holy life, his death, and the glory that he won.

We can know what God has revealed through the teaching of the Catholic Church. "It is through the Church that the subtlety of God's wisdom is made manifest."[284] That is why we must listen to the Church and believe everything that she tells us to believe.

[283] Cf. Jn 6:53-69

[284] Eph 3:10

Without the grace of God, we are not able to believe. St. Paul said: "It was grace that saved you, with faith for its instrument; it did not come from yourselves—it is God's gift."[285] So we should often pray for God's grace. In baptism, we are given, through the Holy Ghost, the gift of faith. It is a sort of extra eye with which we can see the truth of God's mysteries.

What we see now only by the eyes of faith we shall one day see directly. In our everlasting home, God will show himself to us face-to-face, and we shall see for ourselves with boundless joy how glorious and good he is.

*Consider.* 1) Through whom has God chiefly revealed himself? 2) Why must we believe everything that the Church teaches us? 3) Why should we pray for faith? 4) When shall we see for ourselves what we only believe now?

117. **What must we believe?**
We must believe everything that God has revealed.

118. **Why do we believe everything that God has revealed?**
We believe everything that God has revealed because God is eternal truth: he cannot be mistaken and cannot lie.

119. **Who teaches us what God has revealed?**
The Catholic Church teaches us what God has revealed.

*For my life.* By faith I can see the hidden glory of God. I will never make myself blind by unbelief.

*From holy scripture.* "Blessed are they that have not seen and have believed."[286]—"At present we are looking at a confused reflection in a mirror; then we shall see face-to-face; now I have only a glimpse of knowledge; then I shall recognize God as he has recognized me."[287]

*An explanation.* Sometimes we use the word *believe* when we merely mean "think" or "guess" as when we say: "I believe it is going to rain." But when we say: "I believe what my friend told me," then the word *believe* means "holding

[285] Eph 2:8
[286] Jn 20:29
[287] 1 Cor 13:12

something to be true on the word of another." This is the meaning of the word when we say: "I believe what God has revealed." For we are holding something to be true because God, who is eternal truth, has told it to us.

*Things to do.* 1) Why is Abraham a model of faith? 2) On what occasion did our Lady show her faith? 3) How did the apostles and the first Christians show their faith? 4) Name some martyrs, and describe how they witnessed to their faith.

## *LESSON 65*

## *The Life of Faith*

St. Paul wrote to the Colossians: "Our prayer is that you may be filled with that closer knowledge of God's will which brings all wisdom and all spiritual insight with it. May you live as befits his servants, waiting continually on his pleasure; may the closer knowledge of God bring you fruitfulness and growth in all good."[288]

In the faith, we must not remain always as ignorant children; we must ever learn more and more about God. Especially must we grow in knowledge of Christ our Lord; "in him the whole treasury of wisdom and knowledge is stored up."[289]

To grow in our faith, we must keep on learning more about it. So we must be attentive at sermons and instructions, be eager to learn in our catechism classes, and to read our Bible, catechism, missal, and stories about the saints. We can grow in our faith also by reading good books and Catholic papers or magazines.

It is not enough if we believe only in our hearts; we should freely and openly let others see that we believe. Christ said: "Everyone that shall confess me before men, I will confess him before my Father who is in heaven. But he that shall deny me before men, I will also deny him before my Father who is in heaven."[290]

[288] Col 1:9-10
[289] Col 2:3
[290] Mt 10:32-33

We should protect our faith by leading a good Christian life and avoiding everything that might put our faith in danger. If anyone makes close friends of people who are enemies of the faith, or if he reads books or papers against the faith, then he puts his own faith in danger. If anyone is very proud or leads an impure life, he may easily lose his faith. If anyone cannot avoid living in an atmosphere of unbelief, he should pray a great deal, take pains to learn his religion especially well, and go often to the sacraments.

If anyone neglects his faith or puts it in danger without any necessity, he commits a sin against faith. He would do this if, for instance, he deliberately avoided hearing sermons or religious instructions, or read books against the faith, or made close friends of people who make fun of religion. Above all, it is a sin against faith willfully to doubt something which the Church teaches, or willingly to believe something which is false. But the worst sin against faith is to fall away altogether from the Church and deny the faith by refusing to be a Catholic anymore.

Anyone who is really filled with faith lives by his faith. He puts his whole life trustfully in God's hands, loves God with all his heart, and does everything that God wants of him. Faith is like a root from which all the other virtues grow.

*Consider.* 1) Why must we keep learning more and more about our faith? 2) How can we get to know more about our faith? 3) By what means should we protect our faith? 4) What puts our faith in danger? 5) If someone has to live in an atmosphere of unbelief, what should he do? 6) What things would be sins against faith? 7) Why can we liken faith to a root?

120. **In what words did Jesus require that we confess our faith?**
Jesus said: "He that shall confess me before men, him also will I confess before my Father who is in heaven. But he that shall deny me before men, I will also deny him before my Father who is in heaven."

*For my life.* There are others who have to search with great efforts for the truth which God has revealed. But my faith has been given to me from my childhood. I will get to know it so well that I can pass it on to others.

*From holy scripture.* "Body separated from spirit is a dead body; and faith separated from good works is a dead faith."[291]

*Doubts, temptations, and difficulties against faith.* Thoughts against the faith that we do not consent to are not sins; they are only temptations against faith. But suppose someone thinks that one of the truths of the faith seems to contradict some other truth of the faith, he has neither a doubt, nor a temptation, but only a difficulty against faith. He should try to find the answer to this difficulty. Of course, we can never understand fully the mysteries of our faith while we are on earth.

*Things to do.* 1) What things might lead to the loss of our faith? 2) What books about the faith can you find in your home? 3) What Catholic papers or magazines do you know? 4) What things in our house show that we are Catholics? 5) On what occasions do we confess our faith? 6) By what external actions do we confess our faith? 7) What words can we use to arouse our faith?

## *LESSON 66*

## *Hope*

Shortly before his death, St. Paul wrote from prison to his disciple Timothy: "As for me, my blood already flows in sacrifice; the time has nearly come when I can go free. I have fought the good fight, I have finished the race, I have redeemed my pledge: I look forward to the prize that is waiting for me, the prize I have earned. The Lord, the judge whose award never goes amiss, will grant it to me when that day comes; to me, yes, and to all those who have learned to welcome his appearing…The Lord has been at my side; he has endowed me with strength; he has preserved me from every assault of evil; he will bring me safely into his heavenly kingdom; glory be to him through endless ages, Amen."[292]

[291] Jas 2:26
[292] 2 Tm 4:6-8, 17-18

God has "bestowed on us his children high and treasured promises."[293] He is all-powerful and good and always keeps his promises. Therefore, we trustfully await from him all that he has promised to us: we hope in God.

A certain guarantee that our hope will be justified is our Savior Jesus Christ. We find the guarantee in his words, his death, and his resurrection. "He gives us all our confidence, bids us come forward emboldened by our faith in him."[294]

In order that we may be able to hope from God the good things of heaven, we have been given the power or gift of hope; God gave us this through the Holy Ghost at our baptism. The Holy Ghost then gave us the strength to dare and to endure everything for the prize of victory which awaits us in heaven.

The chief things which God has promised to us are heavenly treasures. "He himself has made us a promise, the promise of eternal life."[295] Therefore, we have hope that one day he will give us eternal happiness, and that even now he will forgive our sins and give us his grace.

God will also give us whatever earthly things we really need on our way to heaven. So we have hope that he will grant us whatever health, food, clothing, and other things may be best for the good of our soul; even in poverty, sickness, and want, we trust that God will turn everything to our advantage; we just put our whole lives trustfully into his hands.

Anyone who does not trust God as he should is committing a sin of despondency; if he does not trust God at all, gives up all hope, then he commits a sin of despair. If anyone expects from God something that is contrary to God's holiness, then he commits a sin of presumption; for instance, if he boldly commits some sin because he feels sure that God will forgive him.

One who has put his trust in God lives by hope. Already he has something of the joy of heaven in his heart; he prays perseveringly for what he needs; in times of trial, he bears sorrows and troubles patiently; he stands

293 2 Pt 1:4
294 Eph 3:12
295 1 Jn 2:25

up bravely for the kingdom of God and works with all his might to win eternal life.

*Consider.* 1) Who is the most certain guarantee that our hopes will be fulfilled? 2) What may we hope from God besides heavenly treasures? 3) What has God given to us that we may be able to hope for his heavenly gifts? 4) Give examples of the sin of despondency; of despair; of presumption? 5) What does a man do when he is living by hope?

121. **Why do we hope in God?**

We hope in God because he is almighty and good and always keeps his promises.

122. **What do we hope for from God most of all?**

Most of all we hope from God the forgiveness of our sins, his grace, and life everlasting.

*For my life.* In every need and in every fall, I will put my whole trust in God.

*From holy scripture.* "Nothing is impossible with God."[296] "Be not solicitous, therefore, saying: What shall we eat, or what shall we drink, or wherewith shall we be clothed? After all these things do the heathen seek. For your Father knoweth that you have need of all these things. Seek ye, therefore, first the kingdom of God and his justice, and all these things shall be added unto you."[297] "Throw back on God all the burden of your anxiety; he is concerned for you."[298]

*Things to do.* 1) Abraham, Job, David, the mother of the Machabees and her sons all hoped in God. How did they all show their hope? 2) Cain, Moses, and Judas all sinned against hope. In what ways? 3) Why do the psalms call God "my fortress," "my refuge," "my shield," "my light," "my rock"? 4) Draw those symbols of God mentioned in the psalms. 5) Why is the anchor a symbol of hope? 6) With what words can we arouse our hope?

[296] Lk 1:37
[297] Mt 6:31-33
[298] 1 Pt 5:7

# LESSON 67

## *Love for God*

The apostle St. John wrote: "What has revealed the love of God, where we are concerned, is that he has sent his only begotten Son into the world, so that we might have light through him...God is love; he who dwells in love dwells in God and God in him."[299]

God loved us already before we could love him. It was out of love that the Father created us and destined us one day to be happy forever in his kingdom; it was out of love that he gave his own Son to redeem us from our sins; it was out of love that he sent the Holy Ghost into our hearts and made us his own children. All the while God is giving us graces and favors. God is infinitely good and holy; he deserves our love far more than all the men and all the treasures of this earth. Therefore, we must put God before everybody and everything in the world, even before our own parents; we must be ready to lose everything rather than be separated from him by a mortal sin. We must love God above all.

The love and kindness of God have been revealed to us above all in Jesus Christ. It was out of love that Jesus was merciful to sinners; out of love he died for us on the cross; he is our brother and our best friend. Therefore, we should love Jesus more than anybody.

So that we may be able to love God as his children, God gave us in baptism, through the Holy Ghost, the power of love called "charity." "The love of God has been poured out in our hearts by the Holy Spirit whom we have received."[300]

We show our love for God by thinking of him often, talking to him gladly, and always doing his holy will. "Loving God means keeping his commandments."[301] Love of God is shown especially in love of our neighbor; if we do not love others, then we have no true love of God.

[299] 1 Jn 4:9, 16
[300] Rom 5:5
[301] 1 Jn 5:3

Because God is so good and loves us so much, it is a sin to make no return of love, or to dislike him or to hate him. Hatred of God is the worst of all sins.

The love of God, charity, is the greatest of all the virtues. What we believe now we shall one day see; what we hope for now we shall one day possess. There will be an end of faith and of hope. But charity will remain for all eternity. Therefore, we should strive above all things to love God.

*Consider.* 1) In what way has God shown us his love? 2) Why do we love Jesus? 3) What has God given us to enable us to love him? 4) In what way can we show our love for God? 5) What would be sins against love for God? 6) What is the worst of all sins? 7) Why should we strive to love God above all else?

123. **When do we love God above all things?**

We love God above all things when we are ready to lose all things rather than to be separated from him by mortal sin.

124. **Why do we love God above all things?**

We love God above all things: 1) because he has first loved us; and 2) because he is infinitely good and worthy of all love.

*For my life.* God shows his love for me by all the good things he gives to me. So I will often thank him, and will return his love with all my heart.

*From holy scripture.* "We are well assured that everything helps to secure the good of those who love God."[302] — "Things no eye has seen, no ear has heard, no human heart conceived, the welcome God has prepared for those who love him."[303] — "He that hath my commandments and keepeth them, he it is that loveth me."[304]

*Some short prayers.* "Jesus, give me the great grace of thinking of you often, speaking to you gladly, and remaining ever in your love." "My God, I love you." "My God and my all!" "My Lord and my God!" "Lord, thou

[302] Rom 8:28
[303] 1 Cor 2:9
[304] Jn 14:21

knowest all things; thou knowest that I love thee!"[305] "Come, Holy Ghost, fill the hearts of thy faithful and enkindle in them the fire of thy love."

*Things to do.* 1) In what way did the following show their love for God: Mary, Stephen, Francis of Assisi, Francis Xavier, Vincent de Paul, Thomas of Canterbury, Thomas More, Frances Cabrini? 2) With what words can we awaken our love for God?

My God I love thee—though there were
No heaven for me to win,
No hell to punish those who dare
Against thy love to sin.[306]

## LESSON 68

### Love for Our Fellow Man

Jesus once told a parable about a man who fell among thieves. He said: "A certain Samaritan, being on his journey, came near him; and, seeing him, was moved with compassion. And going up to him, he bound up his wounds, pouring in oil and wine; and, setting him upon his own beast, brought him to an inn, and took care of him." Jesus ended his story by saying: "Go and do thou in like manner."[307]

God loves all men. Every man was made in the likeness of God, was redeemed by the blood of Christ, and is called to everlasting happiness. Therefore, we ought to love all our fellow men; we must be good to them and do all we can to help them both in body and soul.

We must love our neighbors (that is, our fellow men) also for the sake of Christ. For Christ regards all of them as his brothers and sisters. He has said: "As long as you did it to one of these my least brethren, you did it

[305] Jn 21:17
[306] Hymn of St. Xavier
[307] Cf. Lk 10:25-37

to me…Amen I say to you, as long as you did it not to one of these least, neither did you do it to me."[308]

We must not shut out anyone from our love, even if he talks another language or belongs to another race altogether or has another religion.

As children of God and disciples of Christ we must love even our enemies. Christ has said: "Love your enemies: do good to them that hate you and pray for them that persecute and calumniate you; that you may be the children of your Father who is in heaven, who maketh his sun to shine upon the just and the unjust."[309] Christ himself prayed for his enemies when he was dying on the cross: "Father, forgive them for they know not what they do."[310] St. Stephen and many others followed this example of our Lord.

If anyone has insulted us, we should be willing to forgive him and be friendly to him; there is much more for which God is ready to forgive us. Once we have forgiven someone, we should never nurse a grudge against him. But if we have offended or insulted someone, we should beg his pardon as soon as we can, and do our best to put right the harm we have done.

All other Catholics are our brothers and sisters in God's family. Therefore, we ought to love them especially. St. Paul says: "Let us practice generosity to all, but especially to those who are of one family with us in the faith."[311] We should remember this when any collections are made for our fellow Catholics.

Our parents, brothers, sisters, relations, friends and benefactors, and also the fellow citizens of our own country are especially close to us; so they also have a particular claim on our love.

It is a sin against love for our neighbor if we have too little, or else no love at all, for our fellow men. People who are guilty in this way never pray for their neighbor or care about what may happen to him; they are uncharitable, unfriendly, and even harsh to others; they injure others and make their lives miserable. If anybody begrudges his neighbor some gift of God,

[308] Mt 25:40, 45
[309] Mt 5:44-45
[310] Lk 23:34
[311] Gal 6:10

for example, health, talents, riches, honor, good fortune, then he is guilty of the sin of envy. If anybody rejoices at someone else's misfortune, he is guilty of the sin of malice. The worst sins against the love of our neighbor are enmity and hatred. St. John writes: "A man cannot hate his brother without being a murderer."[312]

*Consider.* 1) How must we show that we love our neighbor? 2) In what words did Jesus tell us that in loving our neighbor we are loving him? 3) Why should we forgive injuries? 4) What must we do if we have injured someone? 5) Whom may we and should we love especially? 6) Name some sins against love of our neighbor. 7) What do you mean by the sins of envy, of malice, and of revenge?

125. **Why must we love all men?**

We must love all men because every man was created in God's likeness, was redeemed by the blood of Christ, and is called to everlasting happiness.

126. **In what words did Jesus command that we love even our enemies?**

Jesus says: "Love your enemies, do good to them that hate you, and pray for them that persecute and calumniate you: that you may be the children of your Father who is in heaven, who makes his sun to rise upon the good and the bad and sends rain upon the just and the unjust."

*For my life.* Every day I will do a good turn to somebody. And how? In simple ways help others, share what is mine, and give pleasure to others.

*From holy scripture.* "If you love them that love you, what reward shall you have, do not even the publicans do this? And if you salute your brethren only, what do you more, do not also the heathens do this? Be ye therefore perfect, as also your Father in heaven is perfect."[313]—"The man who loves God must also love his brother as well."[314]—"A new commandment I give unto you: that you love one another, as I have loved you, that you

[312] 1 Jn 3:15
[313] Mt 5:46-48
[314] 1 Jn 4:21

also love one another. By this shall all men know that you are disciples, if you have love one for another."[315]—"Do not repay injury with injury."[316]

*The "golden rule."* "All things whatsoever ye would that men should do to you, do you also to them."[317]

*The works of mercy.* Love of our neighbor is shown especially in the corporal and spiritual works of mercy. (See Lessons 118 and 119.)

*Things to do.* 1) How did Mary show her love for her neighbors? 2) From the lives of the saints, give some examples of heroic love of neighbors. 3) Give similar examples from the lives of other men. 4) How can you show love for your neighbor in the parish? 5) How can you show love for your neighbor: a) in your home; b) at school; c) when playing games; d) in the church; e) at work? 6) How can you show love for your neighbor in sickness? 7) What people specially need our love?

## *LESSON 69*

### *Following Christ*

On the day after Jesus had been baptized, John saw him coming along the road. Then John said to two of his own disciples: "Behold the Lamb of God!" When the two disciples heard this, they followed Jesus. Jesus turned round and saw them following him. So he spoke to them and asked: "What do you seek?" And they answered: "Master, where dwellest thou?" But he said: "Come and see!" And they went with him and stayed with him the whole day. It was about the tenth hour.[318]

Christ calls to us also to follow him. He is our master, and teaches us both by his word and by his example. He dwells in us and gives us light and power. He is our best friend and goes with us through all the darkest

[315] Jn 13:34-35
[316] Rom 12:17
[317] Mt 7:12
[318] Cf. Jn 1:35-39

hours of our life. He says: "He that followeth me walketh not in darkness but shall have the light of life."[319]

If we follow Christ, our first concern is for God's honor, our own salvation, and the salvation of our fellow men. Christ says: "Seek ye first the kingdom of God, and his justice, and all these things shall be added unto you."[320]

If we follow Christ, we must belong wholly to him. "No man can serve two masters."[321] Therefore, we must keep his commandments and do all we can to avoid sins, even small ones.

We cannot follow Christ unless we make sacrifices. Christ says: "Whosoever doth not carry his cross and come after me cannot be my disciple."[322] But if we follow him along his way of the cross and persevere bravely, we have his promise: "I will let him share my throne with me."[323]

The follower of Jesus, like his master, does not seek his own glory. He is humble; he sees how small he is before God, and is modest and always ready to help his fellow men. Christ says: "Learn of me, for I am meek and humble of heart."[324] St. Paul writes: "Yours is to be the same mind which Jesus Christ showed; he dispossessed himself and took the nature of a slave."[325]

Christ wants to lead us to perfection. He demands of us: "Be ye perfect as your heavenly Father is perfect."[326] He is himself the greatest example of perfection; he is the image of God's own holiness. Perfection is shown most of all in love for God and love for neighbor.

If we are united with Christ, we bring forth fruit for eternal life. Every good work that we do while we are in the state of grace earns for us an increase of grace here on earth and an everlasting reward in heaven. Christ says: "Be glad and rejoice, for your reward is very great in heaven."[327]

[319] Jn 8:12
[320] Mt 6:33
[321] Mt 6:24
[322] Lk 14:27
[323] Apoc 3:21
[324] Mt 11:29
[325] Phil 2:5, 7
[326] Mt 5:48
[327] Mt 5:12

*Consider.* 1) How does Christ help us to follow him? 2) What is the first concern of the follower of Christ? 3) What must we avoid, as followers of Christ? 4) For what must we be ready? 5) How does the humility of a true follower of Christ show itself? 6) What do we earn by the good works we do while in the state of grace?

127. **In what words does Jesus invite us to be perfect?**
Jesus says: "Be ye perfect as your heavenly Father is perfect."

128. **Who is the greatest example of perfection?**
The greatest example of perfection is Jesus Christ.

*For my life.* Ask yourself often, especially before making any important decision: "What would our Lord do if he were in my place?"

*From holy scripture.* "If any man minister to me, let him follow me; and where I am, there shall my minister be. If any man ministers to me, him will my Father honor."[328]—"If any man will come after me, let him deny himself and take up his cross daily, and follow me."[329]—"I have given you an example, that as I have done to you, so do you also."[330]

*From the teaching of the saints.* "We bear Christ's name in vain if we are not followers of Christ."[331]

*Things to do.* Read Lessons 24 and 25, and write down the chief ways in which you can imitate Christ.

[328] Jn 12:26
[329] Lk 9:23
[330] Jn 13:15
[331] Leo the Great, *Sermon 25*, Ch. 6

# Prayer

Because we are God's children, we may speak with God, just as children speak with their father. St. Paul writes: "To prove that you are sons, God has sent out the Spirit of his Son into our hearts, crying out in us: 'Abba, Father.'"[332]

## LESSON 70

## *Jesus Teaches Us to Pray*

Once Jesus had been praying to his heavenly Father. And afterward, one of his apostles came to him and asked him: "Lord, teach us to pray, as John also taught his disciples." And Jesus said: "When you pray, say:

'Our Father who art in heaven,
hallowed be thy name,
thy kingdom come,
thy will be done on earth as it is in heaven.
Give us this day our daily bread,
and forgive us our trespasses
as we forgive them that trespass against us,
and lead us not into temptation,
but deliver us from evil.'"[333]

When we pray, we raise our heart to God and talk with him. We praise and glorify him, we thank him and ask him for his graces.

So that we may learn how we should pray, Jesus taught us the Our Father. Because this prayer comes from our Lord himself, we call it "the Lord's Prayer." It is the best of all prayers. It consists of an address to God, followed by seven petitions.

[332] Gal 4:6
[333] Cf. Lk 11:1-4; Mt 6:9-13

We begin by addressing God: "Our Father who art in heaven." We are God's children; therefore, we may speak to him confidently even though he is the most holy Lord of heaven and earth.

First, we pray about the honor that is due to God, asking that his name may be praised and glorified; that his kingdom may come so that he alone may rule over us; that his holy will may be done not only by the angels and saints of heaven but also by mankind upon the earth.

Then we pray for the things that we men have need of; that God will grant us our daily bread and all other things necessary for our lives; that he will forgive our sins because we are ready to forgive everybody who may have offended us; finally, we ask that he will be so good as to keep from us any temptations which we have not enough strength to resist, and that he will protect us from all wickedness and evil.

By means of the Our Father, Jesus teaches us that in our prayer we should be concerned first of all with God's honor; and that for ourselves the things we ask for should be those which help us toward our eternal salvation.

It is a great privilege that we may pray to God. For in prayer we are permitted to come before the King of kings and to join in with the praise offered to him by the angels and saints; we are allowed to talk to God as children whom he loves.

But it is also a duty that we should pray. We owe it to God, because he is our Lord and our Father; he has commanded that we should pray to him, and called us to do so especially by our baptism; moreover, unless we do pray, we shall not receive all the graces that we need to reach heaven.

*Consider.* 1) How is it that we are allowed to address God as "our Father"? 2) What do we pray for in the first three petitions of the Lord's Prayer? 3) What do we pray for in the last four petitions of the Lord's Prayer?

**129. What does *praying* mean?**

*Praying* means raising our hearts to God to praise him and thank him or ask something from him.

130. **Why do we pray?**
We pray 1) because God is our Lord and our Father, and 2) because without prayer we shall not be able to reach heaven.

131. **What should we pray for most of all?**
Most of all, we should pray that God may be glorified and that we men may reach eternal happiness.

*For my life.* At least once every day, I will say the Our Father. And often I will repeat one or other of its petitions quite slowly.

*From the teaching of the saints.* "Only he can live well who knows how to pray well."[334]—"One single Our Father said devoutly is better than many prayed in haste and without thought."[335]

*Different kinds of prayer.* 1. We can pray in our own words, just as they come forth from our heart. Or we can say some prayer which has set words, such as the Our Father.

2. We can pray vocally—that is, with our minds, but using words out loud; or else we can pray interiorly—that is, with our minds only, not saying any words out loud.

3. We can also pray by reading slowly and thoughtfully some passage from holy scripture; we can imagine some event in the life of our Lord; we can look at some holy picture; we can admire the works of God in nature and talk to him about any of these things. Prayer of this kind we call "meditation." When we make the stations of the cross or say the rosary, we ought to be meditating.

*About prayer books.* A good prayer book can help us a great deal to pray well. If we never use any prayer book, our prayer is likely to become monotonous and poor. The most important of all prayer books is the missal.

*Things to do.* 1) What prayers of praise and thanks do you know? 2) What hymns of praise and thanks do you know? 3) Name some prayers in which we ask for forgiveness of our sins. 4) Name some prayers in which

334 Augustine

335 Francis de Sales, *Introduction to the Devout Life*, Pt. 2, Ch. 1

we ask for favors. 5) Put in your own words some petition from the Our Father. 6) Write out the Our Father as beautifully as you can in your very best writing or printing.

## *LESSON 71*

### *How We Should Pray*

The night before he suffered, our Lord went with his apostles to the Garden of Olives. When he had arrived there, he said to them: "Pray lest ye enter into temptation." And he was withdrawn away from them a stone's cast; and kneeling down, he prayed, saying: "Father, if thou wilt, remove this chalice from me: but yet not my will, but thine be done." And there appeared an angel from heaven, strengthening him. And being in an agony, he prayed the longer.[336]

When we pray, our minds must be upon God. We must remember to whom we are speaking, and must think of what we say. Then we will be praying attentively. In order to be able to pray attentively, we must bring our thoughts together and avoid anything that might distract us. So long as we are taking trouble to pray attentively, then we are praying well—even when distracting thoughts keep on coming to us.

When we are praying, we must remember that God is our Lord and our Creator, and that we sinful and weak creatures depend entirely upon his grace. Then we will be praying humbly.

When we are praying, we must yield ourselves completely to God and to his holy will, and leave it to him how and when he will hear us. Then we will be praying devoutly.

Because God is our loving Father, we may turn to him in all our needs. He always hears us; though often he grants our prayer in a way very different from that which we expect; for he knows better than we do what is really for our good. If we trust firmly that God will hear us, then we are praying confidently.

[336] Cf. Lk 22:39-44

Often prayer seems to us hard, because we are tired or lazy or because God does not grant our prayer at once. But we ought not then to give up praying; on the contrary, we should pray all the more—we should pray perseveringly. In the Garden of Olives, Christ did not stop praying; he persevered in prayer, although his soul was sorrowful even unto death.

When we pray well, we are in union with God, and we learn to love him ever more deeply. We understand better the arrangements of his divine providence, and we see the things of earth at their true value. We are strengthened against evil and find joy in what is good. In our troubles, we receive comfort, and in our needs, we are given help. But the chief grace which prayers wins for us is that of remaining true to Christ till the end of our lives.

*Consider.* 1) What do you mean by "praying attentively"? 2) What must we do to pray attentively? 3) What do you mean by "praying humbly"? 4) What do you mean by "praying devoutly"? 5) What do you mean by "praying confidently"? 6) What do you mean by "praying perseveringly"?

132. **How ought we to pray?**
We should pray attentively, humbly, devoutly, confidently, and perseveringly.

133. **What are the effects of prayer?**
Prayer unites us with God, strengthens us against evil, and wins us rich graces, especially the grace of remaining true till the end.

*For my life.* Before I pray, I will collect my thoughts and remember that I am about to speak to the great and holy God.

*From holy scripture.* "Persevere in prayer, and keep wakeful over it with thankful hearts."[337]—"The Lord draws near to every man that calls upon him."[338]—"Ask and it shall be given you; seek and you shall find; knock and it shall be opened to you."[339]

[337] Col 4:2
[338] Ps 144:18
[339] Mt 7:7

*Examples.* Jesus teaches us the difference between proud prayer and humble prayer in his parable about the Pharisee and the publican.[340] He teaches us about persevering prayer in his parable of the friend who wanted three loaves in the middle of the night,[341] and in the parable of the unjust judge.[342] Another good example of persevering prayer is the story of the Canaanite woman.[343]

*From the teaching of the saints.* "God gives us either what we ask for, or something which is even better for us."[344]—"All the saints in heaven reached heaven because they prayed; all the damned in hell were lost because they did not pray."[345]

*Outward attitude at prayer.* By our outward attitude, we express our inward mind. Even our bodies should take their part in prayer. By bowing, genuflecting, and kneeling down, we express humility and our reverence before God. By standing, also, we express reverence, as well as joy and readiness to do his will. By folding our hands, we express attentiveness and devotion to God. When we strike our breast, we express our guilt before God.

*The place for prayer.* We can pray anywhere. But we pray best if we go where we are undisturbed and able to collect our thoughts properly; for instance, in church; or, if we are at home, in front of a crucifix or holy picture.

*Recollection before prayer.* To collect our thoughts together, or to "recollect ourselves" (as we say), we should let our thoughts grow still and turn our minds to God. We remind ourselves that the all-holy God is present and is looking down on us with love. Then we can begin to pray.

*Things to do.* 1) What is disturbing, or distracting, in prayer? 2) What can we do when we ought to pray, yet do not feel ready for it? 3) What

[340] Cf. Lk 18:9-14
[341] Cf. Lk 11:5-13
[342] Cf. Lk 18:1-8
[343] Cf. Mt 15:21-28
[344] Bernard of Clairvaux
[345] Alphonsus Liguori, *The Great Means of Salvation and Perfection*, Pt. 1, Ch. 1

happiness can prayer bring to us? 4) Make sure that you have a crucifix or a holy picture over your bed.

## LESSON 72

## The Arranging of Prayer

Aristides, a Christian writer of the second century, wrote of the Christians of his own day: "Every morning and every hour they praise and glorify God for the favors he has bestowed upon them, and they thank him for their food and drink."

There are many occasions for thinking about God and speaking to him. When we feel his greatness and his power, we praise him; if we have sinned, we ask his pardon; before we do anything important, we ask for his help. In our every need, we can turn to him, especially in temptation. Above all we should thank him again and again, for every good thing we have comes from him. St. Paul says: "Never cease praying."[346] There are also particular times for prayer. We should pray in the morning when we get up, and at night before we go to bed. We pray before and after meals; we pray when we hear the *Angelus* bell, and especially at the Church's services.

We pray to God our heavenly Father; he is our Creator and Lord, the origin of all good, and our final goal. We direct our prayers to the Father through Jesus Christ our Lord. We pray in the name of Jesus; he, as our high priest, presents our prayer to the Father.

We pray also to Jesus Christ; he is true God, our Redeemer and Lord, our friend and our brother.

And we pray to the Holy Ghost; he also is true God like the Father and the Son; he dwells in us and makes us holy.

We also pray to Mary the Mother of our Lord, to the other saints, and to the angels. We do not adore them, though we praise them and ask them to intercede with God for us.

[346] 1 Thes 5:17

In our prayers, we should remember our fellow men. We pray for living and dead, friend and foe. We pray for those specially near to us, or who have particular need of our prayers—our parents, brothers and sisters, benefactors, the sick and the dying; for the shepherds of the Church and those who rule the nations; for sinners, for pagans, and for the peace of the world. The Christian is to shut no one off from his prayers, for God loves everyone, and Christ died for all men.

We should love to pray in common with others, especially in our family and at divine service. Jesus said: "If two of you shall consent upon earth concerning anything whatsoever they shall ask, it shall be done to them by my Father who is in heaven. For where there are two or three gathered together in my name, there am I in the midst of them."[347]

*Consider.* 1) On what occasions can we think of God and speak with him? 2) To whom do we pray? 3) Why do we pray to the Father through Jesus Christ our Lord? 4) Why do we pray to Jesus Christ? 5) Why do we pray to the Holy Ghost? 6) Why do we pray to Mary? 7) Why do we pray to the angels and saints? 8) For whom should we specially pray? 9) Why do we pray also in common with others?

134. **When should we pray?**

We should pray often, especially in the morning and the evening, before and after meals, at Church services, and when we have difficulties and temptations.

135. **For whom should we pray?**

We should pray for all men, especially for those who are near to us or who most need our prayers.

136. **What does Jesus say about praying with others?**

Jesus says: "Where there are two or three gathered together in my name, there am I in the midst of them."

[347] Mt 18:19-20

*For my life.* Prayer is for the soul what breathing is for the body. As I do not forget to breathe, I should not forget to pray.

*From holy scripture.* "Amen, amen, I say to you; if you ask the Father anything in my name, he will give it you."[348]—"Now there will be psalms and hymns and spiritual music, as you sing with gratitude in your hearts to God."[349]

*From the teaching of the saints.* "When our Savior took bread, he blessed it, looked up to heaven, and prayed. Thus he teaches us not to taste of our meals before we have thanked God, the provider of the gifts."[350]

*Morning and night prayers.* As soon as we awake, we should bless ourselves with the sign of the cross and greet God at the beginning of the new day. After getting up, we should say our morning prayers. We thank God for his benefits and tell him that, during the coming day, we want to do everything we can for his glory. Then we ask him to guide us by his grace, and to help us to know his will and to do it. We recommend ourselves to God's holy Mother, to our guardian angel, and to the saints.

Before we go to sleep, we say our night prayers. We look back over the day and thank God for all the good things he has given us; we ask his pardon for whatever evil we may have done (examination of conscience). Then we ask his protection for ourselves and all those for whom we want to pray. Finally, we commend ourselves to Mary, our guardian angel, and the saints. It is excellent if our last thoughts before going to sleep can be of God.

As morning and night prayers we can use some form of prayer that we know by heart, or we can make up prayers in our own words, expressing what we want to say to God. A good practice is to change the form of our prayers now and again.

*Ejaculatory prayers.* We can speak to God in little prayers of a mere half a dozen words or less; these are called "ejaculatory prayers." Such a prayer is like a quick glance up to God, a short breath for the soul. For example, when we begin our work, we can say: "All for you, O God!"; if something

[348] Jn 16:23

[349] Col 3:16

[350] Chrysostom, *Homily 42 on John*

very pleasant happens to us, we can say: "Lord, I thank you!"; if we have to make some decision: "Lord, show me what I ought to do!"; in temptation or difficulty or danger: "Jesus, stand by me!" or "Lord, help me!"; if we see a beautiful view: "God, how lovely is the world you made!"; passing by a hospital: "God, help the poor sick people in their pains!"; passing a cemetery: "Lord, give them eternal rest!"

Other ejaculatory prayers that we can use at any time are: "My God and my all!"—"My Lord and my God!"—"Jesus, mercy!"—"Jesus, Son of God, have mercy on us!"—"Lord, may your holy will be done!"—"Come, Holy Ghost!"—"Lord, teach me to pray!"—or we can use as ejaculatory prayers any of the petitions out of the Our Father.

*A visit in the church.* When we make a visit to our Lord in the church, there are several ways in which we can pray: 1) We greet Jesus in the most Holy Sacrament. 2) We talk to God our Father and tell him what we have been doing, or confide in him anything that we have on our minds. 3) We can read some prayers out of a book. 4) We can make the stations of the cross. 5) We can go round the church looking for a few moments at each of the pictures and statues, and pray a while before each one. 6) We can say a mystery of the rosary.

*Family prayers.* When members of the family pray in common, sometimes they can all recite some prayer together, or else one can lead a prayer to which the others make the answers (as in a litany). It is best if the father of the family leads the prayers. Above all, grace before and after meals should be said in common. That such prayer may really give glory to God, it is important that all should keep together and speak clearly and not too fast.

*Things to do.* 1) Make up for yourself a form of morning prayer which expresses everything that you want to say to God at that time. 2) Try to find some prayers or hymns that would be suitable for morning prayer. 3) Make up for yourself a form of night prayers. 4) Try to find some prayers or hymns that would be suitable for night prayers. 5) Do you know grace before and after meals? 6) What prayer could you say: a) if you see a funeral passing by; b) if you see a man sowing seed in a field; c) if you are passing a prison; d) if you hear someone blaspheme; e) if some children are quarreling; f) at the beginning of your work in school; g) if you find yourself hating somebody or wanting revenge; h) in front of a statue of our Lady; i) when you wake up in the morning; j) before you go to sleep at night? 7) Write out some ejaculatory prayers that you could use at any time. 8) Look for some prayers in the Bible.

# The Sacrament of Confirmation

All those who have been baptized should share in the fullness of grace of the Holy Ghost whom Christ sent down upon his Church on the first Pentecost (Whit) Sunday. It is for this purpose that Christ has instituted the sacrament of confirmation.

## *LESSON 73*

### *The Rite of Confirmation*

When the apostles in Jerusalem heard that Samaria had received the word of God, they sent Peter and John to visit the Samaritans. So these two came down and prayed for them, that they might receive the Holy Spirit who had not, as yet, come down on any of them; they had received nothing so far except baptism in the name of the Lord Jesus. Then the apostles began to lay their hands on them, so that the Holy Spirit was given to them.[351]

Holy scripture tells us that the apostles themselves gave this sacrament of confirmation. In the first few Christian centuries, confirmation was usually given immediately after baptism. That is why confirmation is named after baptism in the list of the sacraments.

Confirmation is normally given by the bishop. But the pope can give authority to confirm even to a priest. For example, a parish priest in his own parish can confirm a sick person who is in danger of death.

[351] Cf. Acts 8:14-17

At the beginning of the ceremony for confirmation, the bishop goes up the steps of the altar, and then turns round to those whom he is going to confirm (the candidates). These all kneel down; the bishop stretches his hands over them and calls down upon them the Holy Ghost with his seven gifts: the spirit of wisdom and understanding, the spirit of knowledge and counsel, the spirit of fortitude, piety, and the fear of the Lord.

Next, the bishop lays his right hand on the head of each candidate and, with chrism, makes the sign of the cross upon his forehead. While doing this, he says: "I sign you with the sign of the cross and I confirm you with the chrism of salvation, in the name of the Father and of the Son and of the Holy Ghost." After the anointing, the bishop gives to each one whom he has confirmed a light blow on the cheek with the words: "Peace be with you."

At the end of the ceremony, the bishop prays over all those who have been confirmed, asking that the Holy Ghost may complete in them the work which he has begun. Then the bishop gives them all his blessing. For this blessing of the bishop, all should be present.

*Consider.* 1) Why is it that confirmation comes immediately after baptism in the list of the sacraments? 2) Who can give confirmation? 3) What does the bishop do when he confirms?

137. **What does holy scripture say about confirmation?**

Holy scripture says: "Now the apostles at Jerusalem, hearing that Samaria had received the word of God, sent Peter and John to visit them. So these two came down and prayed for them, that they might receive the Holy Spirit, who had not as yet come down on any of them: they had received nothing so far except baptism in the name of the Lord Jesus. Then the apostles began to lay their hands on them, so that the Holy Spirit was given them."

138. **How is confirmation given?**

The bishop lays his hand on the one to be confirmed, anoints him on the forehead with chrism and says the words: "I sign thee with the sign of the cross and I confirm thee with the chrism of salvation, in the name of the Father and of the Son and of the Holy Ghost."

*For my life.* When I was confirmed, the bishop made a cross on my forehead. I am proud to be a Christian and will never be ashamed of this cross.

*Explanation.* Chrism means "oil for anointing." The word *chrism* is related to the word *Christ*—which means "the anointed." Chrism is a mixture of olive oil and balsam; it is consecrated by the bishop on Maundy Thursday.

*The cross, the anointing, and the blow on the cheek.* The cross which the bishop makes on the candidate's forehead means that he has now become a soldier of Christ, and should confess his faith openly before all the world. The anointing with chrism means that he is armed with the strength of Christ, that is, with the Holy Ghost. The light blow on the cheek is a warning to the one who has been confirmed that, as a soldier of Christ, he must be prepared to suffer insults for Christ's sake.

*Sponsors at confirmation.* The duty of the sponsor (godfather or godmother) is to help the one confirmed, by prayer, word, and example, to fulfill his duties faithfully.

*Confirmation day.* Anyone who is to be confirmed should prepare himself seriously for the day; he should faithfully attend the instructions about the sacrament, pray daily for the gifts of the Holy Ghost, and make a good confession and Communion. On the day itself, he should follow the sacred rite most attentively, thank God sincerely for the gifts he has received, and avoid worldly distractions for the rest of the day.

## *LESSON 74*

## *The Grace of Confirmation*

Jesus warned his disciples that they would be persecuted, but promised them: "When they shall bring you into the synagogue, and to magistrates and powers, be not solicitous how or what you shall answer, or what you shall say. For the Holy Ghost shall teach you in the same hour what you must say."[352]

In confirmation, Christ fills us with the Holy Spirit. The Holy Ghost is to be at our side, so that we may firmly confess our faith with deep conviction, and bravely stand up for it. He is to give us strength for our fight against the enemies of our soul, the devil, our own evil inclinations, and the dangers of the world. He is to make us fit to work with Christ for the sanctification of the world, and to be an apostle in our own family, in our calling, and in our public life.

In confirmation, the grace-life which we received in baptism is brought to maturity. Whereas we were like immature children, we are now soldiers of Christ. Confirmation is the completing of baptism. The very word *confirmation* means "a strengthening."

Confirmation stamps on our soul a mark which it can never lose. By this sign, we are marked out as Christ's warriors, and his fellow workers in his kingdom. And the mark (or "character," as it is called) is also a guarantee that the Holy Ghost will give us the strength needed to fulfill our duties as confirmed Christians.

Everyone who is baptized should be confirmed. The sacrament of confirmation is, indeed, not absolutely necessary for our salvation; but if anyone failed to receive it through his own fault, he would be guilty of sin because he would be despising the Holy Ghost and his gifts.

*Consider.* 1) What does the Holy Ghost do in one who is confirmed? 2) Explain the word *confirmation.* 3) What is stamped on our soul in confirmation? 4) If someone fails to receive confirmation through his own fault, why is he guilty of sin?

139. **What does Christ bring about in confirmation?**

In confirmation, Christ fills us with the Holy Ghost so that we may firmly confess our faith, fight bravely against the enemies of our salvation, and take part with him in sanctifying the world.

[352] Lk 12:11-12

*For my life.* If I have to do battle for my faith or for purity, I will remember that I have been anointed to be a soldier of Christ, and that the Holy Ghost strengthens me.

*From holy scripture.* "We are no longer to be children, no longer to be like storm-tossed sailors, driven before the wind of each new doctrine that human subtlety may propound. We are to follow the truth, in a spirit of charity, and so to grow up into a due proportion with Christ who is our head."[353]

*Things to do.* 1) Compare the first Pentecost with your confirmation day: In which ways are they alike? In which ways different? 2) Name the tasks for which those who are confirmed are especially called. 3) What does a Christian do: a) if the faith is openly attacked; b) when some companion at work becomes interested in the faith; c) when some children in the neighborhood are without any religious instruction; d) when no priest can come to say Mass on a Sunday; e) if a community has no place where a service can be held; f) when there is somebody in a community leading others to corruption; g) if children are making disturbances at Church services; h) when somebody in the community is seriously ill and the parish priest cannot be reached?

## The Holy Eucharist

In the kingdom of our Father, we shall be forever united with Christ in the celebration of the heavenly marriage feast. With unbounded joy, we shall ever sing God's praises; with heartfelt gratitude, we shall ever remember the death of Christ, and we shall be completely filled with divine life. A guarantee and a foretaste of this heavenly marriage feast is the celebration of the Holy Eucharist.

[353] Eph 4:14-15

## *LESSON 75*

### *Jesus Christ Instituted the Holy Eucharist*

On the night before he suffered, Jesus sat at table with his apostles and said to them: "I have long desired to eat this meal with you before I die." During the meal, Jesus took bread, gave thanks, broke the bread, and gave it to his apostles with the words: "Take ye and eat, this is my body which is given for you." Then he took the chalice, gave thanks, and gave it to his disciples with the words: "Drink ye all of this; for this is my blood of the new testament which is shed for you and for many, that sins may be forgiven. Do this in memory of me."[354]

Before Jesus parted from his disciples, he celebrated with them for the first time the Holy Eucharist. He took bread and wine into his hands, looked up to his heavenly Father, spoke the prayer of praise and thanks over the gifts, and handed them to his apostles with the words: "This is my body; this is my blood."

By the words of Jesus, "This is my body; this is my blood," the bread and wine were changed into his sacred body and his precious blood. There remained only the appearances of these things (that is, what we can see of the bread and wine). Under the forms of the bread and wine, Jesus offered himself up to his Father and gave himself to the apostles as food.

At the supper that evening, Jesus made the same offering of himself as that which he was going to make next day on the cross. Under the appearances of bread and wine, he gave himself beforehand for the apostles and for all men.

The body and blood of our Lord thus offered up were received by the apostles as food for their everlasting life. They were inwardly united to him and filled with heavenly grace.

By the words, "Do this in memory of me," Jesus gave to his apostles the authority and power to celebrate the Holy Eucharist; they were to change the bread and wine into his most holy body and blood, offer these gifts to the

[354] Cf. Mk 14:17-25; Lk 22:14-20; 1 Cor 11:23-26

heavenly Father, and give them to the faithful as food. This power has been passed on from the apostles to those who have followed them in the office of the priesthood. They are to celebrate the Holy Eucharist until he comes again.

*Consider.* 1) In what manner did Jesus offer himself to the Father at the last supper? 2) What offering was he then making in advance? 3) What did Jesus give to the apostles? 4) What grace did they receive from this? 5) What power did Jesus give to his apostles at the last supper? 6) To whom was this power handed on? 7) Until when is the Holy Eucharist to be celebrated?

140. **How did Jesus institute the Holy Eucharist?**
At the last supper, Jesus took bread, gave thanks, broke it, and gave it to his disciples saying: "Take ye and eat; this is my body which shall be given for you." Then he took the chalice, gave thanks, and gave it to his disciples saying: "Drink ye all of this; for this is my blood of the new testament which is shed for you and for many, that sins may be forgiven. Do this in memory of me."

141. **What happened when Jesus said: "This is my body; this is my blood"?**
At the words of Jesus, "This is my body; this is my blood," the bread and wine were changed into his body and blood; only the appearances of bread and wine remained.

142. **With the words, "Do this in memory of me," what power did Jesus give to the apostles and to those who would follow them in the priesthood?**
With the words, "Do this in memory of me," Jesus gave to the apostles and to those who would follow them in the priesthood the power to celebrate the Holy Eucharist, and thus to change bread and wine into his holy flesh and blood.

*For my life.* When I take my part in the celebration of the Holy Eucharist, and receive the body of the Lord, I am as close to our Lord as the apostles were at the last supper.

*The names of the Holy Eucharist.* At first the Holy Eucharist used to be called "the breaking of bread." But because praise and thanks are offered to the Father through its celebration, the early Christians soon gave it the name of *Eucharist* (which means "praise" or "thanks"). The celebration of the Eucharist is also called "the Holy Sacrifice" or "the Holy Sacrifice of the Mass" or "Holy Mass." And because in this sacrament Christ is really present in a special way, and because it is celebrated on an altar, we call it also "the most Holy Sacrament of the Altar."

## *LESSON 76*

### *The Church Celebrates the Holy Eucharist*

About the year 150, St. Justin wrote to the emperor a letter in which he describes how the Eucharist is celebrated. First, he tells about the scripture readings, the sermon, and prayers. Then he goes on: "When we have finished the prayer, bread and wine with water are brought forward. The one who presides offers petitions and thanksgiving, and the people give their assent by saying: 'Amen.' Then these things over which the thanksgiving has been pronounced are distributed to those present, and are brought by the deacons to those who are absent."[355]

By command of our Lord, the Church continues to do what Christ did in the supper room. After bread and wine have been brought to the altar, the priest prays over them the great prayer of praise and thanksgiving and offering which we now call the "preface" and "Canon of the Mass"; in the course of this prayer, he speaks the words of consecration which Jesus spoke at the last supper; and the sacred food is distributed.

At the celebration of the Eucharist, Christ himself is our high priest. The priest at the altar is his visible representative and his living instrument.

When the priest says over the bread and wine the words of Christ, "This is my body; this is my blood," the bread and wine actually become the body and blood of Jesus Christ. This part of the Mass is called the "consecration."

[355] Justin Martyr, *First Apology*, Ch. 65

Under the appearances of bread and wine, Christ our high priest, through the ministry of the human priest, offers himself to his Father in sacrifice and gives himself to us as food. Through him and with him and in him we also may offer ourselves to the Father; and we may receive Christ as our heavenly food. The celebration of the Holy Eucharist is a visible sacrifice which we offer through Christ, and also a sacred meal which Christ prepares for us.

*Consider.* 1) How does the Church celebrate the Eucharist? 2) What happens when the priest says the words of Christ over the bread and wine? 3) Why is the celebration of the Eucharist a sacrifice? 4) Why is it a meal?

143. **What is Christ in the Holy Sacrifice of the Mass?**
In the Holy Sacrifice of the Mass, Christ is high priest, sacrificial gift, and food.

*For my life.* At Mass, I will attentively watch and listen, I will take my part in the prayers and the offering, and whenever possible I will receive the body of the Lord.

*From holy scripture.* The prophet Malachy foretold: "No corner of the world, from the sun's rise to the sun's setting, where the renown of me is not heard among the Gentiles, where sacrifice is not done, and pure offering made in my honor."[356]—A type (foreshadowing in action) of the Sacrifice of the Mass was the sacrifice of Melchisedech who offered bread and wine. That is why David foretold of Christ: "Thou art a priest for ever in the line of Melchisedech."[357]

*From the life of the Church.* The great prayer of thanksgiving (Eucharistic prayer) of the Mass begins with the words: "Right indeed it is and just, proper and for our welfare, that we should always and everywhere give thanks to thee, Lord, holy Father, Almighty and eternal God, through Christ our Lord." And it ends with the words: "Through him and with him and in him there is to thee, God, Almighty Father, in the unity of the

[356] Mal 1:11
[357] Ps 109:4

Holy Spirit, all honor and glory forever and ever." To which all the people should answer: "Amen."

*Remembering the saints in the Holy Eucharist.* The Mass is offered to God alone, never to the saints. Yet at Mass we remember the saints, and do so in two ways: we thank God for the graces which he gave to them, and beg that for their sakes he will be gracious to us.

*Things to do.* 1) Compare the celebration of the Holy Eucharist with: a) the sacrifice of Melchisedech; b) the marriage at Cana; c) the multiplication of the loaves; d) the last supper. 2) Why do we praise God and thank him in the different prefaces to the Canon of the Mass?

## *LESSON 77*

### *In the Celebration of the Holy Eucharist, the Sacrifice of the Cross Is Made Present*

St. Paul wrote of the celebration of the Eucharist: "It is the Lord's death you are heralding whenever you eat this bread and drink this cup until he comes."[358]

When the Church celebrates the Eucharist, Christ offers in the midst of us the very same sacrifice which he offered on the cross. The Mass is the same sacrifice as that of the cross because, in both of them, Christ is the high priest and also the sacrificial gift. In the Sacrifice of the Mass, the sacrifice of the cross is made present.

But there are differences also between the Sacrifice of the Mass and that of the cross. The sacrifice of the cross was a bloody offering; that of the Mass is not. The sacrifice of the cross happened only once; that of the Mass happens again and again, and will do so until our Lord comes back on the last day. The Mass is the permanent unbloody sacrifice of the new testament.

[358] 1 Cor 11:26

In the Mass, Christ lets us share in the sacrifice which he offered on the cross. He includes us in his own self-giving to the Father, and fills us with the graces which he won by his death.

Because the Mass is the same sacrifice as that of the cross, it is the most perfect of sacrifices. Through the Eucharist, God is given the greatest possible honor and thanks; through it, there is addressed to him the most powerful petition that he will forgive our sins and give us grace; through it, boundless blessings are drawn down upon the whole world, on the living and the dead. The Holy Eucharist is thus the most perfect sacrifice of praise, thanks, reparation, and petition.

*Consider.* 1) In what ways are the Sacrifice of the Mass and the sacrifice of the cross different from each other? 2) How does Christ in the Mass let us share in the sacrifice which he offered on the cross? 3) Why is the Mass the most perfect of all sacrifices?

144. **What is the Holy Sacrifice of the Mass?**
The Holy Sacrifice of the Mass is the ever-available unbloody sacrifice of the new testament, in which the sacrifice of the cross is made present.

145. **Why is the Mass the same sacrifice as that of the cross?**
The Mass is the same sacrifice as that of the cross because, in both of them, Christ is the sacrificing priest and also the sacrificial gift.

*For my life.* When I am at Mass, I will remember the sacrifice of my Savior upon his cross, and with him I will offer myself completely to the Father.

*Things to do.* 1) Compare the celebration of the Eucharist with the paschal supper of the old testament. 2) In which of the hymns we can sing at Mass is there mention of the sacrifice of the cross? 3) Learn by heart the prayer after the consecration which you will find on page 319.

## *LESSON 78*

### *In the Eucharistic Meal, We Receive the Bread of Eternal Life*

On the day after the first miraculous multiplication of the loaves, Jesus said to the Jews: "The bread that I will give is my flesh for the life of the world." Then the Jews strove amongst themselves saying: "How can this man give us his flesh to eat?" Jesus said to them: "Amen, amen I say unto you: except you eat the flesh of the Son of man and drink his blood, you shall not have life in you. He that eateth my flesh and drinketh my blood, hath everlasting life, and I will raise him up in the last day. For my flesh is meat indeed; and my blood is drink indeed."[359]

In Holy Communion, we receive the body and blood of our Lord Jesus Christ as food for everlasting life. The bread of heaven which we enjoy here on earth is a guarantee that we shall one day rise again and celebrate the eternal banquet in the kingdom of our Father with Christ and all his saints.

In Holy Communion, Christ, who is our Lord in heaven, even now unites himself with us in the most intimate manner. Through him we are also closely united with our heavenly Father. And because we all receive the same bread of heaven, the same body of Christ, we also become one with each other. The Holy Eucharist is the family meal of God's children.

Through Holy Communion, Christ increases the grace-life in us, and gives us new power to live as children of God and to follow him, our master. He fills us with his own love for the Father and for our fellow men. Our evil inclinations are weakened, and we are preserved from many sins.

By Holy Communion, our sharing in the celebration of the Mass is brought to completion. That is why the Church wishes that at every Mass the faithful who are present should receive Communion at the Lord's table. If anyone is unable really to receive Communion, he should at least receive spiritually by awakening his longing for Holy Communion. This is called "spiritual Communion."

[359] Cf. Jn 6:51-58

Whoever is in the state of grace and, with a right intention, desires to eat of the bread of life, may receive Holy Communion every day. If he has committed venial sins, he should be sorry for them beforehand. If he still remains attached to his venial sins, his Communion does not become an unworthy, or "bad," Communion, but he will receive less grace.

If anyone has separated himself from God by mortal sin, he must first be reconciled with God in the sacrament of penance. If he were deliberately to go to the table of the Lord, knowing that he was in mortal sin, then he would be communicating unworthily, and would commit a sacrilege by his bad Communion. St. Paul says: "If anyone eats this bread or drinks this cup unworthily, he will be held to account for the Lord's body and blood;... he is eating and drinking damnation to himself, not recognizing the Lord's body for what it is."[360]

*Consider.* 1) Of what is Holy Communion a pledge? 2) With whom are we united in Holy Communiom? 3) What other graces do we receive in Holy Communion? 4) What does the Church desire of those faithful who are taking part in the Mass? 5) If someone wants to go to Holy Communion, but is in venial sins, what should he do? 6) If someone wants to go to Holy Communion, but has separated himself from God by mortal sin, what must he do?

146. **What has Christ taught about eating his flesh and blood?**
On the day after the first miracle of the multiplication of the loaves, Jesus said to the Jews: "The bread that I will give is my flesh for the life of the world. Unless you eat the flesh of the Son of man and drink his blood you shall not have life in you. He that eateth my flesh and drinketh my blood hath everlasting life, and I will raise him up on the last day. For my flesh is meat indeed; and my blood is drink indeed."

147. **What do we receive in Holy Communion?**
In Holy Communion, we receive the body and blood of our Lord Jesus Christ as food for life everlasting.

[360] 1 Cor 11:27, 29

148. **What does Christ bring about in us through Holy Communion?**
In Holy Communion, Christ unites himself most intimately with us. He increases the grace-life in us and gives us new power to live as children of God.

149. **Who may go to Communion daily?**
Anyone who is in the state of grace and has a right intention may go to Communion daily.

150. **What does St. Paul say about unworthy Communion?**
St. Paul says: "If anyone eats this bread or drinks this cup of the Lord unworthily, he will be held to account for the Lord's body and blood;...he is eating and drinking damnation to himself, not recognizing the Lord's body for what it is."

*For my life.* On the evening before each day when I am going to Mass, I will ask myself: "Why should I not also go to Holy Communion?"

*From the teaching of the saints.* "Receive this one bread, the medicine for immortality, the antidote whereby we do not die, but live forever in Jesus Christ."[361] — "No one should come to the altar carelessly or wearily; all should be filled with enthusiasm, with eagerness, and the fire of love."[362]

*Preparation and thanksgiving.* The best preparation we can make for Holy Communion is to take our due part attentively in the celebration of Mass. First, we unite ourselves with Christ in prayer, and listen in a spirit of faith to the proclamation of his word. Then, we humbly prepare ourselves to join in with the Church's great prayer of praise and thanks, and to offer ourselves completely to the Father with Christ. Shortly before Communion, we call upon Christ the Lamb of God to have mercy on us.

Then, we have a few moments for silent preparation. We may ask ourselves: 1) "Who is coming to me? Jesus, my Lord and my God!" Thus we arouse our faith and adoration. 2) "To whom is this great God coming? To me, a poor sinner!" Thus we arouse humility and sorrow. 3) "Why is he

[361] Ignatius of Antioch, *Epistle to the Ephesians*, Ch. 20
[362] Chrysostom

coming? To unite himself closely with me and shower his heavenly gifts upon me!" Thus we arouse hope, love, and desire.

After Holy Communion, we should remain with Christ in fervent love, thanking him, praising him, and laying our needs before him. We should plunge ourselves into the love of his most Sacred Heart, offer ourselves to the Father with him, and resolve to do the will of God in all things. The more devout our preparation and thanksgiving, the richer will be the graces we shall receive.

*What would you say?* Some people ask: "Why are the faithful not given the chalice also?" We reply: "It is not necessary. For, even if we receive only under the form of bread, we are still sharing in the Eucharistic meal, and receive Christ whole and entire, body, blood, soul, and divinity." Up till the Middle Ages, it was usual to give the chalice also to the faithful. But later on, for various reasons, this was changed; so that now the faithful of the Latin rite receive our Lord only under the form of bread. Those of the Eastern rites still receive the chalice; and if a Latin Catholic attends one of their Masses, he may do so too.

*The rule of fasting.* The Church requires that, out of reverence for the Holy Eucharist, we should not eat anything at all for three hours before we receive Holy Communion. We may drink things which contain no alcohol up to one hour before Communion, and we may drink water at any time. For sick people there are special laws.

*The fifth commandment of the Church.* It is Christ himself who has ordered us to receive Holy Communion. To warn those who are careless about observing this commandment of Christ, the Church has made a law that all the faithful who have reached the use of reason must receive Holy Communion at least once a year, and that about Eastertide. The holy pope Pius X gave some very compelling instructions about the age at which children should make their first Communion and about frequent Communion.

*Things to do.* 1) Try to find some prayers which would be suitable for you to say: a) before Communion; b) after Communion. 2) Make up for yourself a prayer to say before Communion. 3) Make up for yourself a prayer to say after Communion. 4) What hymns could be sung before

Communion, or used as prayers said silently? 5) Draw some symbols of the Holy Eucharist—for example, the manna, the pelican, wheat and grapes, the fish with the basket of loaves.

## *LESSON 79*

### *Honoring Our Lord in the Blessed Sacrament*

When the Blessed Sacrament is put up on the throne above the altar, a hymn called the *Tantum Ergo* is always sung before benediction is given. An English translation of its first verse is:

*Bowed in lowly adoration*
*This great Sacrament revere;*
*Ancient rites of immolation*
*In this new rite disappear;*
*Faith supplies full confirmation*
*Where the senses fail us here.*

From the celebration of the Holy Eucharist, some hosts are kept and put into the tabernacle. So, even after the Mass is finished, Christ remains with us in the Blessed Sacrament. And thus those of the faithful who could not take part in the Mass can nevertheless receive our Lord's body, especially the sick and the dying. And everyone can visit Christ really present in the Blessed Sacrament to adore him and pray to him. He remains present among us as long as the forms of bread and wine are still there.

The Blessed Sacrament is treated with especial reverence. The consecrated hosts are kept in a precious vessel called the ciborium. Before the Blessed Sacrament, we genuflect; and near the tabernacle, a lamp is kept always burning; it shows us that the Blessed Sacrament is kept here, and reminds us to show reverence and devotion.

Often the Blessed Sacrament is exposed for adoration. The faithful kneel down before it in order to adore our Lord, to thank him for his love and ask for his help.

At the end of the exposition, a blessing is given with the Holy Sacrament. When the priest makes the sign of the cross over us with the body of Christ, we receive the blessing of Christ our Lord.

On Maundy Thursday, we celebrate the institution of the Holy Eucharist. On Corpus Christi, we celebrate this sacred mystery again, but with joyful splendor. The words *Corpus Christi* mean "the body of Christ." On this day, after High Mass—or else, on the Sunday which follows the feast—a solemn procession of the Blessed Sacrament is held. In some countries, the procession goes through the streets or the fields of the parish.

*Consider.* 1) Where is the Blessed Sacrament kept? 2) How is the Blessed Sacrament honored? 3) Why is the Blessed Sacrament sometimes exposed on the altar? 4) How is this exposition concluded? 5) On what day do we celebrate the institution of the Holy Eucharist? 6) What do the words *Corpus Christi* mean? 7) How is the feast of Corpus Christi kept?

151. **How long does Christ remain present in the Blessed Sacrament?**
Christ remains present in the Blessed Sacrament as long as the appearances of bread and wine remain.

152. **How should we honor Christ in the Blessed Sacrament?**
We should 1) gladly visit and adore Christ in the Blessed Sacrament; and 2) behave fittingly in his house.

*For my life.* Whenever I am passing a Catholic church, I will greet Christ in the Blessed Sacrament. And when possible, I will gladly go inside for a while in order to speak to him.

*From the life of the Church.* Sometimes the Blessed Sacrament is exposed for adoration throughout the whole of a day or even longer. In some dioceses, parishes follow one another in perpetual adoration, or take turns in having the forty hours' devotions. In the chapels of some monasteries and convents, the Blessed Sacrament is exposed throughout the whole year, day and night.

*Explanations.* The word *host* means "a sacrificial gift." *Tabernacle* means "a tent, or small house." *Ciborium* means "a vessel for food." *Monstrance* means "a container designed for showing something" (in this case, the

Blessed Sacrament). *Procession* means "an orderly going from one place to another, or even back to the same place."

*Things to do.* 1) What prayers can we use when visiting the Blessed Sacrament? 2) What hymns are suitable for exposition of the Blessed Sacrament? 3) Draw the various vessels in which the Blessed Sacrament is placed. 4) Draw a picture of a Corpus Christi procession.

O sacred banquet in which Christ is made our food,
the memory of his passion is renewed,
the soul is filled with grace,
and there is given to us
the pledge of future glory.[363]

## *What We Should Know about the Celebration of Holy Mass*

Because the Mass is the holiest of all her divine services, the Church has made detailed regulations about its celebration.

### The Things Used for the Celebration of Mass

1. *The altar.* The Eucharist is celebrated on a table which we call "the altar." It contains relics, is covered with white cloths, and has upon it a crucifix and some candles.
2. *The gifts.* The gifts which are brought to the altar to be consecrated in sacrifice are round wafers of unleavened bread (hosts) and pure grape wine.
3. *The sacred vessels.* For the large host, there is a plate made of gold or covered with gold, called "the paten." For the wine, there is the chalice. For the small hosts, there is a ciborium or another paten.
4. *The missal.* This is the Mass-book which contains the prayers, readings, and items to be sung during Mass.
5. *The vestments.* To celebrate Mass, the priest puts on: a) the amice, or shoulder-cloth; b) the alb, a white garment; c) the girdle, which gathers

[363] Aquinas, *O Sacrum Convivium*

the alb about him; d) the maniple, which he wears on his left arm; e) the stole, which he wears crossed over his breast at Mass; f) the chasuble.

### The Liturgical Colors

The color of the Mass vestments and of the chalice veil is changed according to the different feasts and seasons of the Church's year. There are two festive colors—white and red.

White, the color of joy and of purity, is used at Christmas, Easter, and on other feasts of our Lord; on feasts of his holy Mother, of the angels, of confessors (saints who were not martyrs) and of virgins.

Red, the color of fire and of blood, is used for Pentecost, feasts of our Lord's sufferings, and on feasts of martyrs.

Violet (purple), the color for penance, is used in Advent and Lent. On the Third Sunday of Advent and the Fourth Sunday of Lent rose-colored vestments may be used.

Green, the color of hope, is used on the ordinary Sundays after the Epiphany and after Pentecost. For Sunday is meant in an especial way to keep alive in us the hope of our resurrection.

Black, the color of mourning, is used on Good Friday and for Masses for the dead (Requiem Masses).

### The Language Used at Mass

Most Catholics in the world are of the Roman rite, in which Latin is used for the celebration of the Mass. But there are some who belong to various Eastern rites in which other languages, such as Greek and old Slavonic, are used.

### The Different Forms of Mass

1. *The Pontifical Mass.* This is the most solemn form of Mass celebration, and is used by a bishop.

2. *The Solemn High Mass.* This is celebrated by a priest, with a deacon and a subdeacon to assist him. The subdeacon sings the epistle, and the deacon sings the gospel. (In England, this form is sometimes referred to simply as "High Mass.")
3. *The High Mass.* The priest sings the prayers and readings, having no deacon and subdeacon to assist him. (In England, this form is sometimes referred to simply as "Sung Mass," but is usually given its Latin name of *Missa cantata.*)
4. *Low Mass.* In this form of the Mass, the celebrant sings nothing, but says everything. Often the people are silent throughout; but the pope greatly encourages them to take an active part by saying in Latin those parts which they would sing if it were a High Mass. This is called "Dialogue Mass." It is lawful for the people to say together translations of some of the Mass prayers at the proper times; also to sing hymns which correspond to the various parts of the Mass. But they are to be special Mass-hymns, and should not be sung during those parts of the Mass when the priest's voice ought to be heard.

### The Various Parts of the Mass

(Those parts of the Mass which change from day to day are here marked with an asterisk: *)

#### A. The Service of God's Word (Prayers and readings)

1. *Prayers at the foot of the altar.* The priest goes to the altar, and, at the bottom of the steps, recites Psalm 42. Then he bows down and says the *confiteor* ("I confess").
2. * *The introit.* The priest goes up the steps, reverently kisses the altar, and reads from the missal at the right-hand side. This is the introit, or entrance song, which in a Sung Mass would be sung by the choir.
3. *Kyrie eleison.* With this appeal, we bow down before our heavenly Lord and ask for his mercy. In a Sung Mass, it belongs to the people.
4. *The Gloria.* The priest intones the *Gloria* ("Glory be to God in the highest"); at a Sung Mass or Dialogue Mass, the people join in. Sometimes there is no *Gloria*, as on penitential days or at Masses for the dead.

5. * *The collect.* This is the prayer, special for each day. The priest stretches out his hands and greets us with the words, *Dominus vobiscum* ("The Lord be with you"), to which we reply, *Et cum spiritu tuo* ("And with your spirit"). Then he invites us to prayer with the word *Oremus* ("Let us pray"). Then he extends his hands and gathers up all our intentions in the collect or prayer of the day. We answer with *Amen* ("So be it").
6. * *The reading.* This is usually from one of the letters written by an apostle; it is then called the "epistle" (letter). But sometimes it is from some other book of the Bible, and is then called the "lesson." In a Solemn High Mass, this reading is sung by the subdeacon. We should follow the reading attentively, for it is God who speaks to us through the sacred writer.
7. * *Gradual.* In a High Mass, this would be sung by the choir, in between the epistle and gospel. On some days, it is called a "tract," according to the time of the year.
8. * *Gospel.* The word *gospel* means "good tidings." The book is carried over to the left-hand side, called the gospel-side. We stand up in reverence; for in the gospel, God is speaking to us through his only begotten Son. In a Solemn High Mass, the gospel is sung by the deacon. After the gospel comes the sermon, in which God's word is explained to us.
9. *Credo.* On Sundays and certain feast days, there follows the Creed. In it we gratefully profess the faith which has been proclaimed to us.

B. THE SERVICE OF THE EUCHARIST (THE SACRIFICE)

First of all, our gifts of bread and wine are made ready for the sacred celebration (offertory, or preparation of the gifts). Next, there is pronounced over these gifts the great prayer of thanksgiving (preface and Canon) during which our gifts are consecrated and offered to God (consecration, or offering of the sacrifice). And after that, we receive these consecrated gifts as food (Communion, the sacred banquet).

THE OFFERTORY, OR PREPARATION OF THE GIFTS

The priest begins by greeting the community with *Dominus vobiscum* and invites them to pray with him.

1. * *The chant for the gift-giving (Offertory verse).* The priest reads the words out of the missal. At a High Mass, the choir sings them. In olden days, the faithful themselves used to bring up their gifts during this chant; sometimes they may do so even today.
2. *Preparation of the bread.* The priest uncovers the chalice, takes the paten on which a large altar-bread is lying, holds it up while saying a prayer, and then puts the host on the altar. Smaller altar-breads for the faithful are also put on the altar in a ciborium or on a paten.
3. *Preparation of the wine.* Now the Mass server brings up wine and water. The priest goes to the right-hand side of the altar, pours some wine into the chalice, and mixes with it a drop of water. Then he goes to the middle, holds the chalice up while saying a prayer, and puts it down on the altar. Thus the bread and wine are withdrawn from man's use and dedicated to God. Through these gifts of bread and wine, we offer to God ourselves together with all that we have. We dedicate our hearts to him. In this way, we make ourselves ready to become a holy offering with Christ.
4. *The washing of hands.* After preparing the gifts, the priest washes his hands. That reminds us that we should be pure of heart when we take part in the celebration of the holy sacrifice.
5. * *Prayer over the gifts.* The priest says, *Orate, fratres* ("Brethren, pray!"); then he sums up all our prayers in the official prayer over the gifts (secret). The last words of this are spoken or sung aloud, *Per omnia saecula saeculorum* ("forever and ever"), to which we answer, "Amen."

THE CONSECRATION, OR OFFERING OF SACRIFICE

1. * *Preface and sanctus.* The priest invites us to lift up our hearts to God and give him thanks. Then, with outstretched hands, he sings or prays the preface. With the priest, we praise and glorify our heavenly Father, thanking him for his countless blessings through Christ our Lord. Then we join in with the song of praise of the angels and saints, saying: "Holy, holy, holy, Lord God of hosts. Heaven and earth are full of thy glory. Hosanna in the highest. Blessed is he who comes in the name of the Lord. Hosanna in the highest."—The preface varies according to

feasts and seasons. It is the first part of the great prayer of thanksgiving, which ends with the "Amen" that comes just before the *Pater Noster*.

2. *Before the consecration.* After the *sanctus*, the priest goes on with the Canon of the Mass. We pray with the priest that God may graciously receive and bless our gifts. Then we pray for the living, especially for those who are present, and for those whom we specially wish to remember. After that, we think of the saints in heaven. Then we ask God that our gifts may be changed into the body and blood of his well-beloved Son, our Lord Jesus Christ.
3. *The consecration.* The priest now pronounces the holy words that Christ himself said over bread and wine at the last supper. Then he genuflects, and lifts up first the sacred host and then the chalice. We look up to see this; with adoration we greet the sacred body and precious blood of our Lord, and unite ourselves with the holy sacrifice which he offers to the Father through the hands of his priest.
4. *After the consecration.* Now the priest prays the last part of the Canon. With the priest, we earnestly ask our heavenly Father to accept this most holy sacrifice which we are offering in memory of the death and resurrection of his Son; we beg also that he will give us every heavenly grace and blessing. Then we pray for the dead, and ask that God will some day receive us also into the company of his saints. Now the priest finishes the Canon in solemn words of praise during which he slightly raises the sacred gifts: "Through him, and with him, and in him there is to thee, God, Almighty Father, in the unity of the Holy Spirit, all honor and glory." Then he sings or speaks the final words: *Per omnia saecula saeculorum*, to which we answer, "Amen."

THE COMMUNION, OR SACRED BANQUET

1. *Pater Noster.* After the great prayer of thanksgiving has been said, we prepare to receive our Lord's body. Before doing so, we pray the Our Father, the prayer of God's children.
2. *The breaking of bread.* The priest breaks the sacred host into two parts; from one of these he breaks off a small piece and drops it into the

chalice with the words: *Pax Domini sit semper vobiscum* ("May the peace of the Lord be always with you"). We answer: *Et cum spiritu tuo.*

3. *Agnus Dei.* Now we pray to Christ: "Lamb of God who takest away the sins of the world, have mercy on us." At the third repetition, we end it by saying: "Grant us peace." Next, there comes a prayer for peace; and at a Solemn High Mass, the kiss of peace is given.
4. *Prayers before Communion.* We pray quietly to prepare ourselves for Communion.
5. *The Communion.* The priest first receives the sacred body and blood of our Savior; then the faithful also receive Communion.
6. * *The chant for Communion (Communion verse).* In a Sung Mass, the choir sings this part during or after the distribution of Communion. The priest reads it from the missal at the epistle side.
7. * *Concluding prayer (Postcommunion).* The priest greets the people with *Dominus vobiscum.* Then, with outstretched hands, he sings or prays the concluding prayer. We ask God that the most Holy Sacrament which we have been permitted to receive may bring forth in us much fruit for time and for eternity.
8. *Dismissal and blessing.* The priest greets us again with *Dominus vobiscum* and then dismisses us with *Ite, missa est* ("Go, the Mass is finished"), or with *Benedicamus Domino* ("Let us bless the Lord"). We answer: *Deo gratias* ("Thanks be to God"). At Masses for the dead, the words are, *Requiescant in pace* ("May they rest in peace"), to which the answer is, "Amen." At a Solemn High Mass, this dismissal is given by the deacon. Now the priest gives us his blessing (except in Masses for the dead) and reads the last gospel (which is the beginning of the gospel of St. John).

*Things to do.* 1) What things would the priest need if he were to celebrate Mass in a room? 2) Draw the vestments of the priest, and write the name of each on your drawing. 3) Draw the things which, when put together, make up a covered chalice. 4) During the Mass, at what points does the priest stand at the right-hand side of the altar? At what points does he stand at the left-hand side? 5) Give the meaning of the following: *Kyrie, eleison; Christe, eleison; Dominus vobiscum; Et cum spiritu tuo; Oremus; Per omnia saecula saeculorum; Gloria tibi, Domine; Sursum corda; Habemus ad Dominum; Gratias agamus Domino Deo nostro; Dignum et justum est; Sanctus; Pax Domini sit semper vobiscum; Ite, missa est; Deo gratias.*

# Dangers Threatening Our New Life

God wills that our time on earth should be a time of testing, so that we may receive the glory of heaven not only as a gift, but also as a prize for victory won. Therefore, he allows us to be tempted; and because of these temptations, it is possible for us to commit sins which put our eternal salvation in danger.

## *LESSON 80*

## *Temptation*

When Jesus was tempted in the desert, "the devil took him up unto a high mountain, showed him all the kingdoms of the world and their glory, and said to him: 'All these things will I give thee if, falling down, thou wilt adore me.' But Jesus answered: 'Begone, Satan! For it is written: The Lord thy God shalt thou adore, and him only shalt thou serve.' Then the devil left him. And behold, angels came and ministered to him."[361]

So long as we live on this earth, we are sure to be tempted again and again. The evil inclinations in us attract us toward sin; other men try to lead us astray; the devil uses his cunning and wickedness to bring us into sin so that we may lose God forever.

God permits temptations because they can be good for us. He wants us to keep control over ourselves in temptation, to recognize our weakness and become humble; he wills, too, that we should gain strength by fighting against temptation and thus win a more glorious reward.

[364] Mt 4:8-11

God helps us when we are tempted. We can always rely on him; whenever he allows a temptation to come to us, he always gives grace sufficient for us to overcome it. He is near to us, even when we feel that we are absolutely abandoned.

When temptation comes, we should resist it at once, and turn to God for help. Often it is enough to say an ejaculatory prayer (see Lesson 72) or to make the sign of the cross. At other times, it is best to take no notice of the temptation, but to turn our attention to something else. We should fearlessly repel, and if possible avoid, any persons who are an occasion of sin or who try to lead us astray.

If ever we consent to a temptation, we commit a sin. But also we sin if we even remain in temptation willingly without necessity, or fight against it only half-heartedly. We have to prepare ourselves for the fight against evil by means of prayer and self-control, and we must always be watchful. Christ says: "Watch and pray that ye enter not into temptation."[365]

*Consider.* 1) What are the sources of our temptations? 2) Why does God allow us to be tempted? 3) How does God help us in temptation? 4) How should we behave when others want to lead us into sin? 5) What does Christ tell us to do, that we may not fall into temptation?

153. **What should we do when we are tempted?**
We should resist the temptation at once and ask God for help.

154. **When does temptation lead to sin?**
Temptation leads to sin when we consent to the evil it suggests.

*For my life.* Whenever I am tempted, I will say to myself, "No! Never!" and I will pray, "Lord, help me!"

*From holy scripture.* "Brethren, be sober and watch well; the devil, who is your enemy, goes about roaring like a lion to find his prey; but you, well grounded in the faith, must face him boldly."[366] — "He who thinks he

[365] Mt 26:41
[366] 1 Pt 5:8-9

stands firmly should beware of a fall."[367]—"He who loves danger falls into it."[368]—"God will not play you false; he will not allow you to be tempted beyond your powers. With the temptation itself, he will ordain the issue of it, and enable you to hold your own."[369]—"Blessed is he who endures under trials; when he has proved his worth, he will win that crown of life which God has promised to those who love him."[370]

*From the teaching of the saints.* "He who is not tempted is not tested; he who is not tested makes no progress."[371]—"The more you fight, the more you prove your love for God."[372]—"If we put our hand into God's hand, we shall conquer the devil; if we fight alone, we shall be conquered."[373]

*Rule of life.* A man is weakest and most likely to give way if he is unhappy and depressed. So try to keep cheerful and brave at all times.

*Things to do.* 1) What was the source of temptation in the case of: a) Eve; b) Adam; c) Cain; d) Joseph in Egypt; e) Job; f) David; g) the Machabee brothers; h) Judas; i) Peter; j) Ananias and Saphira? 2) What would you do: a) if a thought against faith came to you; b) if you were bothered with impure thoughts; c) if someone older than yourself tried to lead you into sin; d) if somebody in your own class were leading others to ruin?

## LESSON 81

## Mortal Sin

At the last supper, Jesus said to his disciples: "Amen I say to you that one of you is about to betray me." And they, being very much troubled, began everyone to say: "Is it I, Lord?" Jesus answered: "Woe to the man by whom the Son of man shall be betrayed! It were better for him if that man had not been born!"[374]

[367] 1 Cor 10:12
[368] Ecclus 3:27
[369] 1 Cor 10:13
[370] Jas 1:12
[371] Augustine, *On Psalm* 69
[372] Teresa of Avila
[373] Augustine, *Homily 4 on First John*, n. 3
[374] Cf. Mt 26: 21-24

All too often we do not listen to God's warnings, but give way and consent to some temptation. We offend against God, against his holy will, against the order he has established. Knowingly and willingly, we break God's law. We sin.

Many go so far that they are willing to turn away from God merely for some passing earthly good. They put pleasure or possessions or power or fame even before God. Such people sin grievously against God—they are committing mortal sin.

A sin can be a mortal sin only if it concerns a matter of great importance. It would be a mortal sin, for instance, to give up one's faith, to hate God or one's fellow man, or to steal something of considerable value.

A sin can be a mortal sin only if he who commits it knows quite clearly that what he is doing is serious, and yet does it with full consent. He alone sins mortally who freely consents, knowingly and willingly, in a matter of grave importance.

Mortal sin is a very serious crime against God. In a mortal sin, the mere creature, man, rebels against his Creator and Lord; he insults God who is so holy, and repays the love of his kind Father and of his crucified Savior with shameful ingratitude.

Mortal sin is also a terrible disaster for man himself; for it robs him of his grace-life, of God's friendship, and of all merits for heaven; it makes him liable to temporal punishments and eternal damnation. And often a man does great harm to others by his sin.

So long as anyone guilty of mortal sin does not repent, he is dead as regards that life by which alone he could enjoy heaven; and thus any good works he may do are useless for earning him any heavenly reward. However, in return for good works that a sinner may do, God sometimes lets him enjoy some earthly reward, or gives him the grace of repentance.

If the same mortal sin is committed many times, it becomes first a habit, and finally a vice. Anyone who is constantly neglecting God's grace, sinning again and again, gradually becomes blind to God's truth and deaf to the promptings of his grace. He becomes blinded and does not recognize his serious condition; he becomes hardened and will not let himself be saved.

He is ever in the greatest danger of dying without contrition and of being cast off by God forever.

*Consider.* 1) What things do some men value even more than they value God? 2) Name some mortal sins. 3) Why do we call this kind of sin a "mortal" sin? 4) What happens if a man often commits the same kind of mortal sin? 5) Why is it so dangerous if a man becomes blinded and hardened in sin?

155. **Who commits a sin?**

One who knowingly and willingly breaks God's commandments commits a sin.

156. **Who commits a mortal sin?**

A mortal sin is committed by one who sins against God:

1. in an important matter;
2. with clear knowledge;
3. with full consent.

157. **Why must we guard against every mortal sin?**

We must guard against every mortal sin because it is the greatest wrong against God and the greatest disaster for us men.

158. **What are the results of mortal sin?**

1) Mortal sin robs us of our grace-life and of all merits for heaven; 2) it puts us in danger of everlasting damnation and of temporal punishments.

*For my life.* I would rather lose everything than turn away from God by a mortal sin and lose my soul.

*From holy scripture.* "There is a sin which kills."[375] — "What doth it profit a man if he gain the whole world and suffer the loss of his own soul."[376]

[375] 1 Jn 5:16
[376] Mt 16:26

*From the teaching of the saints.* "For a little paltry pleasure do not give up your whole dignity."[377] — "A man who zealously and perseveringly prays to God will never commit a mortal sin."[378]

## *LESSON 82*

## *Venial Sin*

In the Apocalypse ("Revelation") of St. John, we read the warning which Christ sent to the community of Ephesus: "I know of all thy doings, all thy toil and endurance; how little patience thou hast with wickedness... yet there is one charge I make against thee: of losing the charity that was thine at first. Remember the height from which thou hast fallen, and repent and go back to thy old ways; or else I will come to visit thee, and when I find thee still unrepentant, I will remove thy candlestick from its place."[379]

Even when we do love God, we allow ourselves quite often to be led into sins. We do not turn away from God, but allow ourselves to become careless in his service. Sins of this kind can be forgiven without confession; they are called "venial sins." They do not bring upon us eternal death, but they do inflict wounds upon our soul. Therefore, they could be called "wounding sins."

One commits a venial sin by offending God in some matter which is of less serious importance, for instance, by stealing something that is not of great value.

There are some who commit sins in a matter of great importance; and yet they do not clearly see how important it is, or else they do not give their full consent. In this case, the sin they commit is venial.

Venial sins can be lesser or greater, just as wounds can be small or great. A venial sin is greater in proportion as we see it more clearly or consent to it more willingly. If we do not know at all that something is a sin, or if we do not consent to it at all, then we commit no sin.

[377] Cyril of Jerusalem
[378] Chrysostom
[379] Apoc 2:2-5

Even venial sins are a wrong done against our infinite and holy God and against our loving Savior. They are a carelessness and an ingratitude against our heavenly Father. Therefore, we should do our best to avoid even venial sins.

Venial sins are also harmful to us, especially if we commit them deliberately. They lose us much grace, and weaken in us love for God and joy in doing good; they put us in danger of committing mortal sins.

Venial sins deserve temporal punishment. God will punish us for them during this life, and, if we have not paid off all the punishment due before we die, he will punish us in purgatory also.

*Consider.* 1) When do we commit a venial sin? 2) Why is this kind of sin called a "venial sin"? 3) Why would another good name for it be "wounding sin"? 4) Name some sins which are venial because they are concerned with less serious matters. 5) Why are venial sins an injustice against God? 6) What harm do venial sins do to us? 7) What punishments do we deserve for venial sins?

159. **Why should we do our best to avoid venial sins?**

We should do our best to avoid venial sins because:

1. they are an offense against God;
2. they lose us much grace and draw God's punishments upon us;
3. because they may gradually lead us to mortal sins.

*For my life.* When I am tempted, and the thought occurs to me, "This is only a venial sin!" I will say to myself: "Our Lord had to suffer on his cross also for venial sins!"

*From holy scripture.* "We are betrayed, all of us, into many faults."[380]—"Sin is with us; if we deny that, we are cheating ourselves; it means that the truth is not in us."[381]

*From the teaching of the saints.* "The man who serves God as a son, not as a slave, fears to displease God even in small things."[382]

[380] Jas 3:2
[381] 1 Jn 1:8
[382] Basil

*Proverbs.* "Give the devil an inch and he'll take a mile." "Many a little makes a mickle." "Who steals pennies will soon steal pounds."

*Things to do.* In what ways can pardon be obtained for venial sins?

# Penance and the Sacrament of Penance

God does not will that we should die in our sins. He warns us to do penance, leads us to repentance, and forgives our sins.

## *LESSON 83*

### *The Virtue of Repentance*

When Peter had denied Christ, the Lord turned and looked upon him. And Peter, going out, wept bitterly.[383]

In his fatherly love, God desires that all sinners should find their way home to him. He wills that we should turn away from our sins, and turn to him, our sovereign Lord and eternal goal. Christ said: "Do penance, for the kingdom of heaven is at hand."[384]

God leads us first of all to recognize how good and holy he is, and how badly we have failed him through our sins. Only one who has grasped to some extent how holy and just and full of love God is can realize how foul a thing is sin.

God wills that we should be sorry for our sins. We should be really sad at the thought that we have sinned against him; we should sincerely wish not to have committed sin. For without sorrow, no forgiveness of sin is possible.

383 Cf. Lk 22:61-62

384 Mt 4:17

All true sorrow contains within itself the intention or firm purpose of not committing sin again. Without such a purpose of amendment our sorrow is not genuine.

If we are sorry for our sins, we may trustfully hope that God will grant us forgiveness. God is infinitely merciful; in order to save us from our sins, he did not spare his own Son.

Our sorrow must be such that it includes the thought of God. For if we are sorry for our sins only for some worldly reason (for instance, because our parents punish us), this mere worldly sorrow does not obtain us forgiveness from God.

Even when we do think of God in our sorrow, it may happen that we are regretting our sins chiefly out of love for ourselves (for instance, because we have deserved punishment from God on their account). This kind of sorrow is called "imperfect contrition."

We ought to try to be sorry for our sins out of the love of God; we should regret them because they are an offense against God who is so holy and so good, and because we have grieved our loving Savior. Sorrow of this kind is called "perfect contrition."

If we have perfect contrition, God forgives our sins at once, even our mortal sins; but it is absolutely necessary that such mortal sins, even though now forgiven, be told in our next confession.

Often we should try to awaken perfect contrition in ourselves; for example, when we make our examination of conscience in the evening, or if we are in danger of death, but most of all if ever we commit a mortal sin.

Our spirit of repentance should show itself in acts of penance. Such acts of penance help us to pay off the debt of punishment which we have deserved for our sins; they help also to overcome our evil inclinations and to strengthen us in well-doing.

Penitential actions are: prayer, fasting, almsdeeds, bearing pains or disappointments with patience, willingly fulfilling any duties of our state of life which we may find hard. But the best of all penitential actions is to go to confession. "A Christian's whole life should be a life of penance."[385]

[385] Council of Trent, Session 14, "On the Sacrament of Extreme Unction," Preface

*Consider.* 1) Why does God warn us to do penance? 2) What things does God make us recognize so that we may do penance? 3) What grounds have we for hoping in God's forgiveness? 4) What kind of sorrow is useless in obtaining forgiveness for sins? 5) When should we arouse in ourselves perfect contrition? 6) Name several penitential actions.

160. **When have we imperfect contrition?**
We have imperfect contrition when the reason for our sorrow is fear of God's punishments.

161. **When have we perfect contrition?**
We have perfect contrition when the reason for our sorrow is our love for God.

162. **What is part of genuine sorrow?**
All genuine sorrow includes a purpose of amendment.

163. **What does God do when we are sorry for our sins through love for him?**
When we are sorry for our sins through love for God, he forgives the sins at once.

*For my life.* At my night prayers, I will examine my conscience to see what sins and faults I have committed during the day, and I will be sorry for them out of love for God.

*From holy scripture.* "There shall be joy in heaven upon one sinner that doth penance more than upon ninety-nine just who need not penance."[386]—"Make not slow work of turning to the Lord; do not put it off from day to day; for swiftly falls his anger."[387]

*From the life of the Church.* On Ash Wednesday, the priest puts ashes on our foreheads and says: "Remember, man, that thou art dust, and unto dust thou shalt return."

[386] Lk 15:7
[387] Ecclus 5:8-9

*Short prayers of sorrow.* "God, be merciful to me, a sinner!" "God, forgive me my sins!" "Lord, have mercy on me!" "Forgive us our trespasses!" "Lord, make me clean!" "My Jesus, mercy!"

*Things to do.* 1) With what words or actions did the following persons show that they were sorry for their sins: a) the brothers of Joseph in Egypt; b) King David; c) the citizens of Nineve; d) Peter after the miraculous catch of fish; e) the sinful woman in the house of Simon the Pharisee; f) Zacchaeus; g) Peter in the court of the high priest; h) the good thief? 2) What prayers of sorrow (acts of contrition) do you know by heart? 3) What do we express when we: a) strike our breasts; b) genuflect; c) bow down; d) receive ashes on Ash Wednesday? 4) Make up for yourself a prayer expressing sorrow for sin. 5) Suppose you were by the side of someone who had had an accident and was dying, what kind of prayer would you suggest to him to say?

A heart that is humbled and contrite
Thou, O God, wilt never disdain.[388]

## *LESSON 84*

## *The Sacrament of Penance*

On the evening of the day when he rose again, Jesus appeared to his apostles and said to them: "Peace be to you! As the Father hath sent me, so also I send you." When he had said this, he breathed upon them and said: "Receive ye the Holy Ghost; whose sins you shall forgive, they are forgiven them; whose sins you shall retain, they are retained."[389]

In his love for sinners, Christ comes to help them in a very special sacrament. During his life on earth, he had often forgiven the sins of people who were sorry, and, on the cross, he had made reparation for the sins of all mankind. And now, on the day when he rose again from the dead, he gave to the apostles and to those who would be priests after them the

[388] Ps 50:19
[389] Cf. Jn 20:19-23

authority to forgive sins in his name. Thus he entrusted to his Church the sacrament of penance.

The sacrament of penance (often referred to as "confession") is necessary for every person who has committed a mortal sin since baptism. Venial sins, indeed, need not be confessed because they can be forgiven in other ways. But it is a very good thing to confess them, because in this sacrament Christ helps us by giving rich graces. The best practice is to confess venial sins regularly.

Christ has arranged that in the sacrament of penance sins should be either forgiven or retained (that is, refused forgiveness). The priest is to be the judge as to whether pardon is to be granted or refused. But as he cannot judge about sins unless he knows what they are, we have to confess them to him.

If the priest judges that we are truly sorry for the sins we confess to him, he absolves us (pronounces us to be freed) from them with the words: "I absolve you from your sins in the name of the Father and of the Son and of the Holy Ghost. Amen." This is called "the absolution."

When the priest absolves us, it is Christ, our Redeemer, who forgives us. If we have separated ourselves from God by mortal sin, Christ reconciles us with his Father, removes the guilt of our mortal sin, and lets us off its eternal punishment. He gives back to us our grace-life, and even gives us the merits which we have lost through committing the sin. If we have committed only venial sins, Christ forgives us those, and lets us off at least a part of the temporal punishment we have deserved by them. Also, he increases in us the power of our grace-life and gives us new strength so that we may not sin again.

In the sacrament of penance, we are indeed let off all the eternal punishment we may have deserved, but not all of the temporal punishment. So the priest orders us to do some penitential act (usually to say some prayers), so that, when we do our penance, we may join it to the saving passion of Christ and thus profit even more from it.

*Consider.* 1) What authority did Christ give to his apostles on the day when he rose from the dead? 2) To whom has this authority been handed on? 3) Why is it a good thing to confess venial sins? 4) Why does the priest give us a penance when we have confessed?

164. **What did Jesus say when he instituted the sacrament of penance?**
Jesus said to the apostles: "Receive ye the Holy Ghost; whose sins you shall forgive, they are forgiven, and whose sins you shall retain, they are retained."

165. **Who must receive the sacrament of penance?**
Every one who, since baptism, has committed a mortal sin must receive the sacrament of penance.

166. **Why do we have to confess our sins in the sacrament of penance?**
We have to confess our sins in the sacrament of penance because this is what Christ decided when he instituted the sacrament.

167. **How is the sacrament of penance administered?**
After the penitent has confessed his sins with sorrow, the priest gives him absolution with the words: "I absolve you from your sins in the name of the Father and of the Son and of the Holy Ghost."

168. **What does Christ bring about in the sacrament of penance?**
In the sacrament of penance, Christ: 1) forgives the sins and their eternal punishment; 2) gives back or increases the life of grace; 3) gives us new strength to help us to avoid sin in the future.

*For my life.* The sacrament of penance is the Easter-gift of our risen Savior. I will gladly wash and refresh myself in this spring of grace.

*What would you say?* Some people say: "God can forgive me even without confession." We answer: "It is for God to decide how he is going to forgive. And by the way in which he instituted the sacrament of penance, Christ made it clear that all mortal sins committed by the baptized must be submitted to the power of judgment which he entrusted to his Church. And this is surely right and just; because the sin of any baptized person is also an offense against the Church, which is a community of those who were made holy in baptism and should thus consist of members who are holy. If we confess our sins, we have to humble ourselves, which is very good for us. Also, the absolution makes us happy in the certainty that God has forgiven us."

*Things to do.* What stories in the gospels tell us that Jesus forgave sins?

## *LESSON 85*

### *How We Should Receive the Sacrament of Penance*

When the prodigal son had to look after swine in a far country and was in great poverty, he said to himself: "How many hired servants in my father's house abound with bread, and I here perish with hunger! I will arise and go to my father, and say to him: 'Father, I have sinned against heaven and before thee; I am not worthy to be called thy son.'"[390]

Before we receive the sacrament of penance, we should examine our conscience. We try to remember what sins we have committed since our last confession; we think of the various ways we have offended God by thought, word, deed, or omission (that is, by not doing things that we ought to have done). If there are any mortal sins, we must try to remember how many they were, and also any circumstances that may be important. Important circumstances are those which might make a mortal sin out of what is usually a venial sin (for example, the value of what was stolen), or which might change the nature of a sin by bringing it also under some other commandment (for example, if the thing stolen was a chalice).

What is most important in receiving the sacrament of penance is our sorrow. Unless we are sorry, we cannot receive forgiveness for our sins. If anyone has committed mortal sins, he has to be sorry at least for these mortal sins. If he is confessing only venial sins, he must be sorry for at least one of them. In this sacrament, it is enough to have imperfect contrition; but it is much better, and we should do all we can, to be sorry for our sins out of love for God.

When we go to confession, we should firmly resolve to avoid sin in the future, to put right any harm we may have done, and to serve God

[390] Cf. Lk 15:11-19

faithfully. We must resolve at least to avoid all mortal sins, and everything which is very likely to lead us into mortal sin. (Such things are called "dangerous occasions of sin.") Also, we must resolve to make good any serious harm we may have caused. Anyone who went to confession without such a purpose of amendment would not receive forgiveness for his sins.

When we are telling our sins, we must mention at least all the mortal sins, together with their number and important circumstances, so far as possible. We should confess clearly and frankly, without trying to hide anything or make it sound not so bad. The priest can never tell anybody about any sins he has heard in confession; he must be ready to die rather than reveal even the least thing he has heard. This is called "the seal of confession."

If anyone has left out something important from his confession, but through no fault of his own (for instance, if he merely forgot), he should not worry; all he has to do is to mention it in his next confession. For the sin was included in the forgiveness he received in the last confession. But if anyone were to leave out a mortal sin on purpose, he would make a "bad confession"; his sins would not be forgiven, and he would be also committing a new mortal sin, called a "sacrilege."

If anyone were to make a bad confession, he should go back and make a good one as soon as possible; in this he would have to tell at least all the mortal sins he committed since his last good confession. A confession in which previous good confessions are repeated is called a "general confession"; anyone can make a general confession of his own accord. It is a very good thing to do when beginning a new way of life (for example, before getting married); it is good also during a mission or retreat, or if one is dangerously ill.

After we have confessed our sins, we receive the absolution. Through the mercy of God, we are set free from our sins and filled with new strength to live a good life. The absolution is the most sacred moment of confession.

After we come out from the confessional, we should do the penance which the priest told us to do. It is a good thing to give ourselves some extra penance of our own free will. We should offer up our penance as a satisfaction, in union with the saving passion of our Lord. And, afterward, we must not forget to put right to the best of our ability any harm that our sins may have done.

*Consider.* 1) About what things should we examine our conscience? 2) What things must we try to remember in connection with mortal sins? 3) What kind of sorrow is sufficient in confession? 4) How do we go to confession? 5) What obligation does the "seal of confession" put upon the priest? 6) If we have left out something important, but through no fault of our own, what should we do? 7) If anyone were to make a bad confession, what must he do? 8) What is the most sacred moment during confession?

169. **What things should we do when receiving the sacrament of penance?**

When we receive the sacrament of penance we should:

1. examine our conscience;
2. be sorry for our sins;
3. make a firm purpose of amendment;
4. tell our sins to the priest;
5. do our penance.

170. **What is the most necessary thing when we receive the sacrament of penance?**

The most necessary thing when we receive the sacrament of penance is to be sorry for our sins: for, without sorrow, we cannot be forgiven.

171. **What resolution should we make when we receive the sacrament of penance?**

When we receive the sacrament of penance, we should resolve to avoid all sins, to put right any harm we may have done, and to serve God faithfully in the future.

172. **What sins must be confessed?**

All mortal sins must be confessed, together with their number and important circumstances.

173. **How do we make satisfaction?**
We make satisfaction by doing the penance given to us and by putting right any harm we have done, to the best of our ability.

*For my life.* If ever I should have the misfortune to commit a mortal sin, I will go to confession as soon as possible. It is better to confess my sin to a priest than to live without peace of mind, to die unhappily, to be put to shame before all the world on the last day, and then to be damned forever.

*The fourth commandment of the Church.* In order to urge sinners not to put off their confession, the Church commands all Catholics to go to confession at least once a year.

*What would you say?* Some people say: "You go so often to confession, but what good does it do you?" We answer: "Confession gives me peace with God, the joy of a good conscience, strength for times of temptation, and help in the battle with my faults. It helps me to know myself better and to make progress in the imitation of Christ. After every confession, I have new joy and courage."

*Things to do.* 1) What do you think of the following confessions: a) Somebody left out a venial sin on purpose. b) Another, when he was in the confessional, forgot about a mortal sin which he had meant to confess. c) A third left out a mortal sin from his confession because he had made such a careless examination of conscience that it had not come to his mind. d) A fourth said to himself: "I will say the act of contrition and will confess that I stole a watch, but I will not give the watch back to its owner." e) A fifth had missed Mass on two Sundays through his own fault, and said in confession: "I was careless at divine service." f) A sixth had told a lie as a result of which someone else was sent to prison; and in confession he said: "I have told a lie." Which of these confessions were valid? Which invalid? What should each of these penitents do now? 2) Name some penances which one might undertake of one's own accord. 3) What shortcomings might there be in one's confession? 4) Through what causes could a confession be invalid? 5) Why is it a good practice to keep on confessing to the same priest? 6) In what order can one confess one's sins?

## *Instruction on Going to Confession*

### I. Before Confession

*Preparatory prayer.* "Come, Holy Ghost, and give me light that I may discover my sins. Help me to be sorry for them, to confess them frankly, and to improve my life."

*Examination of conscience.* We think over what sins we have committed since the last confession. It can be useful to follow one of those sets of questions given for this purpose in a prayer book. Another way is to think of the places where we have been: at home, in school, in church, in the street, on the playing field, and so on.

*Sorrow.* We think of the judgment of God who is so holy and just; of purgatory and of hell; and then we consider what punishment we have deserved.

We think of our Savior in his passion and say: "It was for my sins that he suffered so much. How I have wounded his Sacred Heart. My Jesus, mercy!"

We look up to our heavenly Father and think: "How kind God has been to me! How lovingly he looks down on me from heaven! How holy and good he is! How ungrateful and wicked I have been to offend him!" Then we ask his pardon very sincerely.

*Purpose of amendment.* We promise God that we will do our best not to sin again, and will try always to do his holy will. It is useful to consider how we may best avoid sins in the future. For this purpose, we ask: "What is my chief danger? What can I do against it? In which ways must I behave myself better? Today? Tomorrow? In school? At home?" and so on.

It can also be very useful to make a special resolution; we decide to fight against some particular fault or to practice some particular virtue. We should strive above all to get rid of our chief faults.

### II. The Confession

When we have examined our conscience, awakened our sorrow, and made our good resolutions, we go over by the confessional, but not too close, and wait our turn to go in. We should kneel or stand quietly and keep on praying, either in our own words or from a prayer book.

We go into the confessional and kneel down; the priest gives us his blessing and we make the sign of the cross. We say how long it was since our last confession and then tell our sins clearly and frankly. At the end, we may say: "For these and all my other sins I am very sorry," or something like that, according as we may have been taught at school.

Then we listen carefully to any advice which the priest may give us, and note what penance we have to say. If there is anything we have not understood, we should ask about it.

Then the priest gives us absolution. During this time, we should renew our sorrow for sin, think of Christ who forgives our sins, and make the sign of the cross. Finally, the priest tells us to "go in peace," and we come out.

### III. After Confession

*Thanksgiving.* We find some place in the church where we can pray undisturbed. We thank God for his great mercy, renew our good intentions, and ask God for his grace that we may now serve him with fresh eagerness and loyalty.

*Penance.* When it is possible, we should say our penance before we leave the church. And we should think over what extra penance we can undertake of our own free will.

## *LESSON 86*

## *Indulgences*

Every twenty-five years, the pope declares a "holy year." He invites the faithful to visit the holy city of Rome, to be sorry for their sins, to make a good confession, and to receive Communion. They are to visit the principal churches of Rome and pray for the holy father's intention. To all who do these things he grants a plenary indulgence. During the following year, it is usually possible to gain the holy year indulgence throughout the whole world.

Christ has given to his Church the power to let us off the temporal punishments we have deserved for our sins, and to do this also outside confession. He said: "Whatsoever you shall loose upon earth, it shall be loosed also in heaven."[391] And so the Church can let us off temporal punishments due to forgiven sins through what we call "indulgences." If the sins are not yet forgiven, the punishments due on account of them cannot be let off by an indulgence.

Through his death, Christ earned for us the remission (that is, the "letting off") of all punishments due for our sins. In union with him, and through her saints, the Church is continually performing works which earn remission of punishments due to sin. From the treasures of reparation made by Christ and the saints, the Church offers to God substitutes for the punishments which the faithful have deserved, and so distributes the remission to the faithful by means of indulgences.

A plenary indulgence is one which lets us off all temporal punishments. Such indulgences are, for example, the Portiuncula, the jubilee indulgence, and that granted at the hour of death. Through a partial indulgence, only some of the temporal punishments due are remitted. An indulgence of one year, or of forty days, means that we are let off an amount of punishment corresponding to a year or forty days of "doing penance" in the very strict way that the Church used to impose on sinners many centuries ago. How much that is nobody knows except God. Almost all indulgences can be offered for the souls in purgatory.

To gain an indulgence, we have to be in the state of grace, and must do the good work and say the prayers which are ordered. Anyone who goes to confession regularly every fortnight or is at Communion almost daily can gain all the indulgences which require a confession for gaining them.

*Consider.* 1) In what words did Christ give to his Church the power of letting people off the temporal punishment due to their sins? 2) What sort of temporal punishment can be remitted by an indulgence? 3) To whom do

[391] Mt 18:18

we owe it that God is willing to let us off in this way? 4) What is remitted by a plenary indulgence? 5) What is remitted by a partial indulgence?

174. **What is remitted to us by an indulgence?**
Through an indulgence, there are remitted to us the temporal punishments due for sins that have already been forgiven.

175. **What is needed to gain an indulgence?**
To gain an indulgence, we have to be in the state of grace and perform the works or prayers prescribed.

*For my life.* I will often gain an indulgence for the souls in purgatory.

*What would you say?* Some people say: "If the sin is forgiven, then so is the punishment." We answer: "God forgave David his sin, but did not let him off all the punishments. The prophet Nathan told him: 'The Lord has taken away your sin. But the son that was born to you must die.'"[392] It is also quite a wrong idea to think that the sins themselves are forgiven by an indulgence. And it is a lie to say that the Church sells indulgences or forgives future sins for money.

## The Christian in the Shadow of Death

In serious illness and at the hour of our death, we are in special need of strengthening for soul and body. Therefore Christ, the friend of the sick, comes to help us in the sacrament of the anointing of the sick.

[392] 2 Kgs 12:13-14

## *LESSON 87*

### *The Sacrament of Holy Anointing*

St. James the apostle writes: "Is one of you sick? Let him send for the presbyters of the church, and let them pray over him, anointing him with oil in the Lord's name. Prayer offered in faith will restore the sick man, and the Lord will give him relief; if he is guilty of sins, they will be pardoned."[393]

The words of St. James the apostle show us that the apostles themselves used to give the sacrament of the anointing of the sick. They could not have done this unless Christ had instituted the sacrament.

Every Catholic who is in danger of death through sickness, accident, or extreme old age ought to receive the holy anointing. Even sick children can receive it if they have reached the age when they have begun to use their reason. The anointing of the sick can be repeated during the same illness if the danger of death passed and then came back again.

Anyone who receives this anointing must be truly sorry for his sins; when possible, he should prepare himself for it by a good confession. He should place his trust in Christ, believing that he who conquered sickness and death will bring help, and will turn this illness to the good of the sick person's soul. The sick man or his relatives should call the priest in good time, so that the sacrament may be received in full consciousness.

Using specially blessed oil of the sick, the priest anoints the sick man on the organs of his five senses: on his eyes, ears, nose, mouth, and hands (and sometimes also his feet). At each anointing, he says: "By this holy anointing and through his most tender mercy may the Lord forgive you whatever sins you have committed by your sight (or hearing or other senses). Amen."

Through the anointing of the sick, Christ brings healing to the soul. He strengthens it, so that it may not lose courage in sufferings but may bear them patiently and keep on trusting in God. Christ forgives the sick person's sins and lets him off temporal punishment. Even mortal sins are

[393] Jas 5:14-15

forgiven if the person is too ill to confess them, so long as he is sorry or has been sorry for them beforehand.

Quite often, Christ grants to the sick man some relief in his illness—sometimes even a complete cure when this would be for the good of his soul. But if it be God's will to call the sick man to his eternal home, then Christ strengthens him for his last hour.

Besides being called "holy anointing" or "the anointing of the sick," this sacrament is sometimes called "the last anointing" and also "extreme unction."

*Consider.* 1) How do we know that the apostles used to give the sacrament of holy anointing? 2) Who may receive this sacrament? 3) How often may it be received? 4) How should a sick man prepare himself to be anointed? 5) Why is it so important to send for the priest in good time?

176. **What does the apostle James write about the sacrament of holy anointing?**
The apostle James writes: "Is one of you sick? Let him send for the presbyters of the Church, and let them pray over him, anointing him with oil in the Lord's name. Prayer offered in faith will restore the sick man, and the Lord will give him relief; if he is guilty of sins, they will be pardoned."

177. **When should we receive the sacrament of holy anointing?**
We should receive the sacrament of holy anointing whenever we are in danger of death through sickness, accident, or the weakness of old age.

178. **How does the priest give the holy anointings?**
The priest anoints the senses of the sick person with oil of the sick, at the same time saying: "By this holy anointing and through his most tender mercy may the Lord forgive you whatever sins you have committed by your sight (hearing, etc). Amen."

179. **What does Christ bring about through holy anointing?**
Through holy anointing, Christ strengthens us in sickness and fear of death, forgives our sins and their punishment, and restores our health, if it be for our good.

*For my life.* If any Catholic is very ill in my home or in the neighborhood, I will see that the priest knows about it.

*What would you say?* Some people say: "If a sick person is given the last anointing, he is sure to die." We answer: "It is silly to say that. On the contrary, the prayers used in the sacrament of holy anointing ask God most earnestly that the sick person may get better; and in fact it often happens that, from the time of his anointing, he grows better and sometimes recovers altogether."

*What the sick should do for the kingdom of God.* Sick people can offer up their sufferings in union with the passion of Christ; they can offer them for the conversion of sinners, for the foreign missions, for the peace of the world, or any of the other great intentions of the kingdom of God. This is the "Apostolate of the Sick."

## *How the Sacrament of Holy Anointing Is Given*

### Preparation

Anyone who sends for the priest to come to a sick person should leave at the priest's house exact information about the person's name and where he lives—which street, number of the house, and so on. He should also say whether the sick person is still conscious, and whether there is any danger that he might die quickly. Also, he should mention whether a crucifix, candles, and holy water are available in the sickroom, so that the priest will bring with him whatever may be missing.

In the sickroom itself, a table should be so arranged that the sick man can see it. The table should be covered with a white cloth, and the following things put onto it: a crucifix, two candles in candlesticks, a small vessel of holy water with a sprig of some tree or shrub to be used as a sprinkler, a glass of ordinary water, a spoon, a plate with six small pieces of cotton wool, and a saltcellar with salt in it. The cotton wool and the salt should be thrown into the fire after use.

While waiting for the priest, the sick man should be given opportunity to recollect himself; it may help if someone prompts him in ejaculatory prayers of faith, hope, charity, and contrition.

## When the Priest Arrives

As soon as the priest comes, the candles should be lighted. The priest enters the sickroom, gives the peace-greeting, sprinkles the sick man and all present with holy water, and says certain prayers.

If the sick man is going to confession, all should go out until the priest calls them back.

## The Anointing

If time permits, the priest reads from the gospel the story of our Lord's healing of the centurion's servant or some other suitable gospel story. Then all kneel down and answer the preliminary prayers. Then comes the actual anointing, after which there are other prayers for the sick man to which all should make the answers.

## The Holy Communion

To begin with, all say the Our Father together. Then the priest gives Holy Communion; if this is being given as viaticum, the priest says: "Receive, brother, this food for your journey, the body of our Lord Jesus Christ, that he may guard you from the malicious enemy and lead you into everlasting life. Amen." Viaticum is Holy Communion given to a person who seems to be dying.

## The Plenary Indulgence

Finally, the priest urges the sick man once again to be sorry for his sins, devoutly to say the holy name of Jesus, to offer up his sickness and pains in reparation for his sins, and to give himself up wholly to God's will. Then the priest gives the papal blessing which carries with it a plenary indulgence at the hour of death.

## The Sacraments for the Good of the Church

By the will of Christ there are in the Church two particular ways of life which are sanctified by sacraments, because, from these ways of life, the whole Church benefits. They are priesthood and marriage.

### *LESSON 88*

### *The Ordination of Priests*

Before St. Paul went away from Ephesus, he appointed Timothy to be in charge of the Church there. When all the community had assembled, St. Paul prayed and laid his hands on Timothy. Later on, he wrote to Timothy saying: "I would remind thee to fan the flame of that special grace which God kindled in thee when my hands were laid upon thee."[394]

Christ gave to his apostles the fullness of priestly power; at the same time, he gave them grace to live a priestly life and do the priestly work.

The apostles passed on to others this power and grace which they had received from Christ. They laid their hands on them and called the Holy Ghost down upon them; that is, they ordained them (made them priests).

Ever since the time of the apostles, the laying on of hands accompanied by prayer has been used for ordaining bishops, priests, and deacons. Ordinations are done by a bishop; when someone is to be ordained a bishop (this is called "consecrating" a bishop) it is usual for three bishops to do it together.

[394] 2 Tm 1:6

Through this sacrament of order (as it is called), Christ gives the power of the priesthood together with the grace needed to live and work as a priest should. In the consecration of a bishop, Christ gives full priestly authority. In ordination to the priesthood, he gives power to celebrate the Eucharist, to administer the sacraments of baptism, penance, and anointing of the sick, and also to consecrate and bless. In ordination to the diaconate, Christ gives the power to administer baptism solemnly, to be deacon assisting the priest at the altar, and to distribute Holy Communion to the faithful.

The sacrament of order imprints on the soul a mark that can never be lost. It is called the "character" of the sacrament. A man who has been ordained is united in a very special way to Christ, the heavenly high priest, and is made like to him. Nothing can ever take away his priestly powers; but he may use his powers only when he has been appointed to do so by the rightful authorities in the Church.

Christ calls to his service young men from every nation and condition of life. They must be men of living faith and true piety, ready to make sacrifices in order to be God's servants and work for the salvation of their fellow men. No one can be a priest unless he is called to that holy office. Anyone who thinks that he has been called ("has a vocation," as we say) should not allow any worldly reasons to prevent him from following God's call. The one who makes the final decision about a vocation is the bishop.

*Consider.* 1) What power and grace did Christ give to the apostles? 2) How did the apostles pass on this power and grace to others? 3) How are bishops, priests, and deacons ordained? 4) Who has the fullness of the priestly powers? 5) What powers does a priest possess? 6) What powers does a deacon possess? 7) What is the effect of the character in those who are ordained? 8) If anyone desires to be a priest, what qualities must he have?

180. **What does holy scripture say about the sacrament of order?**

Holy scripture says: 1) that Christ gave to the apostles the full power of the priesthood, and grace to live and work as priests should do; 2) that the apostles passed on this grace and power to others.

181. **What does Christ give through the sacrament of order?**
Through the sacrament of order, Christ gives the priestly power and the grace to live and work as a priest.

*For my life.* I will honor priests because of their holy office; I will pay attention to their teaching and will pray for them. If I am a boy, I will give some serious thought and prayer, before I leave school, to the idea of becoming a priest; and if I think God wants me as a priest, I will talk it over with my parents and with some priest who knows me well.

*From the liturgy of ordination to the priesthood.* "Whatsoever these hands bless shall be blessed; and whatsoever they consecrate shall be consecrated and hallowed."

*Special days of prayer for priests* are the Ember days.

*Care for the training of priests.* All the faithful should help by their prayers and contributions to ensure the education of enough priests for the work of God's kingdom. No one who desires to be a priest should have to give up because his parents are unable to pay for his studies. Priests and people should help him to reach that goal toward which God is calling him. For this purpose, most bishops administer an Ecclesiastical Education Fund. It is a very great grace for a parish and for a family if God calls one of its sons to become a priest.

*Things to do.* 1) In what words did Christ give to his apostles the power to celebrate the Holy Eucharist? 2) In what words did he give them power to forgive sins? 3) What would we have to do without if there were no priests? 4) Where is the seminary (place for training priests) of our diocese? 5) How many priests are there who used to be boys in our parish? 6) How long is it since we had a priest offering his first Mass in our parish?

## *How Priests Are Ordained*

There are several steps to the priesthood: first, a man receives the tonsure, which is not an order but makes him a cleric. Then come four minor orders, followed by the subdiaconate and the diaconate.

When a bishop is ordaining priests, he lays his hands in silence on the head of each deacon and calls down the Holy Ghost upon him; all priests who are present do the same. Then the bishop says the ordination preface.

As a sign of his priestly ordination, the bishop crosses the stole of each one upon his breast and dresses him in his Mass vestments. With holy oil, he anoints the hands of each, and gives him a paten bearing an altar-bread, and a chalice containing wine and water as a sign that he has now the power to celebrate Mass. Then the bishop and all the new priests together celebrate the Eucharist. At the end, the bishop again lays his hand on the head of each of the new priests and says: "Receive the Holy Ghost; whose sins you shall forgive they are forgiven; and whose sins you shall retain they are retained."

## *LESSON 89*

## *The Sacrament of Marriage*

At a wedding, the bridegroom and bride stand before the altar. The priest asks them if they truly want to marry each other. Both of them reply in turn that they do; they join hands and the priest winds his stole round their hands. Now the bridegroom makes a solemn declaration that he takes the bride to be his wife; and she in turn solemnly declares that she takes the bridegroom to be her husband. After this, the priest blesses their marriage in the name of the Church. Then he blesses the wedding ring, which the husband puts onto his wife's hand; and the priest says some more prayers asking God to grant them a happy married life.

The marriage ceremony should, when possible, be followed by the Mass for the bridegroom and bride, usually called the "nuptial Mass." The newly married couple and all their friends take part in the holy sacrifice and receive the body of their Lord. After the *Pater Noster*, the priest says a special blessing over the bride. At the end of the Mass, he calls down God's blessing upon the young couple.

The first two human beings whom God created were a man and a woman, and he brought them together in a holy union. So God instituted marriage itself in paradise.

Christ sanctified marriage by his death on the cross and turned it into a source of grace; he raised it up to be a sacrament. Christian marriage is an image of the grace-filled union of Christ with his bride, the Church.[395]

Those who are going to be married should prepare themselves very carefully for their wedding. They must earnestly ask themselves whether they are really suited to each other, and whether their love is strong enough to keep true to each other till death. To find out whether this is so, they should ask God to enlighten them, and they should seek advice from their parents and their priest. They must keep the time of their engagement holy, and often ask God to bless their intended marriage.

The most important of all things for a couple who intend to marry is that they should be of one faith. Marriage between Catholics and those who are not Catholics (mixed marriages) very frequently turn out to be a misfortune both for the couple and for their children. That is why the Church forbids mixed marriages.

The couple must be in the state of grace when they receive the sacrament of marriage. To make sure of this, they should both make a good confession before their wedding. At the nuptial Mass, both of them should receive Holy Communion.

At the wedding ceremony, they publicly declare before the priest and two witnesses that they take each other for man and wife. It is by this that they become married; they themselves give to and receive from each other the sacrament of marriage.

By means of the sacrament of marriage, Christ binds the two of them together in a holy and unbreakable union. Nothing but death can end their union. This is why Christ condemns the breaking of the marriage bond (divorce) with the words: “Everyone that puts away his wife to marry

[395] Cf. Eph 5:32

another commits adultery; and he that marries her that is put away from her husband commits adultery."[396]

In the sacrament of marriage, Christ gives to man and wife very rich graces. He sanctifies and strengthens them that they may be true to each other until death, and may be able to carry out faithfully the duties of their union.

In the sacrament of marriage, a man and his wife undertake holy duties. They are to live faithfully and lovingly together for the rest of their lives, serve God together and take care of each other. And if God blesses their union by sending them children, they are to bring these up for God, teaching them by word and example and caring for their welfare in this world and in the world to come.

*Consider.* 1) When, where, and why did marriage begin? 2) By what means did Christ sanctify marriage? 3) How should those who intend to marry prepare for their wedding? 4) What sacrament should they receive before their marriage? 5) Who is it that gives the sacrament of marriage? 6) What duties do people undertake when they marry?

182. **How do Catholics marry?**

Catholics marry by declaring before a priest and two witnesses they take each other as husband and wife.

183. **What does Christ bring about in the sacrament of marriage?**

In the sacrament of marriage, Christ joins bridegroom and bride into a holy and unbreakable union and grants them rich graces to fulfill the duties of this union conscientiously.

184. **What does Christ say about breaking the marriage bond?**

Christ says: "Everyone that puts away his wife and marries another commits adultery, and he that marries her that is put away from her husband commits adultery."

[396] Lk 16:18

185. **Why does the Church forbid mixed marriages?**

The Church forbids mixed marriages because, for the most part, they are a great misfortune for the married couple and for their children.

*For my life.* Selfishness and love of pleasure ruin marriages. Whoever wants to be happy in marriage must learn while young to think of others and to care for others.

*From holy scripture.* "You who are husbands must show love to your wives, as Christ showed love to his Church when he gave himself up on its behalf."[397] — "What God has joined together, let no man put asunder."[398]

*The things needed to make a success of a Catholic marriage* are: 1) genuine Catholic faith; 2) true love; 3) reliable character; 4) sufficient bodily health; 5) enough to live on.

*Impediments to marriage.* So that both parents and children may be preserved from temporal and eternal harm, the law of God absolutely forbids marriage in certain cases; for instance, no one may marry a divorced person. For similar reasons, the Church forbids marriages between certain classes of persons by declaring "impediments" or obstacles to the marriage. The Church can, of course, make exceptions to her own laws, and sometimes does so for good reasons. But she can never set aside impediments which are based on the laws of God.

*Mixed marriages.* In a mixed marriage, the parents and children are not united in that which is most important of all, namely, their faith. They cannot go all together to Holy Communion, nor can they live with one accord according to the Catholic religion. Very often, parents and children become careless in the practice of their faith, or else fall away from it completely. The non-Catholic partner to the marriage often has the idea that it will be possible to get a divorce and marry again if desired.

Only for the most important reasons, and with great regrets, will the Church make exceptions to her law forbidding mixed marriages. In such cases, both parties must solemnly promise that they will marry according

[397] Eph 5:25

[398] Mt 19:6

to the Church's rites, and will bring up all their children as Catholics. The non-Catholic party must promise not to interfere with the other's practice of the Catholic faith, nor with that of the children.

*Civil marriage.* Because married people have some responsibilities and privileges in the state which differ from those of the unmarried, the state has the right to know who is married and who is not. Both in the United States and in Britain, Catholics who are going to marry must obtain a certificate or license from a state official, and bring it to the priest before their wedding. After the wedding, in the presence of the priest, they sign certain state papers. In the United States, it is the priest who sends these back to where they should go. In Britain, some priests can do this, but usually an official of the state, called a registrar, comes to the church; and after the wedding, before the altar, the newly married couple make a declaration before the registrar, usually in the sacristy. This is not the actual marriage, but only the recording of the marriage by the state.

These state officials also have offices of their own; in the United States, it is the office of the judge, or the justice of the peace; in Britain, it is the registry office. Non-Catholics get married in these places; but if a Catholic were to try to do so, he would not be truly married; and if, after that, he lives as a married man, he would be living in sin. He could not receive the sacraments nor be buried as a Catholic unless he repents. It is just the same if he tries to marry in a non-Catholic church; moreover, in that case, he is expelled (excommunicated) from the Catholic Church. The reason is that Catholics cannot receive the sacrament of marriage except from the Catholic Church to which Christ entrusted the sacraments.—These laws about the way of getting married apply only to Catholics. So, if non-Catholics marry before a justice of the peace or a registrar or in a non-Catholic Church, theirs is a true and valid marriage.

*Divorce in the civil courts.* There are married people who quarrel and want to end their marriage. They go to a place called a divorce court, and sometimes the judge tells them they are no longer husband and wife and can marry again. This is not true, for it is against God's laws. So, if a judge grants a divorce, this does not end the marriage before God and the Church.

*The Church's marriage courts.* The Church, also, has courts to deal with marriages, and they, too, have no power to end a true marriage. But sometimes it is discovered that a couple who were believed to be truly married are not really married at all; there never was any marriage; and so the marriage which they thought to exist is declared "null"—that is, to have been invalid from the beginning. This is called a "declaration of nullity" and is quite different from a divorce. People whose marriage has been declared null are free to marry.

Sometimes, for very important reasons, people who are truly married are allowed to leave each other and live separately. But they cannot marry again, for they are not free. A valid marriage, even of non-Catholics, can never be ended in God's sight.

*Things to do.* 1) What would you say to a Catholic who says that he intends to be married by a state official and by nobody else? 2) Why does the Church forbid mixed marriages? 3) In those cases where the Church, for grave reasons, does permit a mixed marriage, what things must the couple promise? 4) What is to be said about a civil divorce? 5) What is a declaration of nullity? 6) Explain how a declaration of nullity is not a divorce.

## Religious Orders

Christ wants everyone to follow him and to strive for perfection. A particular way of striving for perfection is to make to God certain very solemn promises called the "vows of religion." So in the Church we find, in addition to those ways of life that are sanctified by sacraments (the priesthood and marriage), yet another way called "religious life," or "life in a religious order."

# LESSON 90

## Vows of Religion

St. Benedict of Nursia, when he was a young man, went to live in a lonely cave in a hillside where he could pray wholly undisturbed and think deeply about the mysteries of God. After some time, he realized that God wanted him to live together with other men who would follow the same way of life. When others came to him, he drew up some rules for them to live by; the house they lived in was called a "monastery" and they were called "monks." According to St. Benedict's rule, the monks lived together like a family, praying together and working together. St. Benedict was the first abbot of his monastery.

From very early times, many Christians—both priests and laity—lived together in religious communities. They devoted themselves to prayer and meditation and the singing of God's praises. Many of them worked also in the care of souls, in the education of the young, in nursing the sick, sometimes in the missions. Such communities are called "religious orders." Many such orders have been founded by saints.

Anyone who serves God in a religious order gives up, for the sake of the kingdom of heaven, many things which are lawful and good. He possesses nothing of his own, but lives on whatever the community or kind people give to him; he gives up his right to marry and found a family in order to live a life of continence and belong to God alone; and he submits himself in everything to the will of his superiors and the rule of his order. He binds himself to all these things by the "vows of religion." However, in some religious communities, the members do not bind themselves by vow, but by promises which are less solemn.

Religious orders are of great importance to the Church and even to the world. They pray and offer sacrifice for us all, even for those who do not honor God but insult him. The religious remind us by their example to love God and our neighbor with our whole heart, and to be ready to give up everything if it be God's will. The work which they do in the service of mankind brings great blessings on the world.

Life in a religious order is a great help on the way to God. Whoever serves God in an order has sure and safe guidance, is free from many worries and temptations, and can give himself with undivided heart to Christ; he lives together with others who help him by their prayers and example to serve God as perfectly as possible.

Anyone who desires to enter an order must be called to it by God. He must have a firm resolve to love God above all things, to follow Christ wholeheartedly, and to strive for perfection. Besides that, he must be willing and able to live in a religious community, to observe its rule, to obey its superiors, to do without possessions of his own, and to remain unmarried all his life. He must also be suitable for the special kind of work undertaken by the order which he desires to enter. For anyone who is called to it, life in a religious order is a very happy one, and is the safest and finest way to become a perfect Christian.

*Consider.* 1) To what tasks do members of a religious order devote themselves? 2) What things do religious give up for the kingdom of heaven's sake? 3) In what ways are religious orders important both to the Church and to the world? 4) What helps toward heaven are obtained from life in a religious order? 5) For what things must a boy or a girl be prepared in order to enter the religious life? 6) And for what things must he or she be suited?

186. **To what things do religious bind themselves by vow?**

Religious bind themselves by vow:

1. to have no property of their own;
2. to live in continence;
3. to obey their superiors.

*For my life.* How many sacrifices the religious make in the service of the sick, the young, the missions, in their lives of prayer and reparation! Do I appreciate that? Do I support their work? Have I ever asked myself whether perhaps God might be calling me to be a religious priest or brother (or a nun)?

*The "evangelical counsels."* In the gospel, we read that Jesus advised some to give up their possessions and their occupations in order to follow him. He said that they would be blessed who would give up marriage for the kingdom of heaven's sake. That is why we give the name of *evangelical counsels* to voluntary poverty, celibacy (remaining unmarried) for the kingdom of heaven's sake, and voluntary obedience.

*What would you say?* Some people ask: "Could not the priests and brothers and nuns in religious orders do more good for mankind if they were married and worked in the world?" We answer: "Firstly, by their prayer and sacrifice and reparation, the religious call down countless blessings on mankind; God alone knows what would happen to us if it were not for all the men and women who pray for us in their religious houses. Secondly, the religious in fact do very great services to mankind by all their work in the care of souls, the missions, the schools and hospitals, and by all that they do as men of learning, writers, research workers, and artists."

*Things to do.* 1) What houses of men or women religious do you know: a) in our own parish; b) not far from our parish; c) in our diocese? 2) What religious orders can you name? 3) Can you name any founders of religious orders? 4) What work do the various orders set themselves to do? 5) Name religious who were famous preachers, missionaries, educators, men of learning, discoverers, artists, benefactors of the sick and the poor.

The religious orders are the jewels on the bridal veil of the Church.[399]

[399] Pius XII

## *SECTION III*

# Of Life in Accordance with God's Commandments

## How God Has Made His Commandments Known to Us

Because God is our Lord and our Father, we must keep his commandments. From the beginning, God made known what he would have us do by means of the order of created things; later on, he gave the ten commandments, and, last of all, the one great commandment. He lets his commandments become known to us through our consciences.

### *LESSON 91*

### *The Natural Law of God's Creation*

St. Augustine writes: "The will of the great Creator manifests itself in the nature of every created thing. It is according to the laws of God that the heavens turn upon their axis, the stars move in their course, the sun gives its light in the day and the moon in the night, and that the whole universe keeps to its appointed order through the days and months and years and the ever-changing seasons."[400]

From the beginning, God has established the world according to a great and varied order. He gave to every creature its own nature, and thus its own laws of behavior.

[400] Cf. Augustine, *City of God*, Bk. 8; *Soliloquies*, Bk. 1, Ch. 4

It is God's will that all creatures should follow this natural law. Those that have no reason follow blindly and of necessity the natural forces and tendencies which God himself put into their natures. But we men should come to know this order of creation and follow it of our own accord. This law which God expressed through the order of creation is called the "natural law."

Because the order of nature comes from God, it is something holy. He designed it with wisdom and love, and through it he makes his will known to us. Anyone who offends against the natural law is sinning against God and attacking the work of his hands.

The Christian should find it easier than others to follow the natural law of creation. For he can know it more clearly than they can through the light of his faith and the teachings of the Church. And because God gives him more abundant grace, he can more easily fulfill what the natural law requires.

*Consider.* 1) In what way did God make his will known to men from the very beginning? 2) How do the creatures which have no reason fulfill the laws of nature? 3) In what way should men observe the laws of nature? 4) What do we call that law which God has implanted in nature by his act of creation? 5) In what ways does the Christian receive special help to observe the natural law?

187. **Why is the natural law of creation holy?**

The natural law of creation is holy because it comes from God and makes known to us his holy will.

*For my life.* When I keep the natural law, I am building up my own earthly and heavenly happiness.

*Things to do.* 1) Name some commandments that we can know directly from the natural law. 2) Why do we commit sin when we offend against the natural law?

# *LESSON 92*

## *The Commandments of God*

From Mount Sinai, God proclaimed ten commandments amid terrifying signs of his power. A thick cloud covered the whole mountain; then there was thunder and lightning, and great peals of trumpets could be heard. The mountain was hidden in smoke, because the Lord came down upon it in fire. Moses led the people of Israel out of their camp to meet God, and out of the fire God proclaimed his ten commandments. The Israelites fell back in terror. And Moses said to them: "God has come here to make trial of your obedience; he would have you possessed with the fear of him, to preserve you from sin."[401]

It was out of his fatherly love that God gave us the ten commandments. By their means, he has clearly and solemnly made his will known to us, and confirmed what he had already written into his creation. The commandments tell us precisely and with certainty what we must do. They are like signposts pointing the way to our happiness in this world and in the next.

Christ confirmed these ten commandments. He warned us that we must keep them; he explained them to us, and showed by his example how we ought to observe them.

Above all, Christ announced to us the commandment of love. He said: "Thou shalt love the Lord thy God with thy whole heart, and with thy whole soul, and with thy whole mind, and with all thy strength. This is the first and greatest commandment. And the second is like to this: Thou shalt love thy neighbor as thyself."[402]

This commandment of love is the chief commandment. If we keep this one, we shall keep all the others. St. Paul writes: "All the commandments (Thou shalt not commit adultery, Thou shalt do no murder, Thou shalt not steal, Thou shalt not covet, and the rest) are resumed in this one saying: Thou shalt love thy neighbor as thyself! Love of our neighbor refrains from doing harm of any kind; that is why it fulfills all the demands of the law."[403]

[401] Cf. Ex 19-20
[402] Mt 22:37-39; Mk 12:30-31
[403] Rom 13:9-10

*Consider.* 1) Why did God give the ten commandments? 2) How did Christ confirm the ten commandments? 3) Why is the commandment of love the chief commandment?

188. **Which are the ten commandments?**

I am the Lord thy God.

1. Thou shalt not have strange gods beside me.
2. Thou shalt not dishonor the name of the Lord.
3. Remember that thou keep holy the sabbath day.
4. Thou shalt honor thy father and thy mother.
5. Thou shalt not kill.
6. Thou shalt not commit adultery.
7. Thou shalt not steal.
8. Thou shalt not bear false witness against thy neighbor.
9. Thou shalt not covet thy neighbor's wife.
10. Thou shalt not covet thy neighbor's goods.

189. **Which is the great commandment?**

Thou shalt love the Lord thy God with thy whole heart, and with thy whole soul, and with thy whole mind, and with all thy strength. This is the greatest and first commandment. And the second is like to this: Thou shalt love thy neighbor as thyself.

*For my life.* God's commandment is always right. Even if others do wrong, I will not do wrong.

*From holy scripture.* Jesus said: "If thou wilt enter into life, keep the commandments."[404]—"He that hath my commandments and keepeth them; he it is that loveth me."[405]—"Loving God means keeping his commandments."[406]

*Things to do.* 1) If God had not forbidden them in the ten commandments, would lying, stealing, and killing be sins? Give reasons for your

[404] Mt 19:17
[405] Jn 14:21
[406] 1 Jn 5:3

answer. 2) What differences would we notice in this world if all men kept the ten commandments?

*From Psalm 118.* "I seek thee with all my heart; let me not wander from thy commandments. Blessed art thou, O Lord; teach me thy statutes. Make me to understand the way of thy precepts, that I may meditate on thy wondrous works. Show me the way of thy law, O Lord, and I will keep it perfectly. How I love thy law, O Lord; it is my meditation all day long. Thy word is a lamp to my feet and a light to my path. Let my tongue chant thy word, for all thy commandments are just."

## *LESSON 93*

## *Conscience*

When Solomon became king after the death of his father David, God appeared to him in a dream and said to him: "Choose what gift thou wilt!" And Solomon answered: "Lord God, thou hast bidden me reign where my father reigned, over a great people; but, Lord, what am I? No better than a little child. Be this, then, thy gift to thy servant, a heart quick to learn, so that I may be able to judge thy people's disputes and discern between good and ill."[407]

God desires that we should do his will from our own understanding of the matter. Therefore, he has given us an ability to recognize what we ought or ought not to do. This ability we call our "conscience."

Before we do anything, our conscience tells us if it is good or warns us if it is bad; after we have done anything, our conscience praises us if we have done well or blames us if we have done ill. Thus we speak of "having a good conscience" or "having a bad conscience" about what we have done.

When conscience tells us quite clearly, "You ought to do this!" or "You must not do that!" we must obey it at once. Anyone who goes against the clear judgment of his conscience commits a sin against God. Therefore, not even orders or threats from other people should make us ever do anything against our conscience.

[407] Cf. 3 Kgs 3:5-9

If we follow our conscience faithfully, we are said to be "conscientious." Then God gives us joy and peace of mind; we are free from the torments of a bad conscience and are glad that we have done what we believed was the right thing.

Anyone who often acts against his conscience blunts it or dulls it. A man who keeps on blunting his conscience by acting against it comes in time to lose it altogether. He falls into sins that grow worse and worse till he ends up with the most wicked vices. He is like a blind man walking toward a precipice.

It is possible, however, for our conscience to make mistakes. It may become darkened through sin. In order to decide properly, it must be guided by the natural law, the ten commandments, the example of Christ, and the teaching and commandments of the Church. If we find this difficult, we should pray to God for light, and should ask advice from our parents, our priest, our teacher, or some other reliable person.

*Consider.* 1) What does our conscience tell us about something we have not yet done? What does it tell us after we have done it? 2) What do you mean when you say someone is "conscientious"? 3) What is the result if someone keeps on acting against his conscience? 4) By what things should our conscience be guided? 5) What should we do in difficult cases, in order to find out what is right and what is wrong?

190. **What do we recognize through our conscience?**

Through our conscience, we recognize what we ought to do or what we ought not to do.

191. **When must we follow our conscience?**

We must follow our conscience whenever it tells us clearly: "You must do this," or, "You must not do that."

*For my life.* When I follow my conscience, I act as a free man and child of God, not as a slave of other men or of my evil passions.

*From holy scripture.* "It is not above thy reach, this duty I am now enjoining thee. It is not a secret laid up in heaven, that thou must needs find someone to scale heaven and bring it down to thee before thou canst hear what it is, and obey it. It is not an art, practiced far overseas, that thou must wait for someone to go voyaging and bring it back to thee before thou canst learn to live by it. No, this message of mine is close to thy side; it rises to thy lips, it is printed on thy memory; thou hast only to fulfill it."[408]

*Things to do.* 1) What signs were there of the working of conscience in: a) Adam and Eve; b) Cain; c) the brothers of Joseph in Egypt; d) David; e) the prodigal son; f) the good thief on the cross? 2) Show how Judas fell into ever-growing sins because he would not follow his conscience.

# The First Commandment of God

Because God is our Creator and our sovereign Lord, it is our exalted and sacred duty to adore him alone, and to serve him with all our powers. God commands: "Thou shalt not have strange gods beside me."

## *LESSON 94*

### *The Adoration of God*

The apostle St. John once received a great spiritual favor from Cod. He was given a vision of heaven, where he saw a throne, and on the throne there sat one who shone in glory like the splendor of precious jewels. Above the throne there was a rainbow; around the throne sat twenty-four elders clothed in white garments. On their heads they wore crowns of gold. Near the throne were four living creatures. Day and night they cried: "Holy, holy, holy is the Lord God, the Almighty, who ever was and is and is still to come." And the twenty-four elders fell down in worship before him who sat on the throne, who lives forever and ever. They threw down their crowns

[408] Dt 30:11-14

before the throne saying: "Thou, our Lord God, claimest as thy due, glory and honor and power; by thee all things were created; nothing ever was, nothing was ever created, but in obedience to thy will."[409]

God is the Creator and Lord of heaven and earth. He is infinitely exalted above everything which he has created. Beside him we are as nothing. The angels of heaven tremble before his majesty. Even more should we bow down in reverence and humility before the infinite greatness of God, to acknowledge and honor him as our sovereign Lord; we must adore God.

We may adore no one but God, for he alone is our Creator and sovereign Lord. If anyone adores a creature as a god, he commits the sin called "idolatry"—the worship of false gods.—It is a sin called "superstition" to ascribe to any creature some hidden power which God has not given to it; for example, to seek knowledge of the future from the stars (astrology) or from playing cards (fortune-telling), or to treat certain things or figures or days as if they decided one's fate.—It is a sin to attempt to work wonders by the help of evil spirits (magic) or to obtain from them knowledge or messages about hidden things (spiritualism).

With all that we have and all that we are, we must praise and honor God; our bodies and all other things were created for the glory of God. Therefore, we should adore God also exteriorly; we do this by vocal prayer and song, by folding our hands, by genuflecting; by the light of candles, the sound of music, the decoration of altars, the beauty of vestments.

Communities also come from God—the family, the state, the Church. Therefore, we must adore God also in community and openly give him worship.

Christ has shown us how we should adore the Father. He warns us that we must adore God not only in an outward way, but also interiorly and from the heart. When we unite ourselves in prayer with Christ, then we are true adorers of the Father.[410]

*Consider.* 1) What is the first commandment? 2) What is the sin of idolatry? 3) What is the sin of superstition? 4) Why should we adore God

[409] Cf. Apoc 4
[410] Cf. Jn 4:23-24

also exteriorly? 5) Why should we adore God in community and publicly? 6) When are we true adorers of the Father?

192. **What does God command in the first commandment?**
In the first commandment, God commands that we adore him alone, because he alone is the Creator and sovereign Lord of heaven and earth.

*For my life.* Sometimes I will go all alone into the church, kneel down, and say: "Holy and great God, you are here! I adore you!"

*Prayers of adoration.* "My God, how great and holy and wonderful you are! You are the Lord of the whole world. Your thoughts are infinitely above all human thoughts, your power is greater than any power on earth, your love is stronger and deeper than anyone can understand. I glorify you; I submit myself to you; with deepest reverence, I adore you, my great and loving Lord and God."

"We praise thee, we bless thee, we adore thee, we glorify thee, we thank thee for thy great glory."[411]

## *LESSON 95*

## *Fulfilling the Will of God*

One day, Jesus said to the people: "Not everyone that saith to me, 'Lord, Lord,' shall enter into the kingdom of heaven; but he that doth the will of my Father who is in heaven, he shall enter into the kingdom of heaven."[412]

If we truly adore God, we submit ourselves entirely to his rule. We are ready to do his will in all things, just as Christ, our master, did. Whatever God wills from us is holy and for our good. It is his will which shows us the right way in every situation throughout our life.

God commands some things and forbids others. What God commands, we must do; what he forbids, we must avoid. Sometimes God encourages us to something which is good without actually commanding it. In these

[411] From the *Gloria* of the Mass.
[412] Mt 7:21

things also we should be ready and glad to do God's will, and we must not allow our own convenience or laziness to prevent us from doing so. The saints always took care to do God's will generously and cheerfully even in the smallest things.

We must also fulfill the will of God when he demands sacrifices from us, or lets us suffer. At such times, we should give ourselves up to the will of God and pray with Jesus: "Father, not my will but thine be done."[413]

God has his special plan for each and every human being. We should try to find out what this plan is, and often pray that God will show us the way he wants us to go, and will give us the strength to serve him truly and perseveringly.

*Consider.* 1) What must we do if we truly adore God? 2) What should we do if God lets us know he would like us to do something which is good, but does not command it? 3) What should we do if God asks sacrifices from us, or lets suffering come upon us?

193. **Why must we do God's will?**

We must do God's will: 1) because he is our sovereign Lord; 2) becuase his will is for our good.

*For my life.* Whenever I know that God wants something from me, I will say: "Yes, Father, I will do it gladly!"

*From holy scripture.* "He that does the will of my Father in heaven is my brother and sister and mother."[414]—Mary said: "Behold the handmaid of the Lord; be it done unto me according to thy word."[415]—"The world and its gratifications pass away; the man who does God's will outlives them for ever."[416]

*From the teaching of the saints.* "There is only one true form of nobility: to do the will of God."[417]

[413] Lk 22:42
[414] Mt 12:50
[415] Lk 1:38
[416] 1 Jn 2:17
[417] Chrysostom

*A prayer.* "Lord, I will what you will; I will it because you will it; I will it the way that you will it; I will it as long as you will it."[418]

*Things to do.* 1) How can you know what God wants of you? 2) What is often the reason why men do not do God's will? 3) When can it be particularly hard to do God's will?

## *LESSON 96*

## *Right Intention*

St. Paul writes: "In eating, in drinking, in all that you do, do everything as for God's glory."[419]

Because we are God's children, we should do for God everything that we do. In all our actions we should have the intention of giving glory to God, of showing him our love and gratitude, and of doing his holy will. We call this attitude "having a right intention."

This right intention sanctifies both our work and our play, our joy and our sorrow; it binds us ever more closely to God. It makes even the most ordinary little thing we may do have great value before God, and it will increase our reward in heaven.

We should often arouse in ourselves this right intention. We should use the right intention especially to sanctify our work, for work occupies most of our time. We can arouse our right intention by such words as: "All for God's glory," "In the name of God," "All for you, my God," "Jesus, all for love of you."

We must beware of doing good things for wrong reasons—that is, with a wrong intention. The Pharisees, for instance, used to do their good works not for God's glory, but in order to be admired by men. Jesus said of them: "Amen, I say to you, they have already received their reward."[420]

[418] Clement XI, *Universal Prayer*
[419] 1 Cor 10:31
[420] Mt 6:5

*Consider.* 1) When do we have a right intention? 2) Why is a right intention of great value? 3) How should we arouse a right intention? 4) When should we form our right intention?

194. **Why should we often form a right intention?**
We should often form a right intention because thereby we honor God, sanctify all we do, and increase our reward in heaven.

*For my life.* Every morning, I will form a right intention and will renew it several times during the day.

*From the teaching of the saints.* "Let your hand be at its work, but your heart with God."[421] — "The Lord does not consider the greatness of what we do so much as the love with which we do it."[422]

Begin with God and with him end,
that is the way your life to spend!

## *LESSON 97*

## *Honoring the Saints*

In the year 156, the Christians of Smyrna wrote a circular letter to other Christian communities announcing that their bishop, St. Polycarp, had died as a martyr. They wrote: "We adore Christ, for he is the Son of God. But we love those who have borne witness with their blood as disciples and imitators of the Lord, because of their unequalled devotion to their King and master. May we also become their companions and fellow disciples!" And they wrote of the relics of their martyr-bishop: "They are more precious to us than jewels, more dear than gold. We have preserved them in an honored place. There we shall assemble in triumphant joy each year, to celebrate the anniversary of his death."

421 St. Zita

422 Teresa of Avila, *Interior Castle*, Mansion 7, Ch. 4, n. 23

The saints are in a special way the friends of God. They are masterpieces of the workings of his grace. The saints loved God above all things and gave him heroic service. God honors them now in heaven, and very often he has glorified them on earth by means of miracles. That is why we love and honor the saints.

We honor the saints by celebrating their memory and by asking them to pray to God for us. At the same time, we thank God for the graces which he gave to the saints, and ask him to be gracious to us in answer to their prayers, and to help us to be like them. The feast of a saint is usually celebrated on the day of his death, because this is his birthday into the kingdom of heaven.

The saints are examples to us in the imitation of Christ. When we read their lives, we get to know the heroic way in which they lived; and thus we feel inspired to follow their example.

We honor also the bodies of the saints, and many things which they made use of while they were on earth. These things are precious reminders of the saints; we call them "relics" (that is, things left by them). We revere also pictures and statues of the saints, because, in doing so, we are honoring the saints themselves. These pictures and statues remind us of the saints, and help us to love them and make us want to imitate them.—God has often worked miracles by means of relics and pictures, and has given to those who honor them many favors.

*Consider.* 1) Why are the saints special friends of God? 2) How does God honor his saints? 3) What is the usual day for celebrating the feast of a saint? 4) How are we helped by reading the lives of the saints? 5) What are relics?

195. **Why do we honor the saints?**

We honor the saints because they are friends of God and because God himself honors them.

196. **How do we honor the saints?**

We honor the saints: 1) by celebrating their feasts and asking them to pray for us; 2) by following their example; 3) by honoring their relics and images.

197. **Why do we honor relics of the saints?**
We honor relics of the saints because: 1) they are precious reminders of the saints; and 2) because God has often honored them by miracles.

198. **Why do we honor images of the saints?**
We honor images of the saints because: 1) we thereby honor the saints themselves; and 2) because these images help us to love and to imitate the saints.

*For my life.* I will get a book of lives of some of the saints, and will gladly read it. Above all, I must learn to know the saint whose name I bear, so that I may pray to him and strive to follow him.

*From the life of the Church.* The patron of the United States of America is the Immaculate Virgin Mother of God. The patron saint of England is St. George; of Scotland is St. Andrew; of Wales is St. David; and of Ireland is St. Patrick.

It is a custom to pray to certain saints in particular circumstances; for instance, if we have family worries, we pray to St. Joseph who took care of the Holy Family; we pray to him too for a happy death because, according to tradition, he died with Jesus and Mary at his side; we pray to St. Francis Xavier for foreign missions because he himself was such a great missionary.

*What would you say?* Some people say: "It is superstitious to honor the relics of the saints." But we answer: "We honor the graves and the photographs of our parents, and other things they have left behind them. And as for relics and images of the saints, God has sometimes honored them by miracles."

Others say: "Doesn't the honor we give to saints take away from the honor we should give to God?" We answer: "Not at all; for in honoring the saints, we are honoring God; for it was only from him that their holiness came. Also, by honoring the saints as we should, we are stirred up to honor God all the more and serve him all the better."

*Things to do.* 1) In what way can you specially imitate the saint whose name you bear? 2) What do you know about the patron saint of our parish church? 3) What do you know of the patron of our diocese? 4) Name some saints to whom we pray in particular circumstances. 5) What saints are patrons and examples for young people? 6) Of what saints do you know the feast days? 7) Name some saints who have been canonized in the past few years. 8) What would you reply if someone said to you: "Catholics adore saints"?

## *LESSON 98*

## *Honoring Mary, the Mother of God*

When the angel Gabriel appeared to Mary, he said to her: "Hail, Mary, full of grace; the Lord is with thee." Soon after that, Mary went over the mountains to visit her cousin Elizabeth. And when Elizabeth heard Mary's greeting, she was filled with the Holy Ghost and cried out with a loud voice: "Blessed art thou among women, and blessed is the fruit of thy womb."[423]

God raised Mary to a dignity above that of all the angels and saints, and filled her soul with grace. She is the Mother of his Son and the holiest of all women. She is also our Mother and continually prays to God for us. That is why we honor Mary in an altogether special way.

Often we say the "Hail Mary." There are two parts to it: one praises her, and the other asks something of her.—The praising-part begins with the greeting of the archangel Gabriel: "Hail, Mary, full of grace, the Lord is with thee." That is why the whole prayer is sometimes called the "Angelic Salutation." While we greet Mary in the words of the angel, we think of the fullness of grace which God gave to her, and remember how near she stands to God.—Then we praise her in the words of Elizabeth, and with her we praise Jesus, her Son and our Savior: "Blessed art thou among women, and blessed is the fruit of thy womb, Jesus."—The asking-part of the prayer has been added by the Church: "Holy Mary, Mother of God, pray for us sinners now and at the hour of our death. Amen." With these words, we ask Mary for her powerful intercession before God.

[423] Cf. Lk 1:26-45

When we say the rosary or the *Angelus*, we say the Hail Mary many times. While we are saying the words, our minds should be dwelling on the mysteries of our redemption.

The two chief feasts of Mary are those of her Immaculate Conception (December 8th) and her Assumption (August 15th).—During the month of May, we decorate her altars with flowers from our gardens, and hold May devotions. During October, we say the rosary every day for the great intentions of the Church. Of the days of the week, Saturday is specially dedicated to our Lady.—In our joys and sorrows, we may also make pilgrimages to shrines of our Lady, of which God has shown his approval by giving many graces.

*Consider.* 1) What do we ask of our Lady in the second half of the Hail Mary? 2) What should we have in our minds when we are saying the Hail Mary during the rosary or the *Angelus*? 3) Which are the two principal feasts of our Lady? 4) Which months are specially dedicated to Mary?

199. **Why do we honor Mary in a very special way?**
We honor Mary in a very special way because she is the Mother of God and also our heavenly Mother.

*For my life.* I will not let a day go by without saying the Hail Mary. Whenever I pass a statue or picture of our Lady, I will greet her.

*From holy scripture.* Mary said to Elizabeth: "Henceforth all generations shall call me blessed."[424]

*Some prayers.* "Hail, holy Queen!"—"We fly to thy patronage"—"Remember O most holy Virgin Mary"—the Litany of the Blessed Virgin.

*Things to do.* 1) Write out the first lines of any hymns to our Lady which you happen to know. 2) In our parish church, where can we find pictures or statues of our Lady? 3) How is she represented in these? 4) Can you name any places to which people make pilgrimages in honor of Mary? Are there any in our own country? 5) Get a picture of our Lady, frame it, and hang

[424] Lk 1:48

it over your bed. 6) Collect some beautiful pictures of our Lady. 7) Get a calendar and mark in it the dates which are feasts of our Lady.

# The Second Commandment of God

Because God is so holy, we must pay reverence to his name, and to everything which is dedicated to him. God commands: "Thou shalt not dishonor the name of the Lord!"

## *LESSON 99*

### *Reverence for the Name of God*

"Praise the Lord, you that are his servants; praise the name of the Lord together. Blessed be the Lord's name at all times; from this day to all eternity. From the sun's rising even until its setting, let the Lord's name be praised continually. The Lord is the sovereign king of all nations; his glory is high above the heavens."[425]

God is infinitely holy and worthy of all possible adoration. Therefore, we must speak of God only with reverence, and make use of his name with the greatest respect. And we should say the name of Jesus and other holy names of persons and things (for instance, the cross and the sacraments) with reverence and thankfulness too. God commands us in his second commandment not to dishonor his name.

It is a sin against this commandment to use the name of God or other holy names in an irreverent way or in anger, especially in cursing.—Some people even go so far as to insult God and say wicked things about him; they blaspheme God. It would be a sin of blasphemy if anyone claimed

[425] Ps 112:1-4

that he should have honors due to God alone. In the old testament, there was a law: "He that blasphemes the Lord's name must die."[426]

No one ever used the name of God with such reverence, devotion, and love as did Jesus, the Son of God. He teaches us better than anyone else how to love and honor God's name.

*Consider.* 1) Give examples of sins against the second commandment. 2) What do you mean by the word *cursing*? 3) What is meant by *blaspheming*? 4) Who teaches us best of all how to honor God's name?

200. **What does God command in the second commandment?**
In the second commandment, God commands us to hold his name in respect.

201. **Why must we hold God's name in respect?**
We must hold God's name in respect because he himself is infinitely holy.

*For my life.* Every time I make the sign of the cross, I will pronounce the names of the three divine Persons slowly and reverently.—If ever I hear anyone pronouncing holy names irreverently, I will say: "Praised be Jesus Christ!" or, "Glory be to the Father and to the Son and to the Holy Ghost."

*Things to do.* Make a list of some of the names by which God is called in holy scripture, in prayers, and in hymns.

## *LESSON 100*

### *Reverence for Things Dedicated to God*

"Jesus once went into the temple and drove out all those who were buying and selling things there. He overturned the tables of the money changers and the stands of those who were selling doves, and said to them: 'It is written: My house shall be called the house of prayer, but you have made it a den of thieves.'"[427]

[426] Lv 24:16
[427] Mt 21:12-13

If we love and honor God, we shall have reverence for those places, things, and persons which are dedicated to God; for instance, the church, the cemetery, the cross, the altar, the sacred vessels, priests, monks, and nuns.

Especially holy are the sacraments, above all the most Holy Sacrament of the Altar. In the sacraments, God, who is so holy, comes specially close to us. Therefore, we should receive them worthily, and be careful to prepare ourselves before receiving them.—The Bible also is holy, because it contains God's word.

Whoever dishonors holy places, things, or persons commits a sacrilege; he deprives God of the honor which is due to him. It is a specially serious sacrilege to dishonor the Blessed Sacrament, for instance, by receiving Holy Communion unworthily. It is a sin to behave badly in holy places, to treat holy things carelessly or irreverently, or to behave without proper respect for priests and religious.

*Consider.* 1) Name some places and things which are dedicated to God. 2) What does respect for the Blessed Sacrament demand from us? 3) Why should we have reverence for the Bible? 4) Why do we show respect to priests and monks and nuns? 5) Give examples of sinful irreverence against what is dedicated to God. 6) What exactly is a "sacrilege"?

*For my life.* I shall treat such things as the rosary, blessed candles, holy water, the Bible and other religious books, with reverence, and will take good care of them.—I will not make or laugh at jokes about Bible-stories or divine service or confession.—Pious objects that are not to be used anymore should not just be thrown away, but should be burned or buried.

*From holy scripture.* "Lay no hand on them, never hurt them, servants anointed and true spokesmen of mine."[428]

*Things to do.* 1) How do we show our reverence: a) in the church; b) when taking holy water; c) when going up to Communion or coming back; d) while waiting for confession? 2) What blessed or consecrated things are in your home? In our church?

[428] Ps 104:15

# *LESSON 101*

## *Oaths*

When Jesus had been taken prisoner, the council of the Jews sought false witness against him so that they might put him to death. But they could prove nothing, for although several false witnesses came in, their testimony did not agree. So the high priest stood up and said to Jesus: "I adjure thee by the living God that thou tell us if thou be the Christ, the Son of God." Jesus answered him: "Thou hast said it."[429]

Sometimes it is necessary for a person to give special force to his statement about what he has seen or heard or done. On these very important occasions, especially in the law courts, he may call on God, who knows all things, as a witness that he is telling the truth. He swears an oath, of the kind called an "oath of evidence."

Also, if a person has to make a solemn promise about something of great importance, he may call on God as a witness of the fact that he truly intends to keep his promise. This, too, is an oath, of the kind called an "oath of promise." The oath which some officials of the state are called upon to take before entering on their office is of this kind. If anyone has promised something under oath, he is absolutely bound to keep his promise under pain of mortal sin.

To swear the truth by God in a very important matter is not wrong, but right; and he who takes such an oath is honoring God. For by his oath he acknowledges that God knows all things and is infinitely just and powerful, and he is submitting himself to God's holy judgment.

But to take a false oath knowingly is to call on God to be witness of a lie; this false oath is called "perjury." A perjurer blasphemes God who knows all things and is infinitely holy; and he destroys the faith and trust which men should have in each other's word. That is why perjury is a great crime. It is a sin, too, to swear an oath lightly—that is, without sufficient reason, or without being absolutely sure of the truth of what one says or

[429] Cf. Mt 26:59-64

of the possibility of what one promises.—If anyone swears that he will do something evil, he sins against God, for he is trying to make God help his sinful action.—If anyone has sworn under oath to do something important, and then does not do it although he could, he sins by breaking his oath.

Christ did not forbid oaths; he himself took an oath before the Jewish council. But his will is that we should normally deal with each other without having to confirm what we say by oaths. He says: "You should not bind yourselves by any oath at all...let your word be Yes for Yes, and No for No; whatever goes beyond this comes of evil."[430]

*Consider.* 1) What is an oath of evidence? 2) What is an oath of promise? 3) How is it that God is honored by an oath? 4) What do you mean by *perjury*? 5) When is it not lawful to take an oath? 6) When is it forbidden to keep an oath? 7) What do you mean by "breaking an oath"?

202. **What is meant by *swearing*?**

Swearing means calling on God to witness that one is telling the truth or intends to keep one's promise.

203. **Why is perjury one of the greatest crimes?**

Perjury is one of the greatest crimes: 1) because the perjurer calls on God to witness a lie and thus blasphemes him; 2) because perjury shatters faith and trust between men.

*For my life.* It would be better to lose everything I have than to swear a false oath.

*From the Bible.* The oath which Herod swore is an example of an oath which he should not have taken, and should not have kept.

*From history.* The emperor Charlemagne considered perjury such a great crime that he made a law according to which perjurers were to be punished by loss of their right hand.

[430] Cf. Mt 5:34-37

# LESSON 102

## *Vows*

When Jacob woke up after his dream about the ladder joining heaven and earth, he said: "Indeed the Lord is in this place, and I did not know it!" Then he made a vow and said: "If God will watch over me on this journey of mine, and bring me safely back to my father's house, I will build an altar to the Lord in this place and offer to him a tenth part of all that I receive."[431]

Some people promise to do some good thing for God in order to honor him in a special way, and they bind themselves to do it under pain of sin. For example, they promise to build a chapel, to make a pilgrimage, to help some fellow man, or to do some other good work that will please God. Members of religious orders promise to have no private possessions, to live in continence, and to be obedient to their superiors. Promises of this kind are called "vows." But merely to undertake some good work is not a vow, only a good intention.

By a vow, we honor God and bind ourselves more closely to him. A vow is a sacrifice which we make to God, and at the same time a help for our own weak wills.

Anyone who has made a vow to God is bound to keep his vow. If he breaks his vow in any important way, he commits a mortal sin. "If thou hast vowed anything to God, defer not to pay it…It is much better not to vow than, after a vow, not to perform the thing promised."[432]

Before anyone makes a vow, he must think it over very carefully. No one should make an important vow without first asking advice from his confessor. And if anyone has made a vow and then finds that he really cannot keep it, he should ask his confessor what to do about it. For grave reasons, the Church can dispense a man from his vow or alter the obligation to which he is bound.

[431] Cf. Gn 28:16-22

[432] Eccles 5:3-4

*Consider.* 1) What kind of thing can one vow to God? 2) What vows do members of religious orders take? 3) What must one do before making a vow?

204. **What is meant by "taking a vow"?**
Taking a vow means promising God to do some good work, and binding oneself to it under pain of sin.

*For my life.* I will never make a vow unless I feel quite sure that I can keep it.

# The Third Commandment of God

Because our whole life belongs to God, we must devote one day in the week to him in a special way. God commands: "Remember that thou keep holy the sabbath day."

## *LESSON 103*

### *Taking Part in Public Worship on Sundays and Holidays*

"We hold the Lord's day in reverence and celebrate it solemnly, because on that day our Savior, like the rising sun, shone in the light of his glorious resurrection after conquering the darkness of hell; this day is called 'Sunday,' because Christ, the rising Sun of Justice, fills it with light."[433]

It was on a Sunday that our Lord Jesus Christ rose gloriously from the dead; it was on a Sunday that he sent down the Holy Ghost upon his Church. That is why Christians, ever since the days of the apostles, have celebrated the Sunday, and not Saturday which was the sabbath of the

[433] Maxim of Turin

Jews. Sunday reminds us of that new creation which began with our Lord's resurrection. It is also called "the day of the Lord" or "the Lord's day."[434]

On feast days or holidays (holy days), the Church celebrates the various mysteries of our redemption, and keeps the memory of Mary and of other saints. The oldest and greatest of all feasts is that of Easter, the day of our Lord's resurrection. The more important feasts are holy days of obligation, which must be celebrated by all the faithful. The Church orders this in the first of her commandments: "You are to observe the Sundays and holy days of obligation."

On Sundays and holy days of obligation, we assemble for the celebration of the Holy Eucharist. On these days, all of us should come together to hear the good tidings of Christ, to take our part devoutly in the Holy Sacrifice of the Mass and, whenever possible, to receive the body of the Lord. It is the second commandment of the Church that we must go to Mass on Sundays and holy days of obligation, and the law is binding on everyone who has reached his seventh birthday. Only very serious reasons excuse us from this obligation: if we are sick or cannot leave someone who is sick; if we cannot avoid going to work on Sunday; if we are very far from the church, especially when the weather is bad.

If anyone, without sufficient reason, fails to attend Mass on Sunday, he commits a mortal sin. He commits a venial sin if he arrives late through his own fault, or deliberately pays no attention at Mass or deliberately disturbs others.—To follow a Mass which is being broadcast or televised does not fulfill the obligation of being present at Mass, though it is a good thing to do if, for sufficient reason, one cannot go in person.

On Sundays, we ought also to hear a sermon, so that we may get to know our faith better and live according to it joyfully. Jesus said: "He that is of God hears God's word."[435] In the afternoon or evening, we should come back to Church to take our part in vespers or other devotions. Although these things are not of obligation, missing them Sunday after Sunday is a sign of slackness in our faith and can be dangerous to our souls.

[434] Cf. Apoc 1:10

[435] Jn 8:47

The Sunday Mass is the most important event in our whole week. For at the Sunday Mass, the parish as a whole, and each individual, offers to God through Christ the glory which is his due, and they themselves receive grace and joy and strength for their everyday life.

*Consider.* 1) Why do we celebrate Sunday as a feast day? 2) What does the Church celebrate on other feast days? 3) Which is the oldest and greatest of all feasts? 4) What is the first commandment of the Church? 5) In what way is the memory of our Savior celebrated on Sundays and feast days? 6) What is the second commandment of the Church? 7) Give some reasons which would be sufficient to excuse you from going to Mass on Sunday. 8) Who commits a sin against the Church's second commandment? 9) Why should we also hear a sermon on Sundays and feast days?

205. **Why do we keep Sunday as the Lord's day?**
We keep Sunday as the Lord's day because it was on a Sunday that Christ rose from the dead and on a Sunday that he sent the Holy Ghost.

*For my life.* I will always regard Sunday Mass as the most important duty of the whole week.—If it is impossible for me to go to Mass on some Sunday, then I will say my Mass prayers at home.—Before taking on some job after I leave school, I will find out whether I would be able to attend Sunday Mass.

*What would you say?* A child says: "My parents do not go to Mass and do not let me go to Mass. What shall I do?" We answer: "Keep on asking them to let you go. If they still forbid you to go, you commit no sin by missing Mass. But also you would commit no sin of disobedience if you could manage to get to Mass without their knowing it."

Some people say: "On Sundays, I can pray better in God's great open spaces in the midst of nature." We answer: "It is good to pray among the beauties of nature. But God requires of us that we adore him on Sundays and feast days above all by coming together as a community for the celebration of Holy Mass. And the Church orders us in the name of Christ to do this. To refuse to take part in this celebration is to reject the will of God, the sacrifice of Christ, and the commandment of the Church."

Others say: "I have no time to go to church on Sundays." We answer: "There are 168 hours in the week. If you will not make even one of these hours free for the service of God, you show that God means nothing to you."

*Proverb.* As your Sunday, so your dying-day.

*Things to do.* 1) Why do you go to Mass on Sunday? 2) Is there any way in which you can help as many children as possible to go to Mass on Sunday? 3) Which days are holy days of obligation in our country? 4) Which days are only civil holidays?

## *LESSON 104*

### *The Sunday Rest*

When God on Mount Sinai commanded that every seventh day should be kept holy, he said: "Six days for drudgery, for doing the work thou hast to do; when the seventh day comes, it is a day of rest, consecrated to the Lord thy God. That day all work shall be at an end, for thee and every son and daughter of thine, thy servants and serving-women, thy beasts too, and the aliens within thy gates."[436]

Sundays and holy days of obligation should be days of rest. On these days, we should free ourselves from the ordinary work of the week. Heavy bodily work ("servile work") is forbidden; we should do work of this kind only when it is absolutely necessary.

On Sundays and feast days, we should find new strength. Both our bodies and our minds should be refreshed, and our souls should turn to higher things. We can, for example, read good books, and enjoy ourselves by means of something beautiful (such as music or scenery) for which we have no time during the week.

On Sundays and holy days, we should gladly enjoy each other's company. It is good when the whole family goes to church together, when all share the same meal, or all enjoy themselves together in some way. We

[436] Ex 20:9-10

should have time for our relations and friends and acquaintances, but above all for people who are sick or lonely.

Anyone, who, without sufficient reason, does heavy physical work on a Sunday, or makes others do it, sins against the Sunday rest. The Sunday is also dishonored by drinking too much, by excess in sport, or sinful amusements. Staying up late on Saturday nights for the sake of pleasure puts the proper Christian celebration of Sunday in danger.

*Consider.* 1) What would be sufficient reasons for doing heavy physical work on Sunday? 2) For what purposes should we make use of Sundays? 3) In what ways can we make Sunday a family day? 4) What things would dishonor the Sunday?

206. **What kind of work is forbidden on Sundays and holy days of obligation?** On Sundays and holy days of obligation, it is forbidden to do heavy bodily work unless it is urgently necessary.

*For my life.* Sunday belongs to God. I will not dishonor Sunday by any kind of sin, nor by too much seeking after worldly pleasures.

*Things to do.* 1) What can we do in our families on Saturday to prepare for a worthy celebration of Sunday: a) by doing needed work beforehand; b) by putting ourselves spiritually in the right mood? 2) Describe some good ways in which a family can spend Sunday. How can I help to do this in my own family?

## *LESSON 105*

## *Sacred Days and Seasons*

### A. The Christian Week

The first and most important day of the week is Sunday. It was on this day that Christ, our Savior, rose again from the dead. And so, on Sunday we come together to celebrate, in the Holy Eucharist, the memory of the passion, death, and resurrection of our Lord Jesus Christ. This Sunday celebration gives us the strength to live as children of God throughout the week which follows.

On Thursday evening, we may well turn our thoughts to the agony of our Lord on the Mount of Olives. On Friday, we call to mind his passion and death. In some countries, the church bells are rung at these times to call the people to prayer.

## B. The Church's Year

The Church's year has two great feasts with other lesser feasts depending on them; these are called "festal cycles" (because they come round again every year). The two festal cycles of the Church's year are the Christmas cycle and the Easter cycle. Between these festal cycles there occur the ordinary Sundays of the year.

### The Christmas Cycle

Before Christmas day comes, we prepare ourselves by the season called "Advent." *Advent* means "coming." During Advent, the Church reminds us of the second coming of Christ at the last day, and also of his first coming on Christmas day. During Advent, there are four Sundays. The liturgical color for the vestments is purple.

In the Christmas cycle, there are two chief feasts. On Christmas day (Dec. 25th), we celebrate the birth of our divine Savior. On the feast of the Epiphany of our Lord (Jan. 6th), we rejoice that Christ, the King of the world, has made himself known to all peoples. Forty days after Christmas (Feb. 2nd), we have the feast of the Presentation of Our Lord in the Temple, which is also called the "Purification," or "Candlemas day." On these days, the liturgical color is white.

From the Sunday after the Epiphany until Septuagesima, there may be as many as six Sundays, all called "Sundays after the Epiphany." On these Sundays, the color is green.

### The Easter Cycle

Because Easter is the greatest of all feasts, we have two periods of preparation for it, called "Pre-Lent" and "Lent." The color until the Wednesday in Holy week is purple, except for any saints' feasts which may occur. In the Masses of these seasons there is no *Gloria*, and, before the blessing, the priest does not say, *Ite missa est*, but he says, *Benedicamus Domino*, instead. During all this time, the joyous word *Alleluia* is not used at all.

Pre-Lent begins nine weeks before Easter. It starts with Septuagesima Sunday and goes on till Shrove Tuesday, the day before Ash Wednesday.

Lent itself lasts forty days. It begins on Ash Wednesday and ends on Holy Saturday. In early times, those who were getting ready for baptism used to receive special training during Lent; and any of the faithful who had committed serious sins used to do their public penance. During this time, we should do all we can to deepen our faith, to turn away from our sins, and to renew our lives. The Church bids the faithful to pray, to fast, to give alms, to listen to Lenten sermons, and eagerly to receive the sacraments; it is against the mind of the Church to go to dances and other public festivities during this time.

On Ash Wednesday, we receive blessed ashes which the priest puts on our foreheads in the form of a cross; the Church reminds us by this that we will all have to die some day, and warns us to do penance.

Fourteen days before Easter is Passion Sunday, the beginning of "Passiontide." During Passiontide, all crucifixes and statues are veiled in purple.

On the Second Sunday of Passiontide (also called "Palm Sunday") we begin Holy Week, the most important week of the year. On this Second Sunday in Passiontide, we hold a procession with palms or other branches, in memory of the procession of our Lord into Jerusalem. By this means we honor and show our faith in Christ our King.

On Maundy Thursday, we remember the last supper at which our Lord instituted the Holy Eucharist. On this day in each church, only one priest usually celebrates Mass; other priests and all the faithful take part in this Mass and receive the body of our Lord, just as the apostles did at the last supper. The church bells are rung and the organ is played during the

*Gloria*, and after that they are silent until the *Gloria* of the vigil Mass on Holy Saturday night. The liturgical color for Maundy Thursday is white.

On Good Friday, we celebrate the memory of the passion and death of our Lord, and of his victory over the powers of darkness. The history of the passion is sung or read; then prayers are offered for all classes of men. After that, the cross is unveiled and honored; we thereby adore Christ, our Savior, who conquered sin and death. At the end of the service, the priest receives the body of our Lord which was kept on a special altar since the night before; and we may all receive with him. This is not a Mass, but only a Communion service. No Mass is offered on Good Friday. The color for this day is black.

On Holy Saturday,[437] we should be quiet and thoughtful, turning our minds to our Lord resting in his tomb. In the evening comes the great celebration of Easter called the "Paschal Vigil." Outside the door of the Church, new fire is blessed and the paschal candle is blessed and lighted. This burning paschal candle is a symbol of the risen Christ; it is carried before us into the darkened church, and from it the candles of the priest, the servers, and the faithful are all lighted. The paschal candle is put on a stand in the middle of the sanctuary and the deacon sings a festive song in praise of it (the "Exsultet"), proclaiming the good news of this most blessed night. Then four passages are read from holy scripture, the priest blesses the water that is to be used for baptism during the remaining year, and the whole community renews its baptismal vows. Then the first Easter Mass is celebrated; the proper time for it is just about the middle of the night, though for good reasons it is lawful to start the Paschal Vigil earlier. In this Easter Mass, we celebrate with great joy and solemnity the mystery of our redemption. At the *Gloria*, the bells and the organ peal out in joyful sound. After the epistle, the joyful word *Alleluia* is solemnly sung.—The feast of Easter is the greatest of all feasts; and the liturgical color throughout all the Easter season is white.

[437] Editor's note: The bishops here describe the revised rites for the Easter Vigil, first introduced *ad experimentum* by Pope Pius XII on February 9th, 1951.

Forty days after Easter, we keep the feast of the Ascension. Because Christ left the earth on this day, the paschal candle is extinguished after the gospel of the principal Mass.—Just before Ascension day, there are three Rogation days—that is, days of special prayer.

Fifty days after Easter, we celebrate Pentecost (Whitsunday). This is the day on which Christ sent the Holy Ghost down upon his Church, and poured out upon it the graces of his redemption. Pentecost is the last of the paschal celebrations. The color for the entire week is red.

With the Saturday after Pentecost, the Easter season ("Paschaltide") comes to an end. From the First Sunday after Pentecost until the end of the Church's year, there may be anything between twenty-four and twenty-eight Sundays. They are called the "Sundays after Pentecost," and the liturgical color for them is green.

### Other Feasts

The First Sunday after Pentecost is kept as a feast of the Blessed Trinity. The Thursday which follows it is the feast of Corpus Christi; eight days later, on the Friday, comes the feast of the Sacred Heart. On the last Sunday in October, we keep the feast of Christ the King.

The principal feasts of our Lady are her Immaculate Conception (Dec. 8th), her Birthday (Sep. 8th), the Annunciation (Mar. 25th), and the Assumption (Aug. 15th).

There are also some important feasts of saints: St. Joseph has his feast on March 19th, St. John the Baptist on June 24th, Sts. Peter and Paul on June 29th, and All Saints on November 1st.—On November 2nd, we keep All Souls' day.

Every country should keep the feasts of its own national patrons and its own saints; all dioceses and parishes should keep the feasts of their patrons and of the dedication of their churches.

## LESSON 106

### *The Fast Days of the Church*

After his baptism in the Jordan, Jesus was led by the Holy Spirit into the desert, where he was tempted by the devil. Because Jesus had been fasting for forty days and forty nights, he was hungry. And the tempter came and said to him: "If thou be the Son of God, command that these stones be made bread." But Jesus answered: "Not by bread alone does man live, but by every word that proceeds from the mouth of God."[438]

Following the example of Christ and his saints, we Christians also should sometimes fast. We deny ourselves food in order that our spirit may be raised up to God; we do without something which is allowed so as to join ourselves to the sacrifice of Christ and thus do penance for our sins; we prevent ourselves from doing things we want to do, in order to strengthen our wills and weaken our evil inclinations.—During Lent, the Church prays: "By this bodily fasting thou dost curb vice and uplift the mind, bestowing on us virtue and its rewards, through Christ our Lord." (This comes from the preface of the Lenten Masses.)—Whatever we save by our fasting, we should give to the poor as alms.

In order to make sure that the faithful do sometimes fast, the Church has made a law about fasting. It is the third commandment of the Church: "Thou shalt keep the appointed days of fasting and abstinence."

On fast days, we are allowed to eat as much as we want only at one meal; apart from that we may have (usually morning and evening) just a little nourishment. Besides the weekdays of Lent, there are a few other fast days; and we can know which they are by listening carefully to the announcements in church. When we fast during Lent, we do it to prepare ourselves for a worthy celebration of the passion and resurrection of our Lord.

Every Catholic is bound to observe the law of fasting between his twenty-first and his sixtieth birthday. But people who are sick, convalescent, or weak can be excused from it; also such as have to do heavy work or would

[438] Cf. Mt 4:1-4

be unable to fulfill the duties of their state of life if they were fasting. If we think we have grounds for being excused, we should ask the advice of our confessor.

On abstinence days, we must abstain from flesh meat. *Abstinence* means "doing without." Abstinence days are all the Fridays of the year, Ash Wednesday, and the days of fasting unless we are told to the contrary in the announcements given in church. When we abstain, we give up the pleasure of eating meat in memory of the passion and death of our Lord.

Every Catholic who has reached his seventh birthday is bound by the law of abstinence. But again, there are some people who are excused: sick people, and those who cannot obtain anything but meat if they are on journeys, in hotels, or lodgers in the houses of non-Catholics whose food they must share; also, people who have to do hard work, or must eat in their factory-canteen or otherwise find it impossible to abstain. As before, anyone in doubt should ask advice from his confessor.

*Consider.* 1) What ought we to do with the money that we save by fasting? 2) What is the third commandment of the Church? 3) How do we know which days are fast days? 4) Which people are bound to fast? 5) Which people can be excused from fasting? 6) Why do we abstain from meat on Fridays? 7) Which people are bound to observe the days of abstinence?

207. **What is the Church's law about fast days?**

On fast days, we may eat our fill only once: in addition, we may take just a little nourishment on two other occasions.

208. **What is the Church's law about abstinence days?**

On abstinence days, we may not eat any meat.

209. **What blessings does God give us through fasting?**

Through fasting, God weakens our inclinations to sin, lifts up our minds, grants us strength for virtue, and gives us rewards.

*For my life.* On Fridays and fast days, I will gladly do without sugar or sweets or some other pleasure for the love of God.

*Things to do.* 1) What sacrifices can we make on fast days? 2) What are the fast days in our diocese? 3) What are the abstinence days in our diocese?

# The Fourth Commandment of God

God has put us in the communities of the family, the Church, the state, and the human race as a whole. And he has given us the fourth commandment to impress on us the most important of our duties within the community: "Thou shalt honor thy father and thy mother."

## *LESSON 107*

### *The Common Life of Mankind*

Pope Leo XIII writes: "The community of mankind should be like a body having many members; some of them are indeed more important than others, but all of them need each other and are meant to contribute to the common good."

God has made man in such a way that he has to live together with other men. He said: "It is not good for man to be alone."[439] Only in the community of other men can each of us develop the powers which lie within us, subject the outer world to our control, and attain our goals both in this life and the life to come.

By the very fact of our birth, we become members of several communities; we belong to a family, to a village or town, to a state, to a nation, and to the whole family of mankind. By our baptism, we become members of the Church. The family, the state, and the Church are the most important communities. There are also other communities founded by men for certain purposes, such as societies, unions, clubs.

[439] Gn 2:18

The members of any community have certain duties toward each other. Each should have a friendly regard for other members, give them what is their due, and be concerned for their welfare. "Study the welfare of others, not your own."[440]

The members of any community have also duties toward the community itself. They must fit themselves into the structure of the community, acknowledge its leaders and follow them, and work for the general good. No one should think only of his own interests; everyone must be ready to make some sacrifices for the sake of the community.

The community also has duties toward each and every member. It must respect the dignity of man, and see to it that each one gets his rights; it should also help each one to obtain what he needs but is unable to attain by his own unaided efforts.

The greatest and most wonderful of all communities is the "communion of saints." In it, men of every race and age are united in Christ, and they all work together for the glory of God and the salvation of each individual.

*Consider.* 1) Why is it not good for man to be alone? 2) Name the communities of which you are a member. 3) What duties have members of a community toward each other? 4) What duties have the members toward the community itself? 5) What duties has a community toward its individual members? 6) Name the greatest and most wonderful of all communities.

210. **Why do we live together with other people?**
We live together with other people, because God has created us in such a way that we can reach our earthly and eternal goals only in community with others.

*For my life.* I will do my best to see that any schoolmates of mine who are poor or weak shall have their rights.—I will not despise anybody because of his speech, his race, or his religion.

[440] Phil 2:4

*From holy scripture.* "Pay to every man what is his due; respect if he should have respect; honor if he should have honor."[441]

*Things to do.* 1) What human beings must work together in order that you: a) may have bread to eat; b) may have shoes to wear; c) may be able to eat a piece of chocolate; d) may have an atlas? 2) Why is a small child dependent on the love of others? 3) What can you do to ensure that you and all your classmates may live together in peace and good will? 4) Is there anything which has disturbed or endangered the community life of your class during the past six months?

Bear the burden of one another's failings;
then you will be fulfilling the law of Christ.[442]

## *LESSON 108*

### *Father and Mother*

As a child, Jesus lived with Mary and Joseph at Nazareth. When he was twelve years old, he went with them on pilgrimage to Jerusalem for the feast of the Pasch. After the feast, he went back with them to Nazareth and was subject to them.[443]

In his great love, God has given us our parents. It was they who gave us life; they look after us and are responsible for bringing us up. Our parents are God's representatives and have given us countless benefits; they are appointed by God to show us the way to heaven. Therefore we must give to our parents reverence, love, and obedience, and should ever be deeply grateful to them.

We show reverence to our parents when we have a high regard for them, speak to them or about them respectfully, and behave ourselves politely and modestly toward them.—It is a sin against this due reverence to despise our parents or be ashamed of them, to act insolently, or to talk

[441] Rom 13:7
[442] Gal 6:2
[443] Cf. Lk 2:41-51

disrespectfully about them. In the old law, it was ordered: "Death is the penalty for one who kills his father or mother; death is the penalty for one who curses his father or mother."[444]

We show love for our parents when we often pray for them, do our best to please them and to help them, especially if they be old and ill. They have already done so much to provide for us while we were small and unable to fend for ourselves. "My son, when thy father grows old, take him to thyself."[445]—Even if our parents do not live according to God's laws, we should still love them. Through our love and our prayers, we should try to help them to find the right way again.—We sin against the love which we owe them if we are indifferent to our parents, do not pray for them, do not bother about them, wish them evil, or refuse to help them, especially if they be ill or in need.

It is God's will that we should obey our parents, gladly, readily, and exactly. "Children must obey their parents in every way; it is a gracious sign of serving the Lord," as St. Paul says.[446] Unless children are obedient, no family can live together happily. But if ever our parents should order us to do something against any of God's laws, we should not obey them on that occasion.

The duty of obedience toward parents comes to an end when children have fully grown up and live no more in their parents' home. But the duties of reverence and love never come to an end. Jesus loved his mother right till the end; even when he was dying on the cross he provided for her.

*Consider.* 1) For what benefits do we have to thank our parents? 2) How should we show reverence to our parents? 3) Explain what things would be sins against the reverence due to our parents. 4) How should we show love to our parents? 5) What things would be sins against the love which we owe to our parents? 6) How should we obey our parents? 7) What things would be sins against the obedience we owe to our parents? 8) On what occasions should we refuse to obey our parents?

[444] Ex 21:15, 17
[445] Ecclus 3:14
[446] Col 3:20

211. **What does God command in the fourth commandment?**
In the fourth commandment, God commands that we show reverence, love, and obedience toward our parents.

212. **Why must we show reverence, love, and obedience toward our parents?**
We must show reverence, love, and obedience toward our parents:
1. because they are God's representatives;
2. because they have given us countless benefits;
3. because it is by them that we should be led to heaven.

*For my life.* I will try to please my parents as much as I can. And I will not forget to pray for them every day.

*From holy scripture.* "Give thy mother her due while her life lasts; do not forget what hazard she underwent to bear thee in her womb."[447] — "Proud looks that tell of a father mocked, a mother's pangs despised? That eye the raven shall pick out on the hillside, the vulture's brood shall prey on it."[448]

*Things to do.* 1) How can I show due reverence for my parents? 2) What can I do to give them pleasure? 3) How did Absalom, Tobias, and the sons of Heli behave toward their respective fathers? 4) See if you can estimate how many slices of bread you have received from your parents! If you built them all up into a tower, how high would it be?

## *LESSON 109*

### *Brothers, Sisters, Relations, and Friends*

When Joseph's brothers came to Egypt, Joseph wanted them to leave Benjamin behind. Then Juda stepped forth and said: "I have pledged myself for the boy before my father. I therefore, my Lord, would be left here as thy servant, to wait upon thee in his stead; let the boy go home with his brethren; without him I coud not go home to my father." Then Joseph

[447] Tb 4:3-4
[448] Prv 30:17

could no longer contain himself; he let his brothers know who he was, and, weeping, threw his arms around them.[449]

Our brothers and sisters stand nearest to us after our parents. Therefore, we should love them deeply, help them in every way we can, and behave ourselves well toward them; we should pay heed to them and see that each one gets his rights. The older brothers and sisters should look after the younger ones. It is a great blessing from God when we have brothers and sisters to grow up with.

Our relations, too, stand closer to us than other people. We should show our affection for them and be glad to help them, especially if they are in any need; and to those of them who are old, we ought to show special respect.

Good friends are a gift from God. True friends value each other highly, and remain faithful both in joy and in sorrow; they pray for each other and help each other.

Christ became our brother and our friend and loved us so much that he went to his death for us. Thus he shows us how much we should love our brothers and sisters and relations and friends.

*Consider.* 1) What duties have we toward our brothers and sisters? 2) How should we behave toward our relations? 3) What should good friends do for each other?

*For my life.* If my brothers and sisters and I sometimes quarrel with one another, I should ask myself: "Why does this happen? What can we do so that each may have his rights, and so that we can all get along well together?"

*Things to do.* 1) What can older brothers and sisters do for the little ones? 2) Why is it a great blessing from God to have several brothers and sisters to grow up with? 3) What can a boy expect from his best friend? What can a girl expect from hers?

How good and pleasant it is for brethren to dwell together in unity![450]

[449] Cf. Gn 44-45

[450] Ps 132:1

## LESSON 110

### *Respect for Those in Authority and for Old People*

"Every human community must necessarily have over it someone in authority; for without a head and a directing authority, it would fall to pieces. Moreover, it could not attain the purpose for which it came into being or was founded."[451]

It is by the will of our parents that teachers and masters instruct us and train us. Therefore, we should show respect to them, listen to them willingly, and work diligently. We commit sin if we are disrespectful or impertinent to them, refuse to follow their directions, and are lazy and careless in our work.

All those who are employed in some work or profession should respect those set over them and fufill their duties conscientiously.—If anyone has employment as a member of a household, he has his part to play in the life of the family. Therefore, he should fit in with the family arrangements and have regard for their welfare and their reputation.

Old people have a special dignity. In the course of their lives, they have had great experience, and often have worked very hard. Therefore, we should always show respect toward them, treat them courteously, be concerned for their comfort, and help them whenever possible. Holy scripture says: "Rise up from thy seat in reverence for grey hairs."[452]

*Consider.* 1) What are our duties toward those who teach and instruct us? 2) What things would be offenses against these duties? 3) What does God require of a person who is in employment or has a profession? 4) Why should we show particular respect to old people? 5) What duties have we toward old people?

*For my life.* I will do my best to make lessons a pleasure both to those who teach and those who are taught.

[451] Leo XIII
[452] Lv 19:32

# LESSON 111

## The Duties of Parents and Those in Authority

When King Antiochus was persecuting the Jews because of their faith, he commanded that a certain mother with her seven sons should be brought before him. In spite of terrible torments, not one of these sons would deny his faith. To the youngest, Antiochus promised that he would make him rich and happy if only he would abandon the law of his fathers. But his mother spoke to him: "My dear child, whom I carried nine months in my womb, whom I nourished and brought up with much pain, I beg you: look round on earth and in heaven; God has made it all out of nothing, and he made us men too. Therefore, do not be afraid of this butcher; accept death willingly, so that I may find you again with all your brothers in everlasting life."[453]

Parents have the sacred duty of loving their children and caring for their welfare in this world and in the next. They must feed and clothe their children, look after their health, guide them into suitable work, and plan for their future. Above all, they must often pray for their children, and by word and example must train them for the Christian life. They must not spoil and pamper their children, but should bring them up with love, justice, and firmness.

Catholic parents are bound (except when it is impossible) to send their children to a school in which they will be brought up in the Catholic faith. They must carefully watch that their children do not come to any harm through bad company or bad books and papers.

As the children grow up, parents should help them by their advice and their prayer to choose a suitable career in life and especially, if they are going to marry, to choose a suitable life's partner; but they should not force them into any particular career or marriage.

Those who are in authority are to exercise care over those under them, must treat them with justice, and seek their welfare. They must allow them

[453] Cf. 2 Mc 7

time to go to Mass on Sundays and feast days; they should give them sufficient leisure for recreation and further training that they may advance themselves; they must protect them from evils of body and soul.

Parents and those in authority have God the Father as their model. From him they can learn to be just, loving, kind, and yet firm with their children and those under their care.

*Consider.* 1) What are the duties of parents toward their children? 2) To what kind of school must Catholic parents send their children? 3) How should parents help their children in their choice of a career or of a marriage partner? 4) What are the duties of those in authority toward those under their care?

*For my life.* I will make it as easy as possible for my parents to fulfill their dutes toward me.

## LESSON 112

### The State and the Community of Nations

"Pilate said to Jesus: '…Knowest thou not that I have power to crucify thee and I have power to release thee?' Jesus answered: 'Thou shouldst not have any power against me, unless it were given thee from above.'"[454]

According to the will of God, the state has the task of solving the difficulties which individuals, families, or lesser communities cannot solve for themselves. It must consider the general good. It must, for example, make laws, see that justice is done, punish evildoers, make treaties with other states, protect the country from attacks by its enemies and from economic disaster. In all this, it must protect the rights of individuals and distribute burdens fairly.

The subjects of the state must follow the laws of the state, give due respect to the authority of its ministers, and do all they can to promote the general good. For instance, they should always vote in elections; and they should vote only for those persons who are suitable for holding office and

[454] Jn 19:10-11

have given some guarantee that they will stand up for God's laws; they must pay their just taxes, and, in times of danger, must be ready to defend their country even at the cost of their lives.—If, however, the authorities of the state should ever command something which is a sin, then they must not be obeyed. St. Peter writes: "God has more right to be obeyed than men."[455]

Those in authority must rule in accordance with the laws of God and of the state. Anyone who becomes a state official must carry out his duties conscientiously, give justice to every man, and put the general good before his own personal welfare.

Every nation is a member of the great family of nations, and is responsible before God for working for the good of the whole human family. Therefore, every nation should have due regard for other nations and states and for all those who belong to them.

*Consider.* 1) How does the state take care of the general good? 2) Name some of the duties of citizens toward the state. 3) What are the duties of state officials? 4) Why should a Christian have regard for peoples other than his own?

213. **What is the task of the state?**

The state has the task of caring for the general welfare.

214. **What are our duties as citizens of the state?**

As citizens of the state, we must: 1) keep the laws and regulations of the state; 2) give due respect to public authority; 3) strive for the general welfare according to our ability.

215. **When should we disobey the authority of the state?**

We should disobey the authority of the state if it should ever command something sinful, for "God has more right to be obeyed than men."

[455] Acts 5:29

*For my life.* I will love my own people and my country, and be grateful for everything good and fine that I have received. But I will also have respect for other peoples and countries, and acknowledge their good points.

*From holy scripture.* "Render to Caesar the things that are Caesar's, and to God the things that are God's."[456]

*Prayer for the rulers of states.* "Almighty, everlasting God, in whose hand lie all government and the rights of every nation, look graciously upon our rulers, so that all over the world religion and public safety may stand whole and unimpaired under the shelter of thy hand; through Christ our Lord. Amen."[457]

*Things to do.* Answer the following questions as well as you can: 1) How can good people help to bring it about that in our country and among our people the will of God may be done? 2) Sometimes the authority and power in a country fall into the hands of evil men. Whose fault is that? How does it come about?

## *LESSON 113*

## *The Rulers in the Church*

About the year 107, the bishop of Antioch, Ignatius (who was martyred later on) wrote a letter to the Christian community of Smyrna, and in it he said: "All should obey their bishop as Jesus Christ obeyed his Father; they should obey priests as if they were apostles...Let no one do anything touching the Church apart from the bishop...Where the bishop appears, there let the people be; just as where Jesus Christ is, there is the Catholic Church."[458]

The pope, the bishops, and the priests have authority to rule over us in the name of Christ. It was through them that we received our grace-life in baptism; it is they who give us the "bread of heaven" and bring us up

456 Mt 22:21

457 From the liturgy of Good Friday [as found in the Pian version of 1955].

458 Ignatius of Antioch, *Epistle to the Smyrnaeans*, Ch. 8

as God's children. They stand in the place of Christ and are our spiritual fathers. We should honor, love, and obey them.

The rulers of the Church, the pope and bishops, make laws in order to regulate the Church's life, to warn the faithful against sin and indifference, and to guide them in the Christian way of life. It was Christ who gave to the apostles and their successors the authority to do this when he said: "Whatsoever you shall bind upon earth, it shall be bound also in heaven."[459] God wills us conscientiously to obey the pope and the bishops.

We are all to be living members of the mystical body of Christ. Therefore, all of us, especially the confirmed, should support the work of the bishops and priests. The confirmed Christian should always be ready to defend his faith, be eager to take an active part in the Church's services, to receive the sacraments, and to help in every possible way with the work of saving souls. The Christian has also the duty of giving money, according to his means, to make it possible for the Church to fulfill her task.

*Consider.* 1) Why should we honor, love, and obey the pope and our bishops and priests? 2) For what purpose do the rulers in the Church make laws? 3) Why should we conscientiously do whatever the Church commands us? 4) In what ways should we support the work of the bishops and priests?

216. **Which are the five chief commandments of the Church?**

The five chief commandments of the Church are:

1. To observe the Sundays and holy days of obligation.
2. To take part attentively in the Mass on Sundays and holy days of obligation.
3. To observe the days of fasting and abstinence appointed by the Church.
4. To go to confession at least once a year.
5. To go to Communion at least once a year, and that at Eastertide.

*For my life.* The Church is guided by the Holy Ghost; therefore, I will never say: "But this is only a commandment of the Church!"

[459] Mt 18:18

*From holy scripture.* "Brethren, we would ask you to pay deference to those who work among you, those who have charge of you in the Lord and give you directions; make it a rule of charity to hold them in special esteem, in honor of the duty they perform, and maintain unity with them."[460]

*Other commandments of the Church.* The Church commands all her members that, when they desire to marry, they are to do so before a priest and two witnesses; they are to cause their children to be baptized soon after birth, and bring them all up as Catholics. They are to observe Advent and Lent as closed seasons (times when weddings may not be celebrated with solemnity), and to receive the sacraments if in danger of death. The Church forbids her members to read books or papers contrary to faith or morals, to take part in non-Catholic religious services, to belong to sects or societies hostile to the Church, to marry non-Catholics, to be cremated or to join a cremation society. (*Cremation* means burning the body of a dead person instead of burying it.)

# The Fifth Commandment of God

God has given us our body and soul, as also the various powers of our body and soul, in order that we may use them properly for his glory and our salvation. God protects life through the commandment: "Thou shalt not kill."

## LESSON 114

### Our Body and Its Life

"Surely you know that your bodies are the shrines of the Holy Spirit, who dwells in you. And he is God's gift to you, so that you are no longer your

[460] 1 Thes 5:12-13

own masters. A great price was paid to ransom you; glorify God by making your bodies the shrines of his presence."[461]

It was God who made our body, equipped it with wonderful powers, and made it live by means of our soul. The Son of God took to himself a human body. The Holy Ghost sanctified our body in baptism and made it his temple where he dwells. On the last day, God will raise our bodies in glory from the dead. Therefore, we should always treat our body and its life as sacred.

We must take care of our body, and of its life and health, because God has entrusted it to us and will require an account of it from us. We are to keep our body clean, and to feed it and clothe it properly; we are to exercise, develop, and train it, and give to it both reasonable rest and recreation.

To neglect our health or to put it into danger without a serious reason is a sin. Not to observe proper limits in eating, drinking, and smoking, and to overdo sport can all harm the body seriously. For children and young people, drinking and smoking can be harmful even in small quantities.—It is more serious still to risk one's life without sufficient reason.—The worst of all sins against the body is deliberately to take one's own life. The man who kills himself (suicide) is trespassing on the rights of God, for God alone is the Lord of life and death. The suicide is refusing to continue in God's service, throwing away the cross that God bids him carry with Christ; he withdraws from his responsibilities toward others and brings shame and sorrow on his family. And he is casting himself into hell.

But we may not judge everyone who kills himself. Only God knows whether a suicide was voluntary, or whether the person was too ill in mind to know what he was doing.

However, the body and its life are not the greatest and most precious of all treasures. Sometimes it is right, or even a duty, to sacrifice health or life; examples would be for the sake of the faith or the good of one's neighbor or the defense of one's country in a just war. Christ said: "Greater love than this hath no man, that he should lay down his life for his friends."[462]

[461] 1 Cor 6:19-20
[462] Jn 15:13

*Consider.* 1) In what ways must we care for our bodies? 2) What things would be sins against one's health? 3) What things would be sins against one's life? 4) Why is suicide a specially serious sin? 5) When may we or should we risk our health or our life?

217. **Why should we respect our body?**
We should respect our body because God created it, sanctified it, and will one day raise it in glory.

218. **Why must we take care of our life and our health?**
We must take care of our life and our health because God has entrusted them to us and requires that we give an account of them.

219. **Who is the master over life and death?**
God alone is master over life and death.

*For my life.* My life and health should be much more important to me than pleasures or breaking records in sport.

*From holy scripture.* "A poor man sound and strong of body is better off than a rich man enfeebled and racked with disease."[463]

*From the life of the Church.* Anyone who deliberately takes his own life cannot have Christian burial.

*Things to do.* 1) What are the most important rules for health? 2) In what ways do many young people damage their health?

## *LESSON 115*

### *Mental Powers and Talents*

One day, Jesus told the following parable: "A man going into a far country called his servants and delivered to them his goods; and to one he gave five talents, to another two, and to another one, to every one according to

[463] Ecclus 30:14

his proper ability; and immediately he took his journey. And he that had received five talents went his way and traded with them and gained other five. And in like manner, he that had received the two gained other two. But he that had received the one, going his way, digged into the earth and hid his lord's money. And when the lord came back from his journey, he rewarded those that had used the money well, but punished the one who had been lazy."[464]

More valuable than the powers of our body are the powers and talents which God has given to our minds, especially our intelligence, our willpower, our memory, and our feelings. It is through these that we men are greater than all the other creatures God put upon this earth. They are extremely precious gifts of God.

We ought to be specially grateful for our mental powers and talents; we should train them and make good use of them. That is why we must go to school and learn all we can there, so that we may conscientiously prepare ourselves for our task in life. We must open our minds and hearts to everything that is true and good and beautiful; we should listen carefully to those who teach us, and try to follow the example of men who have done great things.

Anyone who neglects his mental powers and talents out of laziness or carelessness commits sin. For he is despising the gifts of God, and has only himself to blame if he is a failure in life after leaving school.

*Consider.* 1) What powers and talents of mind can you name? 2) Why are they especially precious? 3) Why must we train them? 4) In what way can we sin in respect of these powers and talents of our mind?

*For my life.* I will not go through life stupidly, but will see, judge, and act.

*Things to do.* 1) How can I use my free time to improve my education? 2) How can I obtain the use of good books? 3) How can I find out whether a particular film would profit me mentally?

[464] Cf. Mt 25:14-18

# LESSON 116

## Work and Our Occupation

God had planted paradise as a garden, and put Adam into this garden of delights that he might cultivate and tend it. And after God had made Eve and led her to Adam as his helper, he blessed them and said: "Fill the earth and make it your own; take command of the fishes of the sea, all that flies through the air, and all the living things that move upon the earth."[465]

Even before he fell from grace, man had been told by God to cultivate and tend the earth and make it his own. We ought, therefore, to use our bodily and mental powers to make the forces and treasures of nature useful to us. It is God's will that we should work. By our own work, we are privileged to share in God's creative work.

Work brings to us blessings both for time and eternity. It gains for us and for others the food which we need each day, and leads us to prosperity; it exercises and develops our powers, and keeps us healthy in mind and body; it prevents us from being bored and discontented, and protects us from many temptations and sins; it is a source of happiness, and it earns for us also a heavenly reward.

But since the fall of Adam, work is not always a joy; it can be and often is a burden. God said: "In the sweat of thy brow, thou shalt earn thy bread."[466] Nevertheless, we ought to work diligently and perseveringly. Hard work is a part of that test which we have to undergo during this life, and it is good for us as a penance for our sins.

Men work in all sorts of different occupations. We ought to choose some walk of life for which God seems to have fitted us by giving us the particular powers and inclinations and circumstances which we actually have. So that we may be able to recognize which this is, we should ask God to enlighten us, think about the matter very carefully, and obtain advice from our parents, our teachers, and experts in vocational guidance.

[465] Cf. Gn 1-2
[466] Gn 3:19

Our highest calling is to give glory to God. And this can be done in any walk of life, even if we fall ill or find ourselves without work.

*Consider.* 1) What did God mean us to do when he said: "Make the earth your own"? 2) What blessings for time and eternity can we obtain through work? 3) Since when did work become wearisome? 4) Why should we work even if it is wearisome? 5) What points should we remember when making up our minds what we are going to be? 6) What is our highest calling?

220. **Why must we work?**

We must work because God wills it, and because work brings blessings upon us.

*For my life.* I will work diligently and conscientiously both in school and at home. If I develop habits of laziness and carelessness now, I shall probably never learn to work properly.

*From holy scripture.* "Let everyone work and earn by his own labor the blessings he will be able to share with those who are in need."[467]

*Proverbs.* "The devil finds work for idle hands to do."—"God gave us nuts, but he did not crack them for us."

*Principle for choosing work in life.* "Look within you, look about you, ask, and pray."

## *LESSON 117*

## *Care for Our Eternal Salvation*

A student once told St. Philip Neri that he was just about to take an examination and had every hope that he would pass it. St. Philip asked him what he intended to do after that. The young man answered: "I will become a barrister; everybody says I am fitted for it." "And then?" "I shall make a name for myself at the bar; then I shall marry and build myself a house

[467] Eph 4:28

and be a rich man." "And then?" "After that I might become a judge." "And then?" "Then one day I shall be able to retire on a good pension!" "And then?" "Then what? Then I suppose the day will come when I have to die." St. Philip then grasped the young man by the shoulder and said to him very earnestly: "And then?" The young man never forgot that final question!

Our eternal salvation is more important than anything else in the whole world. "Seek ye first the kingdom of God and his justice."[468] Therefore everything that we do on earth ought to help in some way toward saving our soul: our thinking and striving, our praying and working, our eating and drinking, our playing and resting.

We should never put our eternal salvation in danger. Hence, we must never be so concerned about our earthly happiness as to damage our chances of eternal happiness. We have got to fight against our inclination to evil and overcome ourselves. We have to be ready to lose our fortune, our reputation, our freedom, even our life, rather than risk our salvation. Christ said: "What doth it profit a man if he gain the whole world, but suffer the loss of his own soul?"[469]

So that we may learn to keep our passions under control, we must learn and practice self-denial. For example, we should quite often deny ourselves something which is perfectly lawful. Anyone who lets himself be mastered by his impulses is just opening the door of his soul to the devil. There can be no Christian life without self-denial.

In order to reach eternal life, we must live as children of God. We must do our utmost to avoid sin, and, by means of good works, earn merits for heaven.

*Consider.* 1) What is the purpose toward which everything we do on this earth should be made to help? 2) When are we concerned in a wrong way about our earthly welfare? 3) What must we be ready to do for the sake of our eternal salvation? 4) Why must we train ourselves in self-control? 5) What must we do in order to save our souls?

[468] Mt 6:33
[469] Mt 16:26

221. **What does Jesus say to teach us that saving our soul is more important than anything else?**

Jesus says: "What doth it profit a man if he gain the whole world, but suffer the loss of his own soul?"

*For my life.* When I have to make any important decision, I will ask myself: "What will most help me to save my soul?"

*From holy scripture.* "It is better for thee to go into life maimed or lame, than having two hands or feet, to be cast into everlasting fire."[470]—"You know well enough that when men run in a race, the race is for all, but the prize is for one; run, then, for victory."[471]

*Exercises in self-control.* To get up as soon as you are called; to bear pain without showing it; to remain calm when annoyed; not to drink immediately when you feel thirsty; to interrupt your game or other occupation immediately if called by your parents or teachers; to stop reading a very interesting book while you are in the middle of it; if you have interesting news, not to tell it at once. Suggest other things of this kind which you might do to train yourself in self-control.

## *LESSON 118*

## *The Body and Life of Our Neighbor*

In the year 1619, St. Vincent de Paul took up the care of souls in the prisons of Paris. When he saw the terrible misery of those in prison, he set himself first to work for their bodily welfare. He organized soup kitchens for the prisoners, cleaned out their filthy cells, bound up their festering sores, and saw to it that those who were ill were freed from their chains and put into hospital.

The body and the life of every man are precious in God's sight. Therefore, we must respect the body and the life of our neighbor, and concern ourselves for his physical well-being.

[470] Mt 18:8
[471] 1 Cor 9:24

We ought to have special care for those who are in physical need. We should practice what are called "the seven corporal works of mercy": to feed the hungry, to give drink to the thirsty, to clothe the naked, to give shelter to the homeless, to visit the imprisoned, to visit the sick, and to bury the dead. On the last day, Christ will judge us according to the way in which we have done these things.[472]

It is a sin against the life of our neighbor if we do not bother ourselves at all about his needs; it is likewise wrong to strike him unjustly, to wound him, to injure his health, or to put his body or his life in danger. It is also a sin against the life of our neighbor to shorten his life or embitter it by unkind, unjust, or harsh treatment. If anyone kills another unjustly, he commits a sin which cries to heaven for vengeance. God said to Cain: "The blood of thy brother Abel has found a voice which cries to me from the ground."[473]

God does not mean, however, that we are to let ourselves be attacked unjustly without defending ourselves. Everyone has the right to defend himself or his neighbor against unjust attack even to the extent of wounding or killing the aggressor if this be necessary.—The state has the right to punish a serious crime by death.—And soldiers fighting in defense of their country in a just war may kill the enemy in battle.

If anyone unjustly injures the health of another, or wounds him or kills him, then he is bound to put right the harm he has done to his victim or the victim's family as far as he is able.

We are allowed to kill animals if this be necessary or useful; but we may not cause them unnecessary pain in doing so. If anyone deliberately tortures an animal, he commits a sin. We should have regard for all living things, for they are all the work of God's hands.

*Consider.* 1) Why must we respect the bodies and the lives of our fellow men? 2) Which of our fellow men have a right to special care? 3) Who sins against the life of his neighbor? 4) Explain what acts would be sins against the life of our neighbor. 5) If anyone has injured his neighbor in body or life what must he do?

[472] Cf. Mt 25:34-46
[473] Gn 4:10

222. **What are the seven corporal works of mercy?**
The seven corporal works of mercy are: to feed the hungry, to give drink to the thirsty, to clothe the naked, to shelter the homeless, to visit the imprisoned, to visit the sick, to bury the dead.

*For my life.* When I eat, let me take care that no one nearby is hungry.

*From holy scripture.* "Let us practice generosity to all, while the opportunity is ours; and above all, to those who are of one family with us in the faith."[474] — "Blessed are the merciful, for they shall obtain mercy."[475]

*From the life of the Church.* There are many religious orders in the Church which devote themselves to caring for the sick, the poor, and others in bodily need. For the laity there is the Society of Vincent de Paul, besides many other charitable organizations.

*Things to do.* 1) Can you think of any other corporal works of mercy besides those seven which were mentioned above? 2) Describe what things you should bear in mind when visiting a sick person. 3) What works of mercy were done by: a) Tobias; b) the widow of Sarepta; c) the Christians of the early Church in Jerusalem? 4) What sins could be committed against the fifth commandment: a) while playing games; b) in sport; c) in traffic on the roads?

## *LESSON 119*

## *Care for the Salvation of Our Neighbor*

St. Ignatius of Loyola once called on a worldly man who was expert at billiards. The man challenged Ignatius to a game and wanted to bet on it. Ignatius had never played the game in his life, but said: "I will play on condition that the one who loses shall do for a month whatever the winner tells him to do." The man agreed; they played, and Ignatius won the game! He then made the man do the spiritual exercises (a kind of retreat made of meditations and prayers) for a whole month, and thus converted him from his bad life so that he served God faithfully afterward.

[474] Gal 6:10
[475] Mt 5:7

The Son of God became man and died on the cross so that all mankind might be saved. Therefore, we should earnestly desire the salvation of others besides ourselves. St. Paul warns us: "You must befriend one another as Christ has befriended you, for God's honor."[476]

We can help our fellow men on their way to God by our prayers, by words of encouragement, by our example, and by our actions. The Church recommends to us what are called "the seven spiritual works of mercy"; they are: to convert the sinner, to instruct the ignorant, to give advice to the doubtful, to comfort the sorrowful, to bear wrongs patiently, to forgive injuries, to pray for the living and the dead.

There are many who are guilty of sin as regards the salvation of their neighbor. Some of them do not care at all whether their neighbor lives a good life or a bad one. Others even draw their neighbor into sin; they talk evil, they tell dirty stories, give bad example, lend filthy books and pictures, lead others into bad company.—There are some who share in the guilt of other's sins; they do not prevent the sin even when they can, or they keep quiet about it, or praise the bad action and encourage the one who does it, or help him to do it.—It is even worse deliberately to lead someone else into sin. If anyone leads another into mortal sin, he is guilty of a terrible sin himself. Jesus said: "He that shall scandalize one of these little ones that believe in me, it were better for him that a millstone should be hanged about his neck, and that he should be drowned in the depth of the sea."[477] Anyone who gives occasion to another to sin, or actually leads him to sin, is said to "scandalize" him. That is why we call this the "sin of scandal." (*Scandal* comes from a Latin word that means "an obstacle put in somebody's path to trip him up.")

Anyone who has done harm to his neighbor's soul must undo the harm as far as possible. He must try, by persuasion and example, to bring back to the right path the one whom he has led astray. If he cannot succeed in that, he must at least pray for him.

[476] Rom 15:7
[477] Mt 18:6

*Consider.* 1) Why must we desire to help others to save their souls? 2) In what ways can we help others on their way to God? 3) Explain what things would be sins against the salvation of our neighbor. 4) If anyone has injured his neighbor's soul, what efforts should he make to undo the harm he did?

223. **What are the seven spiritual works of mercy?**
The seven spiritual works of mercy are: to convert the sinner, to instruct the ignorant, to give advice to the doubtful, to comfort the sorrowful, to bear wrongs patiently, to forgive injuries, to pray for the living and the dead.

224. **What did Jesus say to warn us against scandalizing others?**
Jesus said: "He that shall scandalize one of these little ones that believe in me, it were better for him that a millstone should be hanged about his neck, and that he should be drowned in the depths of the sea."

225. **If anyone has injured his neighbor in body or soul, what must he do?**
Anyone who has injured his neighbor in body or soul must put right the harm he has done according to his ability.

*For my life.* Are there any of the spiritual works of mercy which I could do today?

*From holy scripture.* "Let us keep one another in mind, always ready with incitements to charity and to acts of piety."[478]

*From the teaching of the saints.* "An ounce of good example is worth more than a ton of words."[479]

*Other spiritual works of mercy.* To take someone to Mass; to encourage someone to go to confession and Communion; to help the spread of Catholic papers; to lend people good books; to give pleasure to others by visiting them, playing, or talking with them; to introduce someone to good people; to tell stories about God to small children; to invite others to your youth club.

[478] Heb 10:24
[479] Francis de Sales

*Things to do.* 1) What should you do if you find one of your classmates reading a bad book? Or if he were going with bad company? 2) What can you do to help pagans to save their souls? 3) See if you can find in holy scripture examples of the seven spiritual works of mercy.

If I see an offense I can maybe impede
But say nothing, then I have committed the deed.

# The Sixth and Ninth Commandments

God protects the great human benefits of marriage and of purity by the sixth and the ninth commandments: "Thou shalt not commit adultery."—"Thou shalt not covet thy neighbor's wife."

## *LESSON 120*

### *The Duties of Husbands and Wives toward Each Other*

When God had created Adam, he said: "It is not well that man should be without companionship; I will give him a mate of his own kind." Then God made Adam fall into a deep sleep, and took one of his ribs and formed it into a woman and brought her to Adam. And he blessed them both and said: "Increase and multiply and fill the earth!"[480]

God made man and woman to his own image and likeness, and he gave to each of them a special nature and a special task. Therefore, men and women should respect each other, behave courteously toward each other, and be helpful to each other.

Most people are called by God to marry. In marriage, husband and wife are to live together in love and faithfulness to each other, and give life to

[480] Cf. Gn 2:18-24; 1:28

children. Their love should make themselves and their children lead a happy life, all traveling together toward heaven.

Christ said: "What God has joined together, let no man put asunder."[481] It is a serious sin and a great tragedy if married people break faith with each other. This sin is called "adultery." God orders in the sixth commandment: "Thou shalt not commit adultery."[482] Adultery always begins with evil thoughts and desires. Christ said: "Whosoever shall look on a woman to lust after her has already committed adultery with her in his heart."[483]

Boys and girls should therefore be determined that they will grow up into men and women of fine character. They should behave simply and naturally toward each other, and yet at the same time treat each other with a respectful reserve. Light-hearted flirting between people who are too young can often destroy the freshness and strength of genuine love later on. Love is no mere plaything; an undisciplined and irresponsible boy-and-girl friendship can ruin an entire human life. Anyone who seriously wants to make a happy marriage must be prepared to wait and hold himself in control until he is sufficiently mature for the responsibilities of marriage.

Some people remain unmarried because of some circumstance in their life—for example, through lack of health, lack of means to marry, or through duty to their family. But they also have from God a task which will give to their lives a purpose and content. They can find happiness, even without marriage.

Yet others remain unmarried of their own free will because they want to give themselves wholly to Christ, and be at his disposal for some special service in the kingdom of God. They are living in consecrated virginity. God loves particularly those who live virginal lives.

*Consider.* 1) How should men and women behave toward each other? 2) What tasks have husband and wife in marriage? 3) What is the sixth commandment? 4) What is the ninth commandment? 5) How should teen-age boys and girls behave toward each other? 6) For what reasons do many people remain unmarried?

[481] Mt 19:6
[482] Ex 20:14
[483] Mt 5:28

226. **What did Jesus say to command faithfulness in marriage?**
Jesus said: "What God has joined together, let no man put asunder. Whosoever shall look on a woman to lust after her has already committed adultery with her in his heart."

*For my life.* I will be what a boy (or girl) really ought to be.

*Things to do.* 1) What are the special gifts which men have from God?—What special gifts does he give to women? 2) Name callings in life that are usually followed by men. 3) Name some that are specially suited to women.

## LESSON 121

## Modesty and Purity

On account of her faith, St. Perpetua had been condemned to death, and was to be thrown to the wild beasts in the amphitheatre in the sight of all the people. As soon as she came into the arena, she was attacked by a wild cow which rushed at her and threw her to one side with its horns. As she fell, her dress was ripped open. The first thing she did was to gather her dress about her so as to be covered; for she thought more of her decency than of her pains.

Man's body with all its limbs and organs was created by God, and so every part is good—including the sex organs. Our first parents never thought about their nakedness because they were innocent and sinless. But after they had disobeyed God, they were no longer innocent, and they began to feel ashamed of being naked.

A natural instinct of modesty urges us not to uncover our body without reason. God wills that we should not display certain parts before others unless we have to; nor should we handle them or touch them except for purposes of nature and for cleanliness. If we see someone who is naked, we should turn our eyes away. If we observe these rules, we are behaving modestly; if we break these rules, we are behaving immodestly.

This instinct of modesty is given us by God to protect those powers which God has placed within our bodies to serve the making and growth of human life, and the holiness of marriage. God wills us to have great reverence for these powers, and never to misuse them; they are to be kept for use only in the way which will bring about the purposes for which he gave them to us. To use these powers only as God intended is to live chastely; to misuse them is to be unchaste or impure.

Sins against chastity, often called "sins of impurity," are misuses of the powers of generation. It is a sin to use them alone, or with others, or to let another use us to that end. It is also a sin deliberately to keep in one's mind thoughts about unchaste things, or to desire to do them, or without necessity to put oneself in danger of thinking about or desiring such things. So long as we do our best to shake off impure thoughts and desires, we have not sinned; we are still chaste.

Purity is something very fine and noble. It gives a man a special dignity and worth. Those who are pure are favorites of God; to them apply the words of our Lord: "Blessed are the pure of heart, for they shall see God."[484] St. Paul says: "Surely you know that your bodies are the shrines of the Holy Spirit who dwells in you. And he is God's gift to you, so that you are no longer your own masters."[485]

Impurity is a great disaster for man. It defiles the temple of the Holy Ghost and leads to many other sins. Some forms of it cause sickness, misery, and shame, and may lead to an unrepentant death.

To remain chaste, we must above all be modest; for modesty is a kind of protective wall for chastity. We have to keep control over our senses, our thoughts, and our passions. Hard work, a natural and healthy life, and a cheerful disposition can save us from many dangers. Above all, we must pray earnestly, go regularly to confession, and receive Holy Communion often. We must sincerely love Christ our Lord, and have devotion to Mary, our Mother, as good children should.

To remain pure, we must avoid everything that might lead us to lose control; such things are bad books and pictures, suggestive films, exhibitions and dances, bad comrades, bad "gangs," indecent clothes, idleness, and becoming

[484] Mt 5:8
[485] 1 Cor 6:19

sentimental. If ever we are tempted, we should shake off the suggestions at once; it is good to say an ejaculatory prayer and then busy oneself with something else. Without effort, we cannot hope to preserve our chastity.

*Consider.* 1) What does our natural modesty prompt us to do? 2) What does it mean to act modestly? 3) What does it mean to act chastely? 4) Explain what is meant by *impurity*. 5) Why is purity something noble and fine? 6) Why is impurity such a disaster for mankind?

227. **Why should we carefully guard our chastity?**

We should carefully guard our chastity: 1) because it gives us a special dignity and worth; 2) because God has a special love for the chaste.

228. **What must we do to remain chaste?**

To remain chaste, we must: 1) be modest and practice self-control; 2) live close to God; 3) avoid occasions of sin and shake off temptations at once.

229. **What does St. Paul say to urge us to chastity?**

St. Paul says: "Surely you know that you are the shrines of the Holy Spirit who dwells in you?"

*For my life.* I will not think or do anything which I would wish to hide from God.

*From holy scripture.* "Watch and pray, lest ye enter into temptation."[486] — "Who wins the victory? Not the cowards, not those who refuse belief, not those whose lives are abominable; not the murderers, the fornicators, the sorcerers, the idolaters, not those who are false in any of their dealings. Their lot awaits them in the lake that burns with fire and brimstone, and it is the second death."[487]

*Rule of life.* God sees everything. Don't ever think to yourself: "Just once is nothing!" Do not listen to dirty talk. Go with those in your class who are decent. Resist curiosity and the fear of what others may say or think

[486] Mt 26:41

[487] Apoc 21:8

about you. Have nothing to do with dirty books and pictures. When you want to know how human life is passed on, ask only those who understand and have reverence for this wonderful work of God, for example, your parents or your teacher.

*Patrons of chastity.* The most holy Virgin Mary, St. Joseph, St. Aloysius, St. Agnes, St. Maria Goretti.

*Things to do.* 1) Can you remember any examples in the Bible of modesty and chastity? 2) What punishments for unchaste living does the Bible tell us about? 3) To what other sins was David led by his unchastity?

# The Seventh and Tenth Commandments of God

Every man has the right to possess property. God enforces our duties concerning our own and our neighbor's property by the seventh and tenth commandments: "Thou shalt not steal!"—"Thou shalt not covet thy neighbor's goods!"

## *LESSON 122*

### *Our Own Property*

Before St. Margaret came to the court of Scotland, luxury and waste were the rule there; a great deal of money was used for feasts and banquets and entertainment of the courtiers. But after she had become queen, she so raised the ideals of her husband Malcolm, king of Scotland, that he put an end to all this waste. The queen brought the royal household into an orderly state and saw that all debts were paid. She also took the poor and sick into her care, founded monasteries, convents, and hospitals, and, by her example and with the help of wise laws, encouraged both clergy and people to live a better life.

All the things on this earth belong to God, for it was he who created them. God is the Lord of all and has first right to possess things. Yet he allows us to share his rights by possessing things of our own, provided we remember our dependence on him.

According to God's will, every man has the right to possess things. Every one ought to have at least enough property to enable him to care for his own material needs and those of his family. If individuals could not win and hold property, they would be too dependent on others and their liberty would be threatened. Both joy in work and the spirit of initiative in undertaking work would be very much repressed.

We must obtain our property honestly—for example, by our work, or by purchase, exchange, gift, or inheritance. If anyone obtains a thing dishonestly, for instance, by stealing or deception, it does not really become his property.

Whatever we own remains at the same time God's property. We are but his stewards or trustees. Therefore, we must make use of things only in ways which are in accordance with the will of God. We must use our property conscientiously, employ it carefully, be thrifty with it, and apply it to good purposes. And we must always be openhanded toward our neighbor who is in need, and toward the needs of the kingdom of God. We must never forget that God intended the things of this earth to minister to the welfare of the entire human family, and that one day he will demand from us an account of our stewardship.

Our strivings for money and for property should never become the chief interest in our lives. We must be on our guard against greed, avarice, and miserliness. It is much better to be poor on earth and to reach heaven rather than to go hunting after earthly wealth and then lose our souls. Christ said: "Lay not up to yourselves treasures on earth, where the rust and moth consume, and where thieves break through and steal; but lay up to yourselves treasures in heaven...For where thy treasure is, there is thy heart also."[488]

There are some who, of their own accord, give up all personal property for the love of Christ (voluntary poverty). They are following the counsel which Christ gave to the rich young man in the gospel: "If thou wilt be perfect, go, sell what thou hast and give it to the poor, and thou shalt have treasure in heaven."[489]

*Consider.* 1) Why do all things belong to God? 2) Why does every man have a right to own property? 3) How much property is the least which a man should have? 4) In what ways can we acquire property? 5) How should we make use of our property? 6) What must we guard against in our striving for money and property?

230. **Why must we be conscientious in managing our property?**
We must manage our property conscientiously because God is its supreme owner and will require an account of our stewardship.

*For my life.* I will not spend my money on useless trifles, but will start a savings account and put some of it by. Then, later on, I will be able to buy things really worth having, give pleasure to others, or make contributions to good causes.

*From holy scripture.* "The love of money should not dwell in your thoughts; be content with what you have."[490]—"Suppose a man has the worldly goods he needs, and sees his brother go in want; if he steels his heart against his brother's needs, how can we say that the love of God dwells in him?"[491]—"Give much if much is thine; if thou hast a little, cheerfully share that little."[492]

[488] Mt 6:19-21
[489] Mt 19:21
[490] Heb 13:5
[491] 1 Jn 3:17
[492] Tb 4:9

*From the life of the Church.* Popes Leo XIII and Pius XI have explained the Christian teaching about property in two famous encyclicals called *Rerum novarum* and *Quadragesimo anno.*

*Things to do.* Describe some examples of good ways in which men can use their property, and other examples of the bad use of property.

*Ask yourself.* Am I careful enough: a) of my clothes and my shoes; b) of my school bag; c) of my school books; d) of my pocket money?

## *LESSON 123*

## *Our Neighbor's Property*

When Tobias became blind, Anna, his wife, had to earn the living for both of them by her weaving. One day when she was paid for her work, she was also given a young goat as a present, and she brought it home. Tobias heard it bleating and asked where it came from. "You surely have not stolen it? If so, you must give it back, for we may never eat anything that is stolen." But his wife answered: "I was given it as a present over and above what I earned."[493]

Every man has the right that his property should be respected by others. God requires us to respect our neighbor's property.

If we have to manage or keep or make use of the property of another, we must take just as much care of it as if it were our own. Likewise, we must be careful of and have respect for public property belonging to some community such as the town or the state. If we borrow anything, we must give it back in good time, and we must pay our debts punctually. If we find something which obviously belongs to another, we must try to restore it to its owner.

It is a sin against other's rights to property if we acquire something belonging to another by unjust means; examples would be thefts at work, or forceful robbery. Anyone who keeps what he finds without trying to discover its owner, or willfully retains things he has borrowed, or neglects

[493] Cf. Tb 2:10-23

to pay his debts, or keeps back wages due for work done, is little better than a thief. If anyone accepts a gift of what he knows to have been stolen, or sells it, or hides it, he is a "receiver of stolen goods." The receiver is as bad as the thief. It is theft also to deceive another in matters of property, for example, by giving short length or short weight in selling things, passing false money in buying things, doing slovenly work or supplying bad material for which one is paid. Other examples would be claiming more wages than one has really earned, pretending to have delivered more goods than was the case, and profiteering—that is, taking unfair advantage of the necessities of others. Finally, it is a sin to damage or destroy or let another's property perish through one's own fault.

Sins against our neighbor's property always begin in the heart. Anyone who cherishes the desire to acquire unjustly what does not belong to him is sinning against the tenth commandment: "Thou shalt not covet thy neighbor's goods."

Anyone who is in wrongful possession of another's property must give it back at once to the true owner or to his heirs. If he cannot find out who the true owner is, he ought to use it for charitable purposes. Anyone who has damaged his neighbor's property through his own fault must make good the damage as well as he can.

*Consider.* 1) Why must we respect the property of other people? 2) What duties have we toward the property of others? 3) Give examples of things which would be sins against the property of others. 4) Give examples of sins against the tenth commandment.

231. **If a man has damaged another's property, what must he do?**

One who has damaged another's property must make good the damage to the best of his ability.

*For my life.* I will never take the smallest thing that does not belong to me—not even at home.

# The Eighth Commandment of God

Men can live together in a satisfactory way only if they are truthful and able to trust each other. Therefore, God commands: "Thou shalt not bear false witness against thy neighbor."

## *LESSON 124*

### *Truthfulness*

A rather stupid man once thought it would be a joke to fool the learned St. Thomas Aquinas. He went to the window and called: "Come and look, Thomas! There is an ox flying over the garden!" St. Thomas came to look, but said he could see no flying ox. The man then laughed at St. Thomas for believing him so easily. St. Thomas replied: "I find it easier to believe that an ox could fly than that a Christian would lie."

God has given us the power of expressing our thoughts in words and thus passing them on to other people. If our words and actions always correspond with our inward thoughts, then we are truthful or trustworthy.

Truthfulness is something very valuable. God himself is infinite truth. Truthfulness makes us noble and worthy of respect; it is a solid foundation for trust and certainty among men. That is why God requires of us that we be truthful.

It is a sin against truthfulness to tell a lie—that is, to say something false when we know it is false. We must never lie, even to help somebody else or to get ourselves out of trouble. Some people seem to think it is all right to say untrue things if they are only joking; but if the other person cannot know it is a joke, then it remains a lie. If anyone lies about an important matter, or tells a lie which he knows will cause serious harm, then he sins grievously.—It is also a sin against truthfulness to be a hypocrite—that is, to pretend to be better, or more friendly, or more virtuous than he really is; or to be sly and underhand and cunning, or to flatter people for the sake of getting something out of them.

Untruthfulness is a very great evil. The liar is imitating the devil whom our Lord called "the father of lies";[494] he greatly displeases God. "Lying lips the Lord cannot abide; keep faith if thou wouldst content him."[495] Lying corrupts a man's character, destroys trust and confidence among men, and is the cause of endless trouble in the world.

Truthfulness does not demand that we should always blurt out everything we are thinking. Sometimes it is only prudent or charitable to keep silent—for instance, to keep a secret or to avoid offending somebody.

If ever we have promised something, or made an agreement, we are bound to keep our promise and abide by our agreement. We must be trustworthy, or faithful. God himself is infinitely faithful (see Lesson 5); he keeps his word, and abides by the covenant he has made with us. Untrustworthiness and double-dealing set men against one another; fidelity draws them together.

*Consider.* 1) Why is truthfulness of such great value? 2) Give examples of sins against truthfulness. 3) What does "being a hypocrite" mean? 4) Why is untruthfulness such a great evil? 5) When should we be silent about what is true? 6) What must we do if we have promised something or made an agreement with somebody?

232. **What do you mean by a "truthful person"?**

A truthful person is one whose outward speech and actions correspond with his inward thoughts.

233. **Why should we be truthful?**

We should be truthful: 1) because God is truthful; 2) because truthfulness makes us noble; 3) because truthfulness leads others to trust us.

[494] Jn 8:44

[495] Prv 12:22

234. **What are the consequences of lying?**
Lying corrupts the character, ruins trust, and causes much evil in the world.

*For my life.* Truth before all else!

*From holy scripture.* "Let your word for Yes be Yes, and No for No."[496]—"Away with falsehood! Let everyone speak the truth to his neighbor, for membership of the body binds us to one another."[497]

*Things to do.* 1) On what occasions does it require special courage to tell the truth? 2) What are the reasons why so many people tell lies? 3) What circumstances make some people behave as hypocrites? 4) See if you can find in the Bible examples of: a) truthfulness; b) lying; c) hypocrisy.

## *LESSON 125*

## *Our Good Name*

When Jesus had given his answer to the high priest in the presence of the Jewish council, one of the servants standing by gave him a blow, saying: "Answerest thou the high priest so?" Jesus answered him: "If I have spoken evil, give testimony of the evil; but if well, why strikest thou me?"[498]

If we make a real effort to fulfill our duties faithfully, we have a right to the respect and due regard of our fellow men. This respect which we have from others is called "our honor," or "our good name," or "our reputation."

A good name is something of great value. "Precious beyond all measure is good repute."[499] Therefore, we must value our reputation. We must not risk it lightly, and, whenever necessary, we should defend it. Above all, we must behave in a manner such that we really deserve a good reputation. To seek a reputation greater than that which we deserve is the sin of ambition.

But the reputation we have among men is not the most important thing of all; it matters a great deal more what God thinks of us. No one can ever

[496] Jas 5:12
[497] Eph 4:25
[498] Jn 18:22-23
[499] Prv 22:1

take away our inner repute before God. When it is necessary for God's sake to lose our reputation before men, we must sacrifice it. Christ said: "Blessed are ye when men shall revile you and persecute you and speak all that is evil against you, untruly, for my sake; be glad and rejoice, for your reward is very great in heaven."[500]

*Consider.* 1) What is reputation or good name? 2) Why should we be concerned for our reputation? 3) In what way should we be concerned about our reputation? 4) What do you mean by the "sin of ambition"? 5) What is even more important than our reputation before men?

*For my life.* Be, rather than seem!

*From holy scripture.* Christ said to the Jews: "How can you believe, who receive glory from one another; and the glory which is from God alone, you do not seek?"[501]

*Things to do.* 1) What is the right way to defend our good name? 2) Give some instances when it is necessary to give up one's reputation before men.

A man is what he is in the sight of God—this and nothing more.[502]

## *LESSON 126*

### *Our Neighbor's Good Name*

St. Augustine, the great bishop and doctor of the Church, had these words put up in the dining room of his house: "In my house, no one may ever speak ill of another."

A good name is more valuable than wealth for our neighbor, too. Therefore, we should respect our neighbor's reputation even more than our own. We should both think and speak well of him, and show him the honor which is his due. If anyone else attacks his reputation unjustly, we should boldly speak out in his defense. We ought not to speak about our

[500] Mt 5:11-12
[501] Jn 5:44
[502] Francis of Assisi

neighbor's faults except for important reasons—for instance, to help him to improve, or to protect others.

It is a sin against the reputation of our neighbor if we think ill of him without sufficient reason. This is the sin of rash judgment, or suspicion. It is a worse sin to tell others about his hidden faults without reason (detraction), to cast suspicions on him, to exaggerate his faults, or to say that he has faults which, in fact, he does not have (calumny). To insult somebody or put him to shame publicly is also a sin against our neighbor's reputation; likewise, to listen with pleasure to talk against others.—If the damage done to someone's reputation is serious, then the sin also is serious.

Anyone who has damaged his neighbor's reputation must put right the harm he has done to the best of his ability. Calumny must be admitted as false; and if an insult was given in public, the apology should also be made in public.

*Consider.* 1) Why must we respect the reputation of our neighbor? 2) Give examples of sins against our neighbor's reputation. 3) What do you mean by a "sin of rash judgment"? 4) What do you mean by *detraction*? 5) What do you mean by *calumny*?

235. **How are we to respect our neighbor's good name?**

We are to respect our neighbor's good name:

1. by thinking and speaking well of him;
2. by not talking about his faults except for important reasons.

236. **If anyone has injured his neighbor's reputation, what must he do?**

Anyone who has injured his neighbor's reputation must put right the harm he has done to the best of his ability.

*For my life.* If I hear talk about a serious fault of someone else, I will first ask myself whether it can be true. If I think that probably it is true, I will then think over carefully whether I had better speak about it to the person himself, or to someone who could speak to him better than I could, or whether I had better keep quiet about it altogether.

*From holy scripture.* "Why seest thou the mote that is in thy brother's eye, but seest not the beam that is in thine own eye?...Cast out first the beam from thine own eye, and then thou shalt see to cast out the mote from thy brother's eye."[503]

*Things to do.* 1) How can I express my respect for grown-up people, and how my respect for children? 2) How could I put right the harm I have done: a) if I told others, without any good reason, of someone's real faults; b) if I told others of someone's imaginary faults—faults which were merely my own invention?

[503] Mt 7:3, 5

## *SECTION IV*

# The Four Last Things

"The resurrection of the body and life everlasting. Amen."
(11th and 12th Articles of the Creed.)

## The Last Things of Mankind

Our time of testing here on earth will end with death and a personal judgment for each of us. After that, our soul will go to heaven, to purgatory, or to hell.

### *LESSON 127*

### *Death and Personal Judgment*

When St. Thomas More, Lord Chancellor of England, was condemned to death for his faith, he thanked the messenger who brought him the news. Before being taken to the scaffold, he dressed himself in his best suit. As an old man, he found it difficult to climb the ladder, and said to the Lord Lieutenant: "I pray thee, see me safely up; as for my coming down, I will shift for myself!" He made a short speech saying: "I die loyal to God and to the King, but to God first of all!" He embraced the executioner and gave him a gold piece, as one who was about to do him a favor. He bound up his own eyes, knelt to lay his head on the block, but pulled aside his beard which had grown in prison saying: "It should not be cut, for it cannot have committed any treason!" Then the axe descended, and the brave martyr went joyfully to meet his God.

All men have got to die because Adam, who was the first man, committed sin. "It was through one man that guilt came into the world; and since death came owing to guilt, death was handed on to all mankind by one man."[504] Christ accepted death in a spirit of perfect obedience and purest love. Following his example, we too should receive death obediently and readily from the hand of our heavenly Father.

By his death, Christ won for us eternal life. He has transformed death. Now it has become the gateway into everlasting life for those who die in Christ.

We do not know when or where or how we shall die. But one thing we do know: if we die as God's children, then we are saved forever; but if we die in mortal sin, then we are lost forever. That is why we must live always—all the time—as God's children. Because then we are always—all the time—ready for death if it should come.

When we die, our soul becomes separated from our body. The body will go back to the earth and go to pieces by returning to dust. But our soul cannot go to pieces, for it is a spirit, and a spirit has no parts.

Immediately after leaving the body, our soul will be brought before God to be judged. It will have to give to God an account of every thought, word, deed, and omission. This will be a personal judgment, often called the "particular judgment." "Man's destiny is to die once for all; nothing remains after this but the judgment."[505] After this personal judgment, the soul enters heaven or purgatory or hell.

*Consider.* 1) In what way did Christ accept death? 2) How should we accept death? 3) Why must we be ready to die at any time? 4) What do you mean by "being ready to die"? 5) What happens when a man dies? 6) What happens to his body? 7) What happens to his soul? 8) Where does his soul go after his personal judgment?

237. **Why must all men die?**

All men must die because Adam, the first man, sinned.

[504] Rom 5:12
[505] Heb 9:27

238. **What happens to the soul immediately after death?**
Immediately after death, the soul comes before God to be judged, to give an account of all thoughts, words, deeds, and omissions of good that should have been done.

*For my life.* I will always be ready to die at any time.—And I will often pray for a good death.

*From holy scripture.* "Blessed are the dead who die in the Lord...The deeds they did in life go with them now."[506]

*A prayer.* "From a sudden and unprovided death, spare us O Lord."

*From the preface of the Mass for the dead.* "The life of those who are faithful to thee, O Lord, is not ended but only changed; and when this home of their earthly life decays, an eternal dwelling place is prepared for them in heaven."

*From the teaching of the saints.* "One who has lived well cannot die badly; but it is very difficult for one who has lived badly to die well."[507]—"It is not death, but the good God, who will take me away."[508]

*Things to do.* 1) What can you do for someone who has had an accident and seems likely to die very soon? 2) Consider how even children can be overtaken by death.

As a man believes, so he lives.
As a man lives, so he dies.
As a man dies, so he stays.

## *LESSON 128*

## *Heaven*

When St. Paul was in prison for preaching the gospel, and was expecting to be put to death, he wrote to the Philippians: "I long to have done with

[506] Apoc 14:13
[507] Augustine, *Sermon 249*, n. 2
[508] Teresa of the Child Jesus

it and be with Christ—a better thing and more than a better thing! And yet, for your sakes, that I should wait in the body is more urgent still."[509]

If anyone dies in the grace of God, free from all sin and from the punishments due to sin, he goes straight to heaven immediately after his death.

The blessed in heaven see God three-in-one in all his glory face-to-face, and are united with him in everlasting love. That is the greatest of all heavenly joys.—The blessed also see Christ, the God-man, in his glorified manhood. They live in the community of the angels and saints. They are free from every evil and unspeakably happy. In heaven, they find again all those relatives and friends of theirs who died in the grace of God.—The joys of heaven are far beyond anything we can possibly imagine. Of them it is true to say what St. Paul said: "Things no eye has seen, no ear has heard, no human heart conceived, the welcome God has prepared for those who love him."[510]

The joys of heaven are not equally great for everyone who is there. "Every one will receive his own wages, in proportion to his own work."[511] Those who have loved God more and served him better while on earth will receive more of God's love in heaven. "He who sows freely will reap freely too."[512]

*Consider.* 1) What joys are given to the blessed in heaven? 2) Why is the degree of happiness in heaven not the same for all those who are there?

239. **Who goes straight to heaven after death?**
He who dies in the grace of God, free from all sin and punishment due to sin, goes straight to heaven after death.

240. **What is the greatest joy of the blessed in heaven?**
The blessed in heaven see God face-to-face and are united with him in everlasting love.

*For my life.* I must have only one purpose in life—to reach heaven.

[509] Phil 1:23-24
[510] 1 Cor 2:9
[511] 1 Cor 3:8
[512] 2 Cor 9:6

*From holy scripture.* "At present we are looking at a confused reflection in a mirror; then we shall see face-to-face."[513]—"Be glad and rejoice, for your reward is very great in heaven."[514]—"Give and it shall be given to you; good measure and pressed down and shaken together and running over shall they give into your bosom."[515]

*Explanation.* The word *heaven* is used to mean: 1) the visible heaven, the sky which we can actually see above the earth; and 2) the invisible heaven, the condition or place in which the blessed see God. Where this invisible heaven is, God has not revealed to us.

## LESSON 129

## Purgatory

After a victory won by Judas Machabaeus over the Syrians, he and his soldiers prayed that God would forgive the sins of those who had fallen. In addition, Judas collected a considerable sum of money and sent it to Jerusalem to have sacrifices offered there for the guilt of his dead companions.[516]

Anyone who dies in the grace of God, but is not free from all sins and all punishment due for sins, cannot go to heaven at once. St. John writes of the eternal city of heaven: "Nothing that is unclean, no source of corruption or deceit can ever hope to find its way in."[517] Those who still have to do penance for their sins go first to a place of cleansing which we call "purgatory" (a word which means "cleansing place").

The poor souls in purgatory are filled with sorrow for their sins, and also a burning desire to be with their great and holy God. They have to undergo in great suffering the punishment still due to their sins. What they feel most is the fact that they cannot yet see God; and what comforts them

513 1 Cor 13:12
514 Mt 5:12
515 Lk 6:38
516 Cf. 2 Mc 12:32-46
517 Apoc 21:27

most is the thought that they are now absolutely certain to see him, and that they are saved forever.

The poor souls in purgatory cannot do anything for themselves to shorten their sufferings. But Christ, their Redeemer, is always speaking to the Father for them, and Mary and the other saints are also praying through Christ and with Christ. But we too can pray and offer sacrifices through Christ that the holy souls may soon be loosed from their pains.

Purgatory will continue to exist until the whole world is judged on the last day. After the judgment, there will be nothing but heaven and hell.

*Consider.* 1) What sufferings do the souls in purgatory have to endure? 2) How can the sufferings of the poor souls be shortened? 3) Until what day will purgatory continue to exist?

241. **Who goes to purgatory?**
Those who die in the grace of God, but still have penance to do for their sins, go to purgatory.

*For my life.* Every day, I will say a prayer for the souls in purgatory.

*Things to do.* 1) On what day should we think especially about our own dead? 2) How can we help the poor souls in purgatory?

May the souls of the faithful departed,
through the mercy of God, rest in peace. Amen.

## *LESSON 130*

## *Hell*

One day, Jesus told the Pharisees the following parable: "There was a certain rich man, who was clothed in purple and fine linen, and feasted sumptuously every day. And there was a certain beggar, named Lazarus, who lay at his gate, full of sores, desiring to be filled with the crumbs that fell from the rich man's table, but no one did give to him…And it came to pass that the beggar died, and was carried by angels into Abraham's bosom.

And the rich man also died; and he was buried in hell. And lifting up his eyes when he was in torments, he saw Abraham afar off, and Lazarus in his bosom; and he cried and said: 'Father Abraham, have mercy on me and send Lazarus that he may dip the tip of his finger in water to cool my tongue, for I am tormented in this flame.'"[518]

It is a most terrible disaster to die in mortal sin. Anyone who, right till the end of his life, has refused to accept the love and mercy of God and so has died in mortal sin, has cut himself off from God forever by his own act. He is damned, and goes to hell forever.

The damned in hell will never be able to see the glory of God, for they are now cast off by him forever. That is the worst of all the punishments of hell. The damned souls are separated from Christ, and shut out from the communion of saints. Besides that, they suffer pains in the fire of hell, are tortured all the while by their own bad conscience, and must endure the companionship of the devils and all the other damned souls. While they were on earth, they thought they could do without God; now they realize that there can be no happiness except with God. They curse themselves and are tortured by unceasing despair. Their punishment will never have an end; it will go on and on for all eternity.

The damned in hell do not all suffer to the same degree; for some it is worse than for others. For God is just; and those who committed the worst sins are given the worst punishments.

Christ taught us about hell not just to alarm us but to warn us and save us. He loves sinners and wants to lead them to repentance so long as there is time.

*Consider.* 1) Why is it the most terrible of all disasters to die in mortal sin? 2) What tortures do the damned have to suffer? 3) Why do some of the damned have worse sufferings than others? 4) Why did Christ teach us about hell?

242. **Who will go to hell?**

All those who die in mortal sin will go to hell.

[518] Lk 16:19-24

243. **What is the worst of the pains of hell?**
The damned will never be able to see God and are cast off by him forever.

*For my life.* If ever I am in danger of committing a mortal sin, I will call to my mind the pains of hell.

*From holy scripture.* "It is a fearful thing to fall into the hands of the living God."[519]—"Then shall he say to those on his left hand: 'Depart from me, ye cursed, into everlasting fire which was prepared for the devil and his angels.'...And these shall go into everlasting punishment; but the just into everlasting life."[520]—"I say to you my friends: Be not afraid of them that kill the body and after that have no more that they can do. But I will show you whom you shall fear: Fear ye him who, after he hath killed, hath power to cast into hell. Yea, I say to you: Fear ye him."[521]

*From the teaching of the Church.* "Woe to him who now treats hell as a matter for joking, and first comes to believe in it when he finds himself there."[522]

*From the life of the Church.* Every day, just before the consecration in the Mass, the Church prays: "Rescue us from eternal damnation!"

## *LESSON 131*

## *Christian Burial*

King Salmanasar had taken the Israelites into Syria where they were in exile. His son Sennacherib persecuted them, killed many of them, and forbade that their bodies should be buried. But Tobias, a devout Israelite, feared God more than he feared the king. He used to hide the bodies of the dead in his house, and then bury them at night. So, he himself was persecuted by the king. God, however, was very pleased with the brave and pious action of Tobias, and sent the angel Raphael to him to say: "When

519 Heb 10:31
520 Mt 25:41, 46
521 Lk 12:4-5
522 Eusebius of Caesarea

thou wert praying with tears, when thou wert burying the dead, I, all the while, was offering that prayer of thine to the Lord."[523]

The body of a Christian is a temple of the Holy Ghost; it serves God and is to be brought to life again in glory on the last day. Therefore, even after death, the body of a Christian is deserving of respect. The Church honors it by the rites of a Christian funeral and lays it to rest in consecrated ground.

The body of a Christian is to be laid in the earth, as was Christ's own body. It is like a seed that is buried in the earth, to rise again on the last day. "What is sown corruptible will rise incorruptible."[524] That is why a cemetery is sometimes called "God's acre."

Some people wish to have their body cremated (burned in a furnace) because they believe that death is the end of everything. To show that she believes the contrary, the Church forbids her children to have their bodies cremated. Death is not the end of everything: the day of resurrection will come. If any Catholic gives orders that when he dies his body is to be cremated, and does not withdraw this order, then he may not receive the sacraments and cannot be given Christian burial.

*Consider.* 1) Why is the dead body of a Christian worthy of respect? 2) In what way does the Church honor the bodies of her dead? 3) Why should the body of a Christian be laid in the earth? 4) Why do some people want to be cremated? 5) Why does the Church forbid the cremation of the bodies of her dead? 6) What is the penalty that falls on a Catholic who gives orders that his body is to be cremated?

*For my life.* I will sometimes visit the graves of my family and of others who have died, and will gladly help to look after them.

*Things to do.* 1) What symbols or carvings do you find on the gravestones of Catholics? 2) What words of holy scripture are very suitable for use as inscriptions on Catholic graves? 3) How can you show your sympathy for the relatives of someone who has died?

[523] Cf. Tb 1:18-23; 12:11-14

[524] 1 Cor 15:42

## *The Church's Funeral Rites*

### In the Home

The priest sprinkles the body with holy water and begins Psalm 129: "Out of the depths I have cried to thee, O Lord." And after a silent Our Father and some prayers which all present should answer, the priest asks God to grant to the soul of the departed forgiveness of all his sins and everlasting life.—This blessing in the home is not customary everywhere.

### In the Church

Wherever it is possible, the body should be taken to the church and placed in the center aisle. Then a special Mass (Requiem Mass) is offered. At the end of the Mass, a solemn prayer of intercession and blessing for the departed soul is said or sung (*Libera*).

### In the Cemetery

If the body has not been taken to the church, it is taken instead to the mortuary or cemetery chapel and blessed there. Then it is accompanied to the grave and buried there. Having blessed the grave (if it is not already blessed) the priest prays for the departed soul, sprinkles the coffin with holy water, and incenses it. In some places, it is the custom for the priest to throw three shovelsful of earth onto the coffin after it has been lowered into the grave. He ends by saying more prayers for the dead and for the living. Then, according to custom, all who are attending the funeral come to the grave and drop a handful of earth onto the coffin, as a sign that they are helping to bury the dead (which is one of the seven corporal works of mercy).

# The End of the World and the Completion of God's Design

God has not yet brought his holy plan to completion. But on the day which the Father has decided, Christ will come back again to judge all mankind and put the finishing touches to God's design.

## *LESSON 132*

### *What Christ Has Foretold about the Time Which Must Elapse until the Last Day Arrives*

Once, the disciples asked Christ what would be the signs of his coming again and of the end of the world. He said to them: "Take heed that no man seduce you; for many will come in my name saying: 'I am the Christ'; and they will seduce many. And you shall hear of wars and rumors of wars... Then they shall deliver you up to be afflicted and shall put you to death; and you shall be hated by all nations for my name's sake. And then shall many be scandalized, and shall betray one another and the charity of many will grow cold. But he that shall persevere to the end, he shall be saved. And this gospel of the kingdom shall be preached in the whole world, for a testimony to all nations, and then shall the consummation come."[525]

Christ has prophesied that his message will be proclaimed throughout the whole world until the last day. All peoples are to hear the good tidings of the kingdom of God before the end comes.

Christ has also prophesied that many men will reject his word, will fight against the Church, will inflict great trials upon Christians, persecute them, and put some of them to death. "If they have persecuted me, they will also persecute you."[526] Again and again the peoples of the world will be

[525] Cf. Mt 24:3-14
[526] Jn 15:20

afflicted by wars, revolutions, famines, and other terrible sufferings. Under these trials, many Christians will weaken and fall away from their faith.

But Christ has also promised that he will always be with his Church through all these troubles: "The gates of hell shall not prevail against it."[527] "I am with you all days, even till the end of the world."[528] He has promised to the apostles and to all the faithful that he will enlighten them by the Holy Ghost, and strengthen them so that they may be able to remain true to him in persecution and distress, and thus witness to the world that Christ lives and conquers.

Shortly before the end, the devil will again unleash all his powers against the kingdom of God. Wicked men will live as if there were no God, no judgment, and no eternity.[529] False prophets will arise; they will lead many astray and bring them to ruin. Finally, there will come Antichrist, "the man of sin, the son of corruption, the adversary who raises himself up above everything else that bears God's name and holds for God's cause." Through the power of Satan, he will perform many deceptive signs and wonders, and seduce many. But Christ, when he returns, will utterly destroy him by his divine power.[530]

All this has been foretold to us, so that if it should happen in our time, we will not go astray, nor lose courage, but will persevere until the end.

*Consider.* 1) Until what day will the good tidings of Christ be proclaimed to all the peoples of the earth? 2) What trials and troubles has Christ foretold for the time which must go by until the last day? 3) What has Christ promised for all time until the last day? 4) What will happen shortly before the end of the world comes? 5) Why did Christ let us know beforehand many things about the end of the world?

*For my life.* When atheism and injustice show themselves without shame in the world, I will not be surprised; for Christ said it would happen.

[527] Mt 16:18
[528] Mt 28:20
[529] Cf. Mt 24:37-39
[530] Cf. 2 Thes 2:3-11

# LESSON 133

## *The End of the World and the Resurrection of the Dead*

When Jesus had foretold to his disciples the trials of the times before the end of the world, he went on: "And after the tribulation of those days, the sun shall be darkened, and the moon shall not give her light, and the stars shall fall from heaven, and the powers of heaven shall be moved. And there shall appear the sign of the Son of man in heaven; and all the tribes of the earth shall see the Son of man coming in the clouds of heaven with much power and majesty. And he shall send his angels with a trumpet and a great voice; and they shall gather together his elect from the four winds, from the farthest parts of the heavens to the utmost bounds of the earth."[531]

It is God who decides when the end of the world is to come. He is the Lord of time and the King of eternity. He alone knows how long this world of time is going to last; he alone has the power to bring it to an end. That is why Christ says: "Watch ye, therefore, for ye know not the day nor the hour."[532]—This day on which the world will end is called "the last day."

On the last day, Christ will come back again and reveal his divine glory before all the world. At his coming, the whole of creation will be shaken. His arrival will show that the old world of time, in which the glory of God was still hidden, has now come to an end, and that a new world, in a new era, is at hand in which the glory of God will fill the whole of creation. That is why the last day is also called "the day of Christ," or "the day of the Lord."

When Christ comes back, he will command, with divine power, that all men shall appear before him. Even the dead will hear his voice and rise again to life. Christ said: "The hour will come when all that are in the graves shall hear the voice of the Son of God. And they that have done good things shall come forth unto the resurrection of life; but they that have done evil, unto

[531] Cf. Mt 24:29-31
[532] Mt 25:13

the resurrection of judgment."[533] The good will hear the Lord's voice with unbounded joy; but the wicked will hear it with terror.

At the resurrection, the bodies of the dead will be eternally united with their immortal souls. The bodies of the wicked will be horrible and loathsome; they will show forth plainly the evil and despair of the wicked souls that live in them. But the bodies of the good will be beautiful and filled with glory; for they will be like the glorified body of the risen Christ.

*Consider.* 1) Who decides when the end of the world will be? 2) What do you mean by "the last day"? 3) How will it be made clear that the old world of time has come to an end? 4) What will Christ do when he comes again? 5) How will men receive the summons of Christ to appear in his presence? 6) At the end of the world, what will the bodies of the risen be like?

244. **What does Christ say about the resurrection of the dead?**

Christ says: "The hour will come wherein all that are in the graves shall hear the voice of the Son of God. And they that have done good things shall come forth unto the resurrection of life, but they that have done evil unto the resurrection of judgment."

*For my life.* "The world and all its pleasures pass away; but he who does the will of God remains for ever."[534]

*From holy scripture.* "We look forward, blessed in our hope, to the day when there will be a new dawn of glory, the glory of the great God, the glory of our Savior Jesus Christ."[535]—"It will happen in a moment, in the twinkling of an eye, when the last trumpet sounds; the dead will rise again, free from corruption, and we shall find ourselves changed."[536]—"Christ will form this humbled body of ours anew, molding it into the image of his glorious body."[537]

533 Jn 5:28-29
534 1 Jn 2:17
535 Ti 2:13
536 1 Cor 15:52
537 Phil 3:21

*What would you say?* The Adventists, the Jehovah's Witnesses, and some other sects say that we can calculate beforehand when the last day will come.—But we answer: "Jesus said: 'The day and the hour no man knoweth, neither the angels in heaven, nor the Son, but the Father.'"[538]

## *LESSON 134*

### *The Last Judgment*

Shortly before his passion, Jesus said to his disciples: "When the Son of man shall come in his majesty, and all his angels with him, then shall he sit upon the seat of his majesty. And all the nations shall be gathered together before him, and he shall separate them one from another, as the shepherd separateth the sheep from the goats. And he shall set the sheep on his right hand, but the goats on his left. Then shall the king say to them that shall be on his right hand: 'Come ye blessed of my Father, possess ye the kingdom prepared for you from the foundation of the world.'...Then he shall say to them also that shall be on his left hand: 'Depart from me, ye cursed, into everlasting fire which was prepared for the devil and his angels.'...And these shall go into everlasting punishment, but the just into everlasting life."[539]

After the dead have risen again, there will follow the judgment of all the world (called "the last judgment" or "the general judgment"). "For God has fixed a day when he will pronounce just judgment on the whole world."[540] The time when God, in his great patience, has borne with sinners, will then have passed. The wicked now meet with the full power of his anger, while the good receive his love.

God will judge the world "through Jesus Christ."[541] "The Father hath given all judgment to the Son."[542] Christ has redeemed the world; he is therefore also to judge it.

538 Mk 13:32
539 Mt 25:31-46
540 Acts 17:31
541 Rom 2:16
542 Jn 5:22

Every single thing which every man has ever done will be made known in the presence of the glorified Lord. "He will bring to light what is hidden in darkness and reveal the secrets of men's hearts."[543] The good will be separated from the bad. Then Christ will pronounce judgment. He will call to himself and award eternal life to all those who have loved God and served him; he will banish from his presence and condemn to hell all those who have turned against God and refused to repent even at their death.

After the judgment, the good will go body and soul into everlasting life, while the bad will be cast body and soul into hell. For man's body is to share the reward or the punishment because, while on earth, it took part in the good or bad deeds which earned them.

At this last judgment, the devil, too, will be finally and definitely condemned. Christ will take away from him even the last remainder of his power, and thrust him back into hell forever.

This general judgment will be held in order that God's holiness, justice, and wisdom may be acknowledged by all men, that Christ may be glorified before all the world, and that the good may have the honor and the bad the shame which they have deserved. Then no one will ever be able to deny God or to complain against him, to reject Christ or strive against him, or to mock, oppress, or torture the good. "Inward remorse will wring a groan from those hearts: Why! These were the men we made into a laughing stock and a byword! We, poor fools, mistook the life they lived for madness, their death for ignominy; and now they are reckoned as God's own children—now it is among his holy ones that their lot is cast."[544]

*Consider.* 1) Who will preside over the last judgment? 2) What will happen at the last judgment? 3) Why will the body share in the eternal reward or punishment? 4) What will happen to the devil at the last judgment?

### 245. What will happen after the resurrection of the dead?

After the resurrection of the dead, there will be the last judgment.

[543] 1 Cor 4:5
[544] Ws 5:3-5

246. **How will the divine judge pronounce sentence?**

The divine judge will say to the good: "Come ye blessed of my Father, possess ye the kingdom prepared for you from the foundation of the world." But to the wicked he will say: "Depart from me, ye cursed, into everlasting fire, which was prepared for the devil and his angels."

247. **For what purposes will the last judgment be held?**

The last judgment will be held:

1. in order that God's wisdom and justice may be acknowledged by all men;
2. that Christ may be glorified before the whole world;
3. that the good may have the honor, and the bad may have the shame, which they have deserved.

*For my life.* In all my actions, I will often ask myself: "At the last judgment, will I be glad or ashamed of having done this?"

*From holy scripture.* "Who will stand with head erect at his appearing? He will put men to a test as fierce as the crucible."[545]—"Behold, he comes with clouds about him, seen by every eye, seen by those who wounded him."[546]—"The kings of the world with their noblemen and their captains, men of wealth and of strength, all alike, slaves and freemen took shelter in caves and in rock fastnesses among the hills. Fall on us, they said to the hills and the rocks, and hide us from the presence of him who sits on the throne, and from the vengeance of the Lamb. Which of us can stand his ground, now that the great day, the day of their vengeance, has come!"[547]

*Things to do.* 1) In which parables does Jesus speak of the last judgment? 2) See if you can find any pictures representing the last judgment, and describe them. 3) Where in the Mass for the dead is there any mention of this general judgment?

[545] Mal 3:2
[546] Apoc 1:7
[547] Apoc 6:15-17

## *LESSON 135*

### *The Transformation of the Visible World*

Through the prophet Isaias, God promised: "I will create new heavens and a new earth; old things shall be remembered no longer, have no place in men's thoughts. But you shall be glad and rejoice for ever in those things which I shall create."[548]

On the last day, when God manifests all his power, the visible world is going to be transformed.[549] It will not fall back into nothing, for God does not destroy what he has made. But "the fashion of this world is to pass away."[550] It will be utterly transformed and brought to perfection in the fire of God's love and holiness. "We have a new heaven and a new earth to look forward to, the dwelling place of holiness."[551]

This transformation of the visible world on the last day will be brought about by the heavenly Father through Christ, his Son. "God has put all things in subjection under his feet."[552]

Christ will free the visible world from all evils and from every kind of disorder that has come upon it as the result of sin; he will fill it with eternal glory. And thus creation, in its own way, will have its part in the glorification of Christ's body.

When the visible world is transformed, it will have become that for which God designed it in the beginning: the radiant dwelling of God among men. And with that, the whole work of the redemption is completed. Christ will have handed over to his Father the entire creation now fully redeemed.[553]

*Consider.* 1) Through whom will God transform the world? 2) What will Christ do when he transforms the world?

[548] Cf. Is 65:17-18
[549] Cf. Mt 19:28
[550] 1 Cor 7:31
[551] 2 Pt 3:13
[552] 1 Cor 15:27
[553] Cf. 1 Cor 15:24

248. **What will happen to the visible world on the last day?**
On the last day, the visible world will be transformed and created anew.

*For my life.* God's beautiful world, which I can already see, is going to be even more beautiful when God transforms it.

*From holy scripture.* "Heaven and earth shall pass away, but my words shall not pass away."[554]

*Things to do.* Why are butterflies and springtime considered as symbols for the transformation of the world? Can you think of any other symbols?

## *LESSON 136*

## *The Kingdom of God in All Its Glory*

In the Apocalypse of St. John, we read: "Then I saw a new heaven and a new earth. The old heaven, the old earth, had vanished, and there was no more sea. And I, John, saw in my vision that holy city which is the new Jerusalem, being sent down by God from heaven, all clothed in readiness, like a bride who has adorned herself to meet her husband. I heard, too, a voice which cried aloud from the throne: 'Here is God's tabernacle pitched among men; he will dwell with them, and they will be his own people, and he will be among them, their own God. He will wipe away every tear from their eyes, and there will be no more death, or mourning, or cries of distress, no more sorrow; those things have passed away.' And he who sat on the throne said: 'Behold, I make all things new.'"[555]

In the new creation, God, three Persons in one, will at last reign alone over us and have his dwelling among us. He will display to us all his glory, and will make us eternally happy in his love. He will surround the whole of redeemed creation with everlasting peace.

Christ, the Son of God made man, will rule over us in this new creation with the Father and the Holy Ghost, and will always be with us. The splendor of divine glory will shine forth upon us from his countenance; he will

[554] Mt 24:35
[555] Apoc 21:1-5

offer to the Father the praise and adoration of the whole world, and will endow us with the fullness of eternal life.

In body and soul, heart and eye, mind and feeling and will, we shall all be filled with the glory of God in this wonderful new world. We shall be thrilled through and through by indescribable happiness, and we shall be united in everlasting love with God, three in one, and with all his angels and saints.

Then everything which belonged only to the world as we know it now will have passed away. Faith will have given way to vision, and hope to possession. Temptations and conflicts, hunger and thirst, suffering and death will all be over and done with; for now the victory has been gained and immortal life has been won. There will be no separation anymore: heaven and earth will be one, and the countless legions of angels and the children of God from every race and age will all be united in God. There will be no more churches: for the whole of redeemed creation will then be one single glorious and radiant house of God. There will be no more days and years; for all will live in God's eternity, and all together will celebrate that feast which the Father had prepared from the beginning of the world.

That is the kingdom of God in its glory, which Christ has proclaimed to us. That is the everlasting home for which our hearts yearn. That is the marriage feast of the Lamb, for which the Church ever sighs like a bride. She says to Christ, her bridegroom: "Come, Lord Jesus!"[556]

*Consider.* 1) Describe what life will be like in the new creation. 2) What things will be no more in the new creation?

*For my life.* I will often thank God from the bottom of my heart that he has called me to his glorious kingdom.

*From holy scripture.* "The just shall shine as the sun in the kingdom of their Father."[557]—"He showed me, too, a river, whose waters give life; it flows, clear as crystal, from the throne of God, from the throne of the Lamb."[558]—"God's throne (which is the Lamb's throne) will be there (in the holy city of God) with his servants to worship him, and to see his face,

556 Apoc 22:20
557 Mt 13:43
558 Apoc 22:1

his name written on their foreheads...The Lord God will shed his light on them, and they will reign for ever and ever."[559]

*From the teaching of the saints.* "We long for the new Jerusalem which is to come; and the more we long for it, the more patiently we will bear all things needed to attain it."[560]

*Things to do.* 1) How is it that not a single one of the seven sacraments will be needed in the new creation? 2) How is it that there will be no more breaking of any of God's commandments? 3) How much of this completed kingdom of God has already come into existence?

*Awaiting Christ's coming.* Cardinal Newman writes: "This earth, which now buds forth in leaves and blossoms, will one day burst forth into a new world of light and glory...It will be that eternal spring for which all Christians are waiting. Come it will, though it delay; yet, though it tarry, it will surely come. Therefore, we say day by day: 'Thy kingdom come!'"

[559] Apoc 22:3-5

[560] Augustine, *Epistle 27 to Paulinus*, n. 1

# Appendix

## *The Christian's Daily Life*

1. As soon as you wake in the morning, make the sign of the cross, turn your mind happily to God, and offer him the new day: "My God, all for you!" If it is time to get up, do so promptly and get dressed. After that, say your morning prayers attentively, and, if possible, on your knees. Never miss your morning prayer! Use the occasion to renew your special resolution.—Whenever you can, go to church and take part in the Holy Mass. You could not possibly spend your time more profitably.
2. Go to your day's work with a happy heart; and do your work as well as you can, industriously and conscientiously.
3. In the course of the day, be glad to think sometimes about God; he is thinking of you all the time! Say a few words of greeting to him now and again; consider often what he wants you to do, and do it for him willingly. "All the days of thy life have God before thy eyes."[561]
4. Every day you will find plenty of opportunities for doing good. It is God who sends them to you; so watch out for them and make good use of them. Carry the love of God and his joy into the world.
5. In your dealings with other people, be polite, friendly, and helpful. Be on your guard against loose or uncharitable talk; avoid bad companions and be careful about strangers—you need to know something about them before giving them your confidence.
6. Never eat a meal without first having asked God's blessing on it. By all means, enjoy the good things God has provided for you, but be moderate; don't be greedy and don't be faddy. And after eating, don't forget to thank God.

[561] Tb 4:6

7. Make good use of your spare time—never waste it in idleness. Try to relieve your parents of some of their work; they do a great deal of work for you. Give your time to your brothers and sisters, and be ready to help friends and neighbors. If you still have time to spare, spend it with good companions and with good books or hobbies.
8. Be patient if you have to bear pain or hardship. Say to yourself: "Christ, my master, suffered for me although he was blameless." Offer up to God anything that you find hard: it will earn you a rich reward in heaven.
9. Be glad to celebrate Sundays and feast days—make them occasions of joy. Never miss Mass through your own fault; and, as far as possible, receive Communion as part of every Mass that you help to offer. "As your Sunday, so your dying-day."
10. Be watchful against temptations. Don't give way to them even in the smallest point. If ever you should be so unfortunate as to commit a mortal sin, be sorry for it at once, earnestly ask God's forgiveness, and go to confession as soon as you can.—Let your confessions be regular; never let more than a month go by without going to confession. Go oftener if you like, but certainly not less often.
11. Before you go to bed, always say your night prayers attentively. Night prayers are very important and you should never miss them. Examine your conscience and tell God you are sorry for any sins you discover. Also take note as to whether you are keeping your special resolution. If you are really very tired, you can make your prayers quite short, but they should never be omitted and should always be sincere and earnest. Before you get into bed, take holy water and make the sign of the cross; and, when in bed, try to think about God or our Lady or to pray until you drop off to sleep.

> Fight the good fight of faith; lay thy grasp on
> eternal life, that life thou wert called to.[562]

[562] 1 Tm 6:12

## *Prayers*

### The Sign of the Cross

In the name of the Father and of the Son and of the Holy Ghost. Amen.

### The Lord's Prayer

Our Father who art in heaven, hallowed be thy name, thy kingdom come, thy will be done on earth as it is in heaven; give us this day our daily bread, and forgive us our trespasses as we forgive them that trespass against us, and lead us not into temptation, but deliver us from evil. Amen.

### The Angelic Salutation

Hail, Mary, full of grace, the Lord is with thee; blessed art thou among women and blessed is the fruit of thy womb, Jesus. Holy Mary, Mother of God, pray for us sinners now and at the hour of our death. Amen.

### The Apostles' Creed

I believe in God the Father Almighty, Creator of heaven and earth, and in Jesus Christ, his only Son, our Lord, who was conceived by the Holy Ghost, born of the Virgin Mary, suffered under Pontius Pilate, was crucified, died, and was buried. He descended into hell, the third day he rose again from the dead. He ascended into heaven, sitteth at the right hand of God the Father Almighty; from thence he shall come to judge the living and the dead. I believe in the Holy Ghost, the holy Catholic Church, the communion of saints, the forgiveness of sins, the resurrection of the body, and life everlasting. Amen.

### The Little Doxology

Glory be to the Father and to the Son and to the Holy Ghost; as it was in the beginning, is now, and ever shall be, world without end. Amen.

## Some Important Mass Prayers

### The Gloria

Glory be to God on high, and on earth peace to men of good will. We praise thee, we bless thee, we adore thee, we glorify thee; we give thee thanks for thy great glory. Lord God, heavenly king, God the Father Almighty. Lord Jesus Christ, only begotten Son. Lord God, Lamb of God, Son of the Father: who takest away the sins of the world, have mercy on us; who takest away the sins of the world, receive our prayer; who sittest at the right hand of the Father, have mercy on us. For thou alone art the holy one; thou alone art Lord; thou, Jesus Christ, alone art the Most High, with the Holy Ghost in the glory of God the Father. Amen.

### The Sanctus

Holy, holy, holy, Lord God of hosts. Thy glory fills all heaven and earth. Hosanna in high heaven! Blessed is he who is coming in the name of the Lord. Hosanna in high heaven.

### Before the Consecration

O God we beg thee to give thy full blessing to these gifts; consecrate and approve of them; make them perfect and pleasing to thyself, so that they may be made for us the body and blood of thy dearly loved Son, Jesus Christ our Lord.

### After the Consecration

Now Lord, we call to our minds the blessed passion of thy Son, our Lord, and also his resurrection and ascension; and to Thy Sovereign Majesty all of us, priest and people together, do offer a sacrifice which is pure, holy, and unblemished—the holy bread that brings us endless life and the chalice that wins us eternal salvation.

### The Great Doxology

Through him and with him and in him, thou, God Almighty Father, in the unity of the Holy Spirit, has all honor and glory forever and ever. Amen.

### After the Communion

May we possess with pure hearts, O Lord, the sacrament we have received as food; may this day's gift prepare our souls for eternity.

## *Daily Prayers*

### Morning Prayer

O Jesus, through the most pure Heart of Mary, I offer thee all the prayers, works, joys, and sufferings of this day for all the intentions of thy divine Heart.

Heavenly Father, I thank thee for keeping me safe through the night which has passed, and for giving me another day in which to serve thee. Thou hast created me, redeemed me through thy Son Jesus Christ, and called me to thy eternal kingdom. Therefore, I want to belong to thee wholly today, for the rest of my life, and through all eternity. May thy holy will be done in me; give me light that I may know what I ought to do for thee during this day. Protect me from all evil; lead me through thy Son Jesus Christ; fill me with the love of the Holy Spirit. All for thy glory! All for love of thee!

*Our Father. Hail Mary. I believe. Glory be.*

My good angel, whom God has sent to be my guardian, watch over me carefully today. In the name of the Father…Amen.

## Night Prayer

*Sign of the Cross. Our Father. Hail Mary. I believe.*

O God, my Father, I thank thee for all the blessings and graces thou hast given me today. I fear that I have not served thee as well as I should have done, and ask now for light to remember where I have failed and grace to be sorry for whatever sins I have committed.

*(Examination of conscience)*

O my God, I am sorry and beg pardon for all my sins and detest them above all things, because they deserve thy dreadful punishments, because they have crucified my loving Savior, Jesus Christ, and most of all because they offend thine infinite goodness; and I firmly resolve, by the help of thy grace, never to offend thee again and carefully to avoid the occasions of sin.

I put myself trustfully into thy loving hands, asking thee to keep me safe throughout the coming night and to let my sleep renew me in strength and courage to serve thee better tomorrow and for the rest of my life. Bless my father and mother, my brothers and sisters, and all those for whom I ought to pray. Reward all those who have been kind to me, comfort those who are in sorrow, strengthen those in temptation, bring sinners to repentance, have mercy on the sick and the dying. Heavenly Father, let all men find their way home to thee through Jesus Christ our Lord and Savior.

May our Lord bless and preserve us and bring us to life everlasting. Mary, my Mother and Queen, take me under thy protection. My good angel, whom God has sent to be my guardian, watch over me during the night.

Jesus, Mary, and Joseph, I give you my heart and my soul.

Jesus, Mary, and Joseph, assist me in my last agony.

Jesus, Mary, and Joseph, may I breathe forth my soul in peace with you.

May the souls of the faithful departed, through the mercy of God, rest in peace. Amen.

In the name of the Father and of the Son and of the Holy Ghost. Amen.

## Table Prayers

*Before meals.* Bless us, O Lord, and these thy gifts which we are about to receive through thy bounty. Through Christ our Lord. Amen.

*After meals.* We give thee thanks, Almighty God, for all thy benefits: Who livest and reignest world without end. Amen.

## The Angelus (Prayed Standing on Sundays)

The angel of the Lord declared unto Mary; and she conceived by the Holy Ghost. *Hail Mary.*

Behold the handmaid of the Lord; be it done to me according to thy word. *Hail Mary.*

And the Word was made flesh; and dwelt amongst us. *Hail Mary.*

Pray for us, O holy Mother of God; that we may be made worthy of the promises of Christ.

Let us pray. Pour forth we beseech thee, O Lord, thy grace into our hearts, that we to whom the incarnation of Christ thy Son was made known by the message of an angel, may by his passion and cross be brought to the glory of his resurrection; through the same Christ our Lord. Amen.

## From Easter to Pentecost (Prayed Standing)

Queen of heaven rejoice, alleluia.
For he whom thou didst deserve to bear, alleluia.
Has risen as he said, alleluia.
Pray for us to God, alleluia.
Rejoice and be glad, O Virgin Mary, alleluia.
Because our Lord is truly risen, alleluia.

Let us pray. O God, who hast given joy to the whole world through the resurrection of thy Son our Lord Jesus Christ; grant that through the prayers of his Virgin Mother Mary we may obtain the joys of everlasting life. Through the same Christ our Lord. Amen.

## Occasional Prayers

### Faith

My God, I believe in thee and in all thy Church teaches, because thou hast said it and thy word is true.

### Hope

My God, I hope in thee for pardon for my sins, for grace during this life and glory in eternal life, because thou hast promised all these things and art ever faithful to thy promises.

### Love

My God, I love thee above all things because thou art so good; and for thy sake I will love my neighbor as myself.

### Sorrow

My God, I am sorry for all my sins because thou art so good; with the help of thy grace, I will do my best not to offend thee again. O God, be merciful to me, a sinner.—Lord have mercy on me.—Lord, if thou wilt, thou canst make me clean.—Jesus, mercy! Mary, help!

### Offering

Take, O Lord, and receive all my liberty, my memory, my understanding, and all my will, whatsoever I have and possess. Thou hast given all these things to me; to thee, O Lord, I restore them: all are thine, dispose of them all according to thy will. Give me thy love and thy grace, for this is enough for me.

### Resignation

My God, I accept death, in whatever way it may come to me according to thy holy will, as a punishment due to my sins; I accept it in union with the death of Christ thy Son, and as the only way in which I can reach my everlasting home with thee.

"The Lord has given; the Lord has taken away; blessed be the name of the Lord."[563] Thy will be done. All for thee, O God.

### Adoration, Praise, and Thanks

My God, how holy and great and wonderful thou art! Thy majesty is exalted above all creation; thy thoughts are above all human thoughts; and thy power greater than all powers in this world. Thy love is stronger and closer to me than I can ever grasp. I am filled with wonder at thy greatness; I bow down before thee; with the deepest reverence I adore thee, my dearest God and Lord.

Holy, strong, immortal God, have mercy on us.—"To the King of ages, immortal, invisible, the only God, be honor and glory for ever and ever. Amen."[564]

## *To Christ Our Lord*

Blessed be Jesus Christ, true God and true man.—"My Lord, and my God."[565] We adore thee, O Christ, and we bless thee, because by thy holy cross thou hast redeemed the world.—O Sacred Heart of Jesus, I implore the grace to love thee daily more and more.—Jesus, meek and humble of heart, make my heart like unto thine.

563 Jb 1:21
564 1 Tm 1:17
565 Jn 20:28

### Anima Christi

Soul of Christ, make me holy.
Body of Christ, save me.
Blood of Christ, fill me with joy.
Water from the side of Christ, wash me.
Passion of Christ, strengthen me.
O kind Jesus, hear me.
Hide me within thy wounds,
And never let me be parted from thee.
Defend me from the wicked enemy.
Call me at the hour of my death
And bid me come to thee
That I may praise thee with thy saints
Forever and ever. Amen.

## *To the Holy Ghost*

Come, Holy Spirit, fill the hearts of thy faithful, and kindle in them the fire of thy love. Send forth thy Spirit, all will be created anew, and thou wilt renew the face of the earth.

Let us pray. O God, who hast taught the faithful by sending the light of the Holy Spirit into their hearts, grant us by the same Spirit that we may relish what is right, and may ever rejoice in his comfort. Through Christ our Lord. Amen.

## *To Mary*

### THE ROSARY

*The joyful mysteries:*

1. The annunciation.
2. The visitation.
3. The birth of our Lord.
4. The presentation in the Temple.
5. The finding in the Temple.

*The sorrowful mysteries:*

1. The agony in the garden.
2. The scourging at the pillar.
3. The crowning with thorns.
4. The way of the cross.
5. The crucifixion.

*The glorious mysteries:*

1. The resurrection.
2. The ascension.
3. The descent of the Holy Ghost.
4. The assumption.
5. The crowning of our Lady in heaven.

### SALVE REGINA

Hail, holy Queen, Mother of mercy, hail our life, our sweetness, and our hope. To thee do we cry, poor banished children of Eve; to thee do we send up our sighs, mourning and weeping in this vale of tears. Turn, then, most gracious advocate, thine eyes of mercy toward us; and after this our exile, show unto us the blessed fruit of thy womb, Jesus. O clement, O loving, O sweet Virgin Mary.

### Sub Tuum Praesidium

We fly to thy patronage, O holy Mother of God; despise not our petitions in our necessities; but deliver us from all dangers, O glorious and blessed Virgin.

### The Memorare

Remember, O most gracious Virgin Mary, that never was it known that anyone who fled to thy protection, implored thy help, and sought thy intercession was left unaided. Inspired with this confidence, I fly unto thee, O Virgin of virgins, my Mother. To thee I come; before thee I stand, sinful and sorrowful. O Mother of the Word incarnate, despise not my petitions, but in thy mercy hear and answer me. Amen.

### Common Collect of the Blessed Virgin Mary

Grant to us thy servants, we beseech thee O Lord God, to enjoy continual health of mind and body; and by the glorious intercession of Blessed Mary ever Virgin, to be delivered from the sorrows of this life, and enjoy the happiness of life everlasting. Through Christ our Lord. Amen.

## *For Special Occasions*

*When in trouble.* Jesus, help me.—"Lord, save us; we perish."[566]—"Father, if thou wilt, let this chalice pass from me! But yet not my will, but thine be done."[567]

*When in temptation.* Lord, help me!—Jesus, mercy! Mary, help!

*For parents and relations.* Heavenly Father, I thank thee for the innumerable benefits thou hast given me through my parents. Reward them for all that they have done for me from the day of my birth until now, and help me always to be grateful to them. Bless them and all the work they do, keep

[566] Mt 8:25
[567] Lk 22:42

them in good health, stand by them in every difficulty. Make them rich in merits and protect them from all evil.

Bless also my brothers and sisters, and all my relations. Do not permit any member of our family to be lost forever, but unite us all finally in the everlasting home of our Father in heaven. Amen.

*For choice of state in life.* Heavenly Father! Thou didst create me in thy love, and didst plan for me a path through life by means of which I can reach my eternal salvation. Let me know what it is that thou desirest from me; show me the way of life which I should choose. Show me in which way I can best use the powers thou hast given me, and how I can best serve thee. Help me now to choose my state of life wisely, to learn well what is needed for it, and to do something worthwhile in it. May my whole life please thee and give thee glory. Amen.

*For a happy death.* From a sudden and unprovided death, deliver us O Lord.—Jesus, Mary, and Joseph, I give you my heart and my soul; Jesus, Mary, and Joseph, assist me in my last agony; Jesus, Mary, and Joseph, may I breathe forth my soul in peace with you.—"Father, into thy hands I commend my spirit."[568]

*For the souls in purgatory.* Eternal rest give to them, O Lord, and let perpetual light shine upon them. May they rest in peace. Amen.

[568] Lk 23:46

# SCRIPTURE CITATION ABBREVIATIONS

| Abbr | Douay-Rheims | Contemporary |
|---|---|---|
| 1 Cor | 1 Corinthians | 1 Corinthians |
| 1 Esd | 1 Esdras | Ezra |
| 1 Jn | 1 John | 1 John |
| 1 Kgs | 1 Kings | 1 Samuel |
| 1 Mc | 1 Machabees | 1 Maccabees |
| 1 Par | 1 Paralipomenon | 1 Chronicles |
| 1 Pt | 1 Peter | 1 Peter |
| 1 Thes | 1 Thessalonians | 1 Thessalonians |
| 1 Tm | 1 Timothy | 1 Timothy |
| 2 Cor | 2 Corinthians | 2 Corinthians |
| 2 Esd | 2 Esdras | Nehemiah |
| 2 Jn | 2 John | 2 John |
| 2 Kgs | 2 Kings | 2 Samuel |
| 2 Mc | 2 Machabees | 2 Maccabees |
| 2 Par | 2 Paralipomenon | 2 Chronicles |
| 2 Pt | 2 Peter | 2 Peter |
| 2 Thes | 2 Thessalonians | 2 Thessalonians |
| 2 Tm | 2 Timothy | 2 Timothy |
| 3 Jn | 3 John | 3 John |
| 3 Kgs | 3 Kings | 1 Kings |
| 4 Kgs | 4 Kings | 2 Kings |
| Abd | Abdias | Obadiah |
| Acts | Acts of the Apostles | Acts of the Apostles |
| Agg | Aggeus | Haggai |
| Am | Amos | Amos |
| Apoc | Apocalypse | Revelation |
| Bar | Baruch | Baruch |
| Cant | Canticle of Canticles | Song of Songs |
| Col | Colossians | Colossians |
| Dn | Daniel | Daniel |
| Dt | Deuteronomy | Deuteronomy |
| Eccles | Ecclesiastes | Ecclesiastes |
| Ecclus | Ecclesiasticus | Sirach |
| Eph | Ephesians | Ephesians |
| Est | Esther | Esther |
| Ex | Exodus | Exodus |
| Ez | Ezechiel | Ezekiel |

| Abbr | Douay-Rheims | Contemporary |
|---|---|---|
| Gal | Galatians | Galatians |
| Gn | Genesis | Genesis |
| Hb | Habacuc | Habbakuk |
| Heb | Hebrews | Hebrews |
| Is | Isaias | Isaiah |
| Jas | James | James |
| Jer | Jeremias | Jeremiah |
| Jb | Job | Job |
| Jl | Joel | Joel |
| Jn | John | John |
| Jon | Jonas | Jonas |
| Jo | Josue | Joshua |
| Jude | Jude | Jude |
| Jgs | Judges | Judges |
| Jdt | Judith | Judith |
| Lam | Lamentations | Lamentations |
| Lv | Leviticus | Leviticus |
| Lk | Luke | Luke |
| Mal | Malachias | Malachi |
| Mk | Mark | Mark |
| Mt | Matthew | Matthew |
| Mi | Micheas | Micah |
| Na | Nahum | Nahum |
| Nm | Numbers | Numbers |
| Os | Osee | Hosea |
| Phlm | Philemon | Philemon |
| Phil | Philippians | Philippians |
| Prv | Proverbs | Proverbs |
| Ps | Psalms | Psalms |
| Rom | Romans | Romans |
| Ru | Ruth | Ruth |
| Soph | Sophonias | Zephaniah |
| Ti | Titus | Titus |
| Tb | Tobias | Tobit |
| Ws | Wisdom | Wisdom |
| Zac | Zacharias | Zechariah |

# ABOUT THIS SERIES

Tradivox was first conceived as an international research endeavor to recover lost and otherwise little-known Catholic catechetical texts. As the research progressed over several years, the vision began to grow, along with the number of project contributors and a general desire to share these works with a broader audience.

Legally incorporated in 2019, Tradivox has begun the work of carefully remastering and republishing dozens of these catechisms which were once in common and official use in the Church around the world. That effort is embodied in this *Tradivox Catholic Catechism Index*, a multi-volume series restoring artifacts of traditional faith and praxis for a contemporary readership. More about this series and the work of Tradivox can be learned at www.Tradivox.com.

# SOPHIA INSTITUTE

Sophia Institute is a nonprofit institution that seeks to nurture the spiritual, moral, and cultural life of souls and to spread the Gospel of Christ in conformity with the authentic teachings of the Roman Catholic Church.

Sophia Institute Press fulfills this mission by offering translations, reprints, and new publications that afford readers a rich source of the enduring wisdom of mankind.

Sophia Institute also operates the popular online resource Catholic Exchange.com. *Catholic Exchange* provides world news from a Catholic perspective as well as daily devotionals and articles that will help readers to grow in holiness and live a life consistent with the teachings of the Church.

In 2013, Sophia Institute launched Sophia Institute for Teachers to renew and rebuild Catholic culture through service to Catholic education. With the goal of nurturing the spiritual, moral, and cultural life of souls, and an abiding respect for the role and work of teachers, we strive to provide materials and programs that are at once enlightening to the mind and ennobling to the heart; faithful and complete, as well as useful and practical.

Sophia Institute gratefully recognizes the Solidarity Association for preserving and encouraging the growth of our apostolate over the course of many years. Without their generous and timely support, this book would not be in your hands.

www.SophiaInstitute.com
www.CatholicExchange.com
www.SophiaTeachers.org